IMAGES
of America

KERNERSVILLE

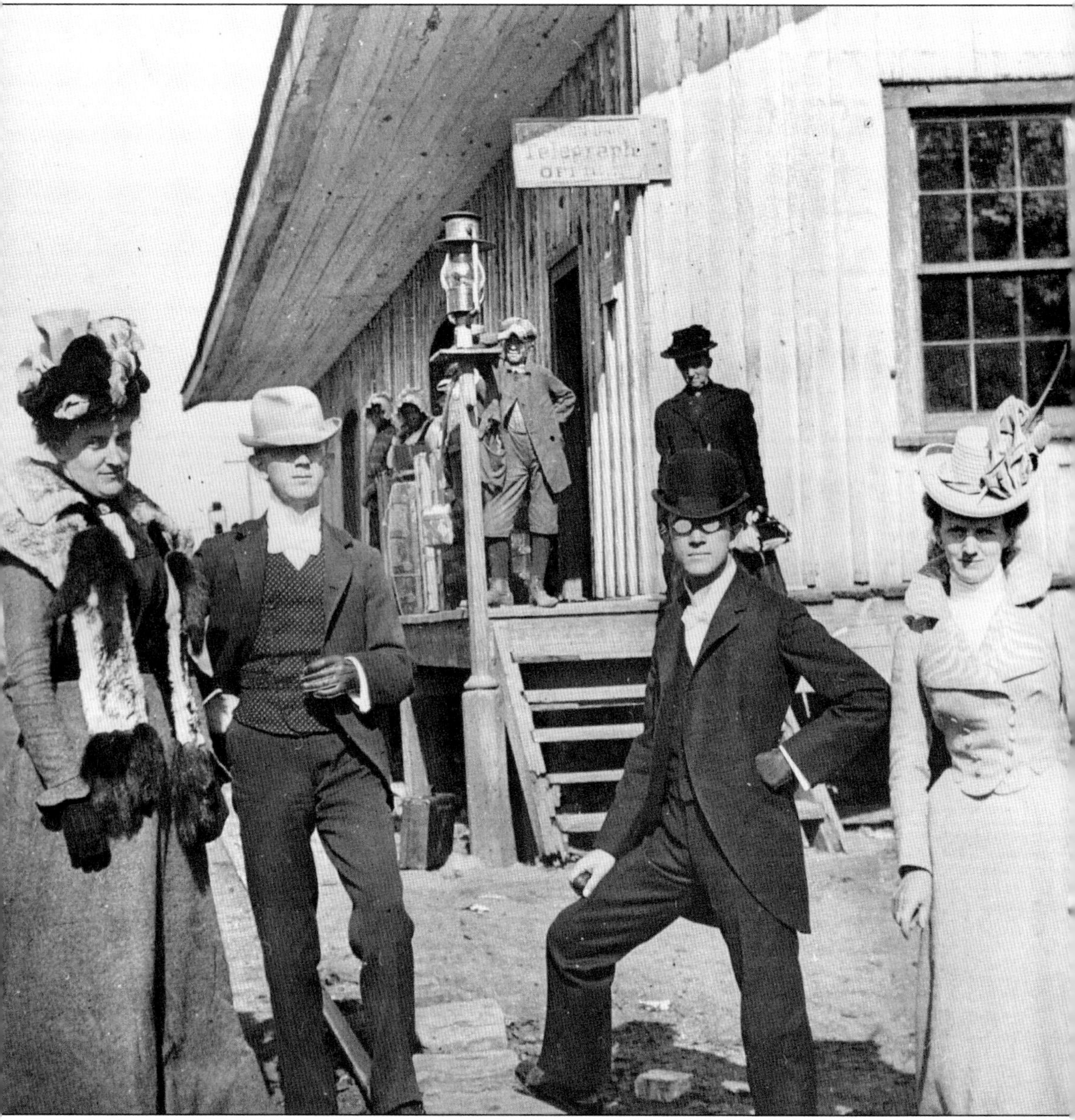

ON THE COVER. Elegantly dressed men and women wait in the railroad yard for the next train. Servants stand on the Old Depot porch. (Photograph courtesy of Old Salem.)

IMAGES
of America

KERNERSVILLE

Alice E. Sink in partnership with the
Kernersville Historic Preservation Society

ARCADIA
PUBLISHING

ISBN 978-0-7385-4159-4

Published by Arcadia Publishing
Charleston, South Carolina

Printed in the United States of America

Library of Congress Catalog Card Number: 2005925651

For all general information contact Arcadia Publishing at:
Telephone 843-853-2070
Fax 843-853-0044
E-mail sales@arcadiapublishing.com
For customer service and orders:
Toll-Free 1-888-313-2665

Visit us on the Internet at www.arcadiapublishing.com

This book is dedicated in honor of Dr. L. B. "Billy" Pope,
neighbor, colleague, friend, gentle spirit.

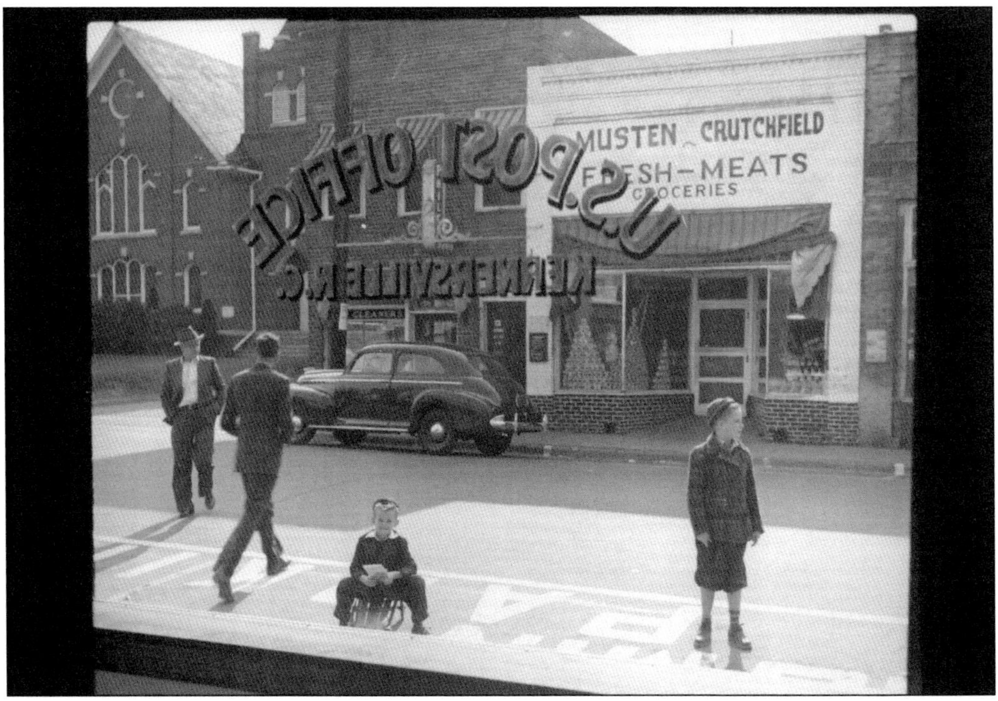

KERNERSVILLE: THE FEELING OF COMMUNITY. Musten and Crutchfield, viewed here through the window of the U.S. Post Office, was established on April 11, 1938. It is the oldest Kernersville grocery store still in operation today. Main Street Baptist Church is on the left. The children in the picture are Robert Stuart (on the sled) and Ned Stuart Jr. (far right). (Photograph courtesy of Mary Ruth Körner.)

CONTENTS

Acknowledgments	6
Introduction	7
1. Historic Overview and Timeline	9
2. Early Houses, Families, and Entrepreneurships	31
3. Körner's Folly	61
4. Community Interests and Involvements	73
5. Friends, Neighbors, and Extracurricular Activities	95

ACKNOWLEDGMENTS

The author wishes to thank the following individuals, organizations, and publications that made possible the publication of this pictorial history:

The Kernersville Historic Preservation Society
Paige Cooke
Bobbie Wolfe (BW)
Jerry Taylor
Charlie Stout
Mary Ruth Körner (MRK)
Mary Körner Hutchins (MKH)
Barbara Bull (BB)
Joe Pinnix (JP)
Barbara Martin (BM)
Dimple Warren (DW)
Edgar Shore (ES)
Martha Vance Brown (MVB)
Solly Coltrane (SC)
Sarah Hamlin (SH)
Alice Thompson (AT)
John Wolfe (JW)
Kernersville Bicentennial Book (KBB)
Kernersville North Carolina Book (KNC)

INTRODUCTION

Kernersville's first pioneers found in its virgin forest cleared areas that Indians had farmed. Arrowheads and broken fragments of pottery surfaced. Early hunters also discovered that the territory was a natural watershed, the source of six rivers or creeks.

Most of the early people were transitory. Some were headed for the Great Lakes region; they passed through after leaving the eastern part of North Carolina. Catawba tribes, who did settle in the area, farmed, made pottery, and wove baskets. Many Cherokees who found their original mountain settlements overcrowded migrated here.

By the mid-1700s, Native Americans were joined by other immigrants. About 1756, Caleb Story, of Scotch-Irish descent, appeared on the scene and, with his land grant from the Royal Colony of Carolina, settled on his newly obtained land. Whether he was frightened away by 1756 French and Indian War activities in nearby Bethabara or he merely decided to move on, no one knows. Story sold all his land to David Morrow for what may have been the common barter—four gallons of rum.

In 1771, Irishman William Dobson bought David Morrow's land and other adjoining property, bringing his tract to 1,133 acres. With "Captain" Dobson, the intriguing history of Kernersville—as we know it today—begins. Dobson built a store and inn at the crossroads. Dobson's Tavern became the first stop for Moravians on their way from Salem to their Bethlehem, Pennsylvania, settlement. According to *Moravian Records,* on June 2, 1791, Pres. George Washington ate breakfast "at one Dobson's." The crossroads had the honor of entertaining our first president.

On November 14, 1817, Joseph Kerner bought the inn and named it Kerner's Crossroads. The real story of Kernersville begins with this man called "Joseph of Kernersville," and the pictorial history continues throughout the pages of this book. Although the age and conditions of some photographs defy clear reproduction, they represent the genuine history of the town. Because of their historical value and intrinsic worth, they have been included in this volume.

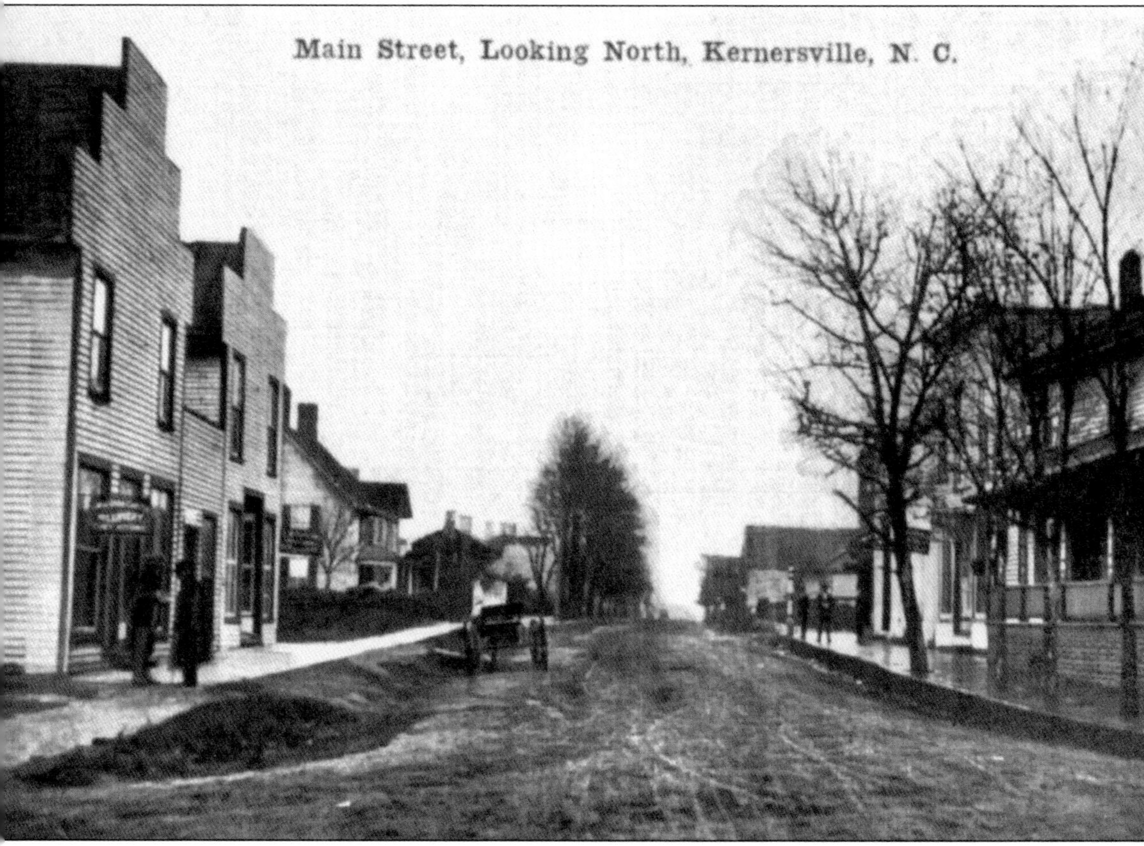

EARLY VIEW. This is a 1909 view of Main Street, looking north. Dobson's Tavern is on the right. (BW.)

One

Historic Overview and Timeline

Kernersville has always been a staunch supporter of schools, churches, civic improvements, and progressive business endeavors. In earlier times, small religious groups, consisting of charter members, met in private homes or schools. Different denominations met only once a month. Congregations staggered individual services during the first four Sundays of each month. A joint meeting brought everyone together on the fifth Sunday.

The Kernersville Academy opened in 1858 with the assurance that "every possible care will be taken to guard those placed under our tuition against those evils so dangerous to the young." Approximately 40 students enrolled, some boarding in private homes for as little as $5 per month. Although work in both the primary and high school was not graded, many students studied so diligently they were accepted into college as sophomores.

When other schools closed during the Civil War, the Academy remained open. Before the fall session of 1864 convened, student fees could be paid in either produce or money. Classes began at 9:00 a.m. and continued until 4:00 p.m., with short recesses and a designated lunch hour. Students completed their writing assignments on slates, cleaning them with water or—as oral history indicates—saliva. Fridays were reserved for special academic events, such as recitations and debates.

Although early facilities were primitive and books scarce, teachers proved to be devoted, educated, and cherished by their charges. General stores opened, mills began operation, and leaders emerged, devoting time, money, and individual and collective wisdom to the business of governing the community.

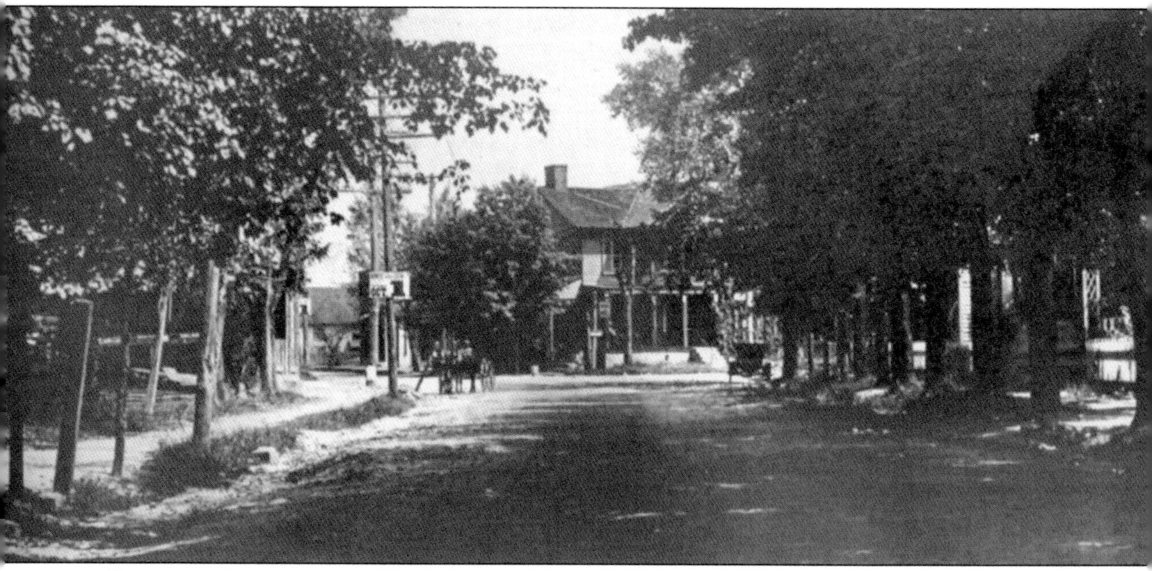

Dobson's Crossroads. In 1771, Irish emigrant William Dobson purchased 400 acres of land from David Morrow and built an inn where the roads crossed. This settlement was called Dobson's Crossroads. (KBB.)

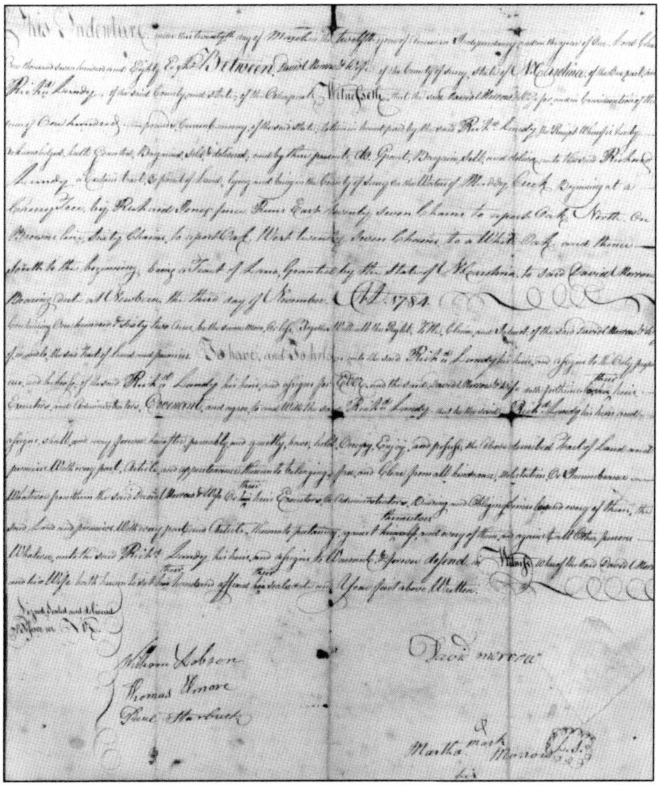

DEED. This is the 1784 deed records transfer of 400 acres from David Morrow to William Dobson for land that would later become Kernersville. (MRK.)

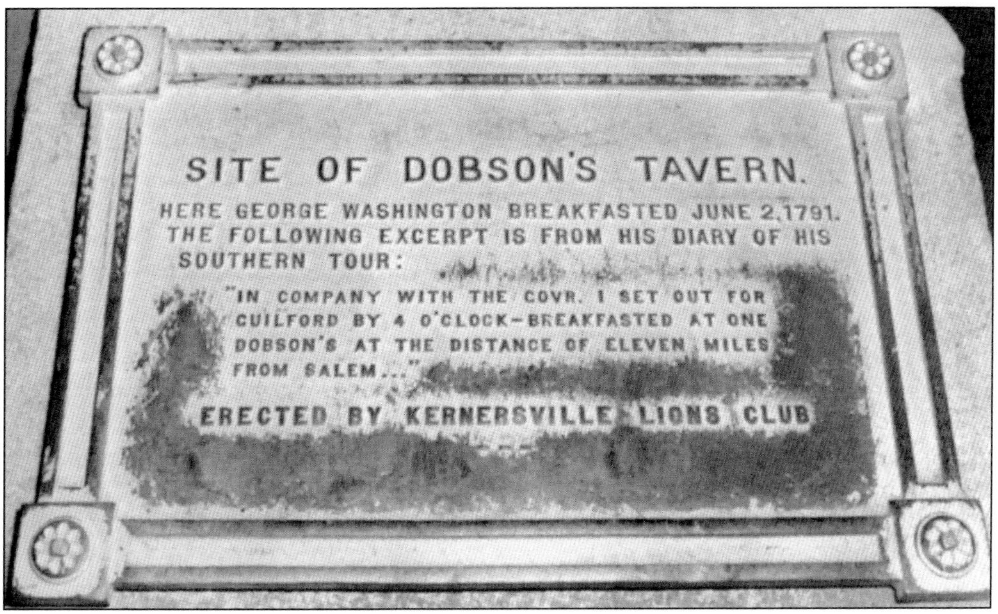

GEORGE WASHINGTON'S VISIT. On June 2, 1791, George Washington and his company left Salem at 4:00 in the morning, traveled 11 miles, and arrived at Dobson's Tavern for a hearty breakfast. The president and his entourage proceeded to Guilford Battleground; on their way, they stopped to drink water from a spring on the J. Carl Beeson farm. A little girl on the property became afraid, but President Washington calmed her fears and dropped a coin in her tin drinking cup. (KBB.)

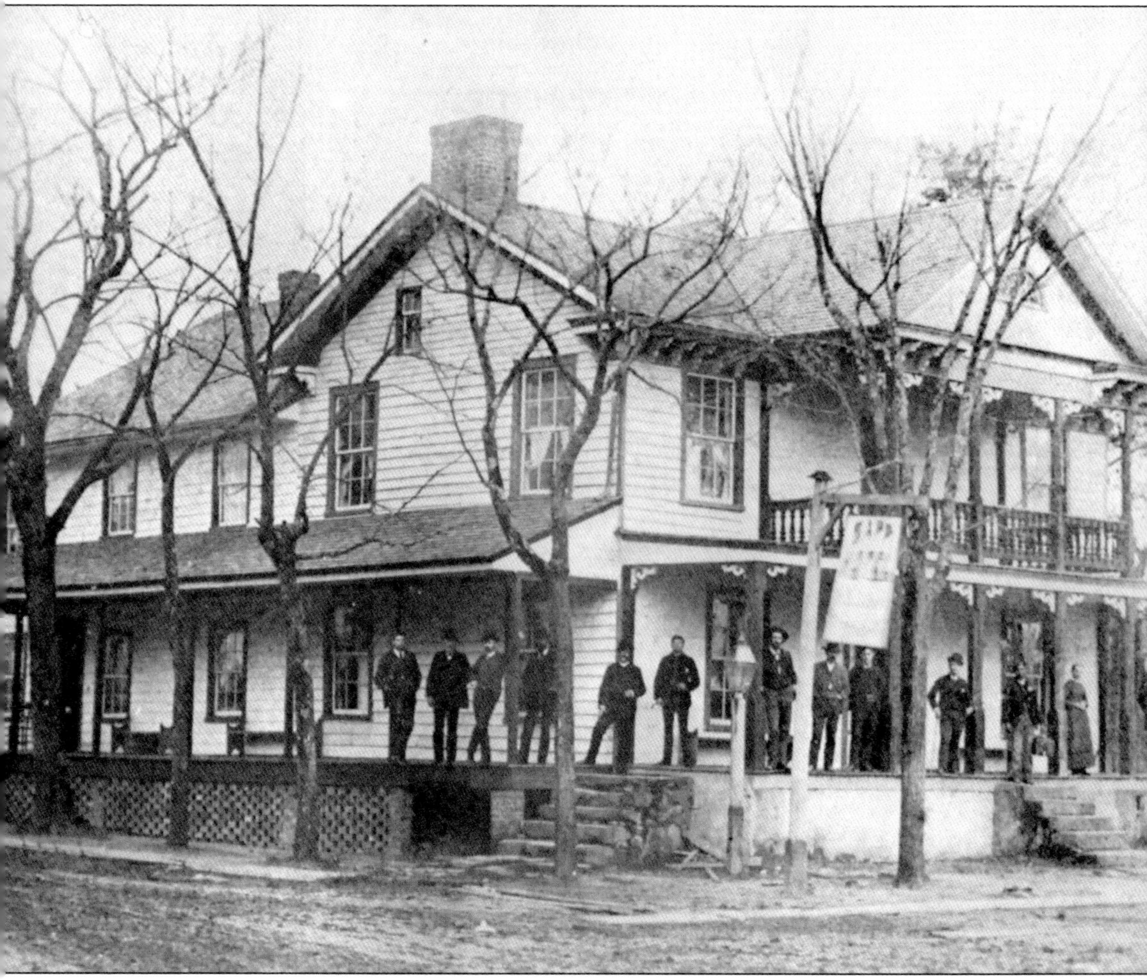

JOSEPH KERNER AND KERNER'S CROSSROADS. In 1797, Joseph Kerner bought the land surrounding Dobson's Crossroads. That same year, he married Christinia Kastner, a Moravian. Three children, John Frederick, Salome, and Philip, were born of this union. In 1817, the family moved to the Crossroads. Joseph continued to operate the inn for those traveling between the Moravian settlements of Salem and Bethlehem, Pennsylvania. The name of the village changed from Dobson's Crossroads to Kerner's Crossroads. A multi-talented individual, Joseph was a farmer, clock maker, hardware manufacturer, and miller. He also established a fan factory that manufactured machines that blew chaff from threshed wheat. (KNC.)

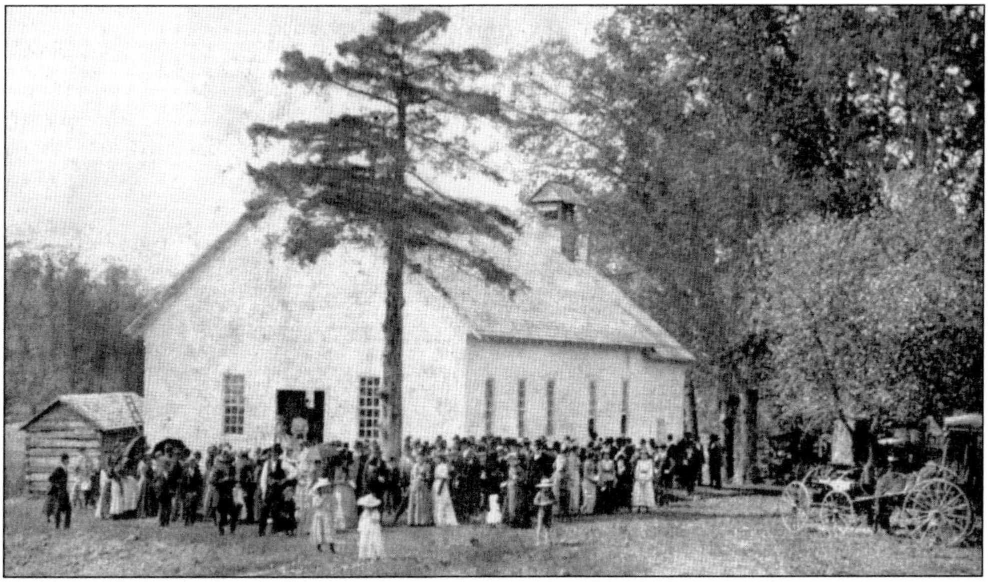

OLD FRIEDLAND MORAVIAN CHURCH. Joseph Kerner died at the age of 61, and his funeral was held at Old Friedland Moravian Church in Friedland, North Carolina, where his wife and children were members. An overflow crowd of mourners heard the funeral sermon from the churchyard because the church was too small to seat everyone present. After Joseph Kerner's death in 1830, his children divided their father's land. In 1848, William Penn Henly bought the inn. Other families migrated to the area, which by the beginning of the Civil War was becoming a thriving community. (BW.)

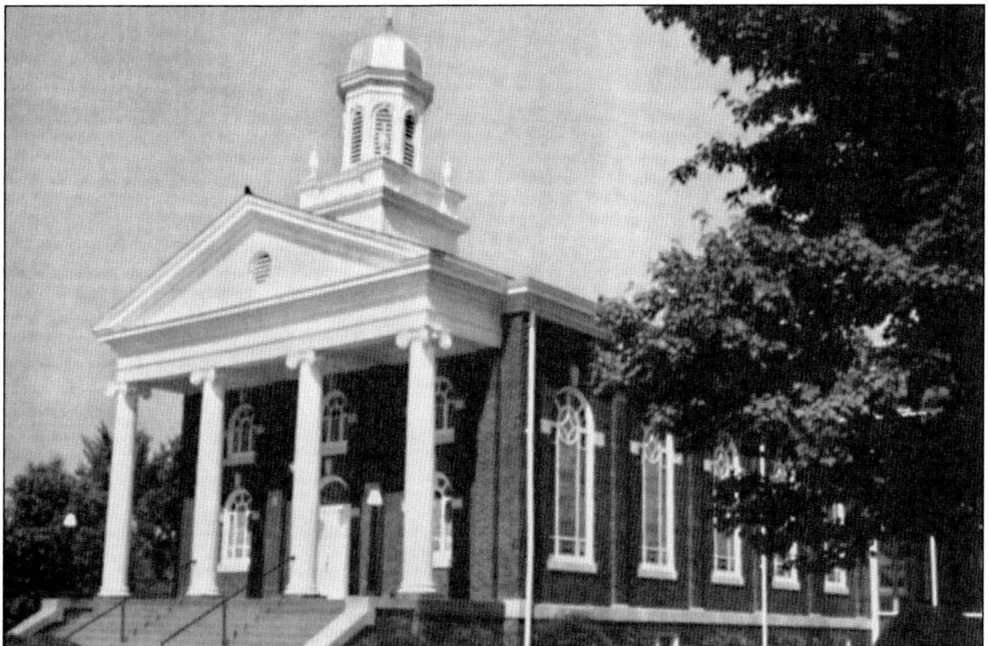

MAIN STREET UNITED METHODIST CHURCH. This first church was organized in 1837 and built on land donated by John Frederick Kerner. Builder John Ross used hand-hewn timbers, mortised and held together with pegs. The present church was constructed and dedicated in 1932. (MRK.)

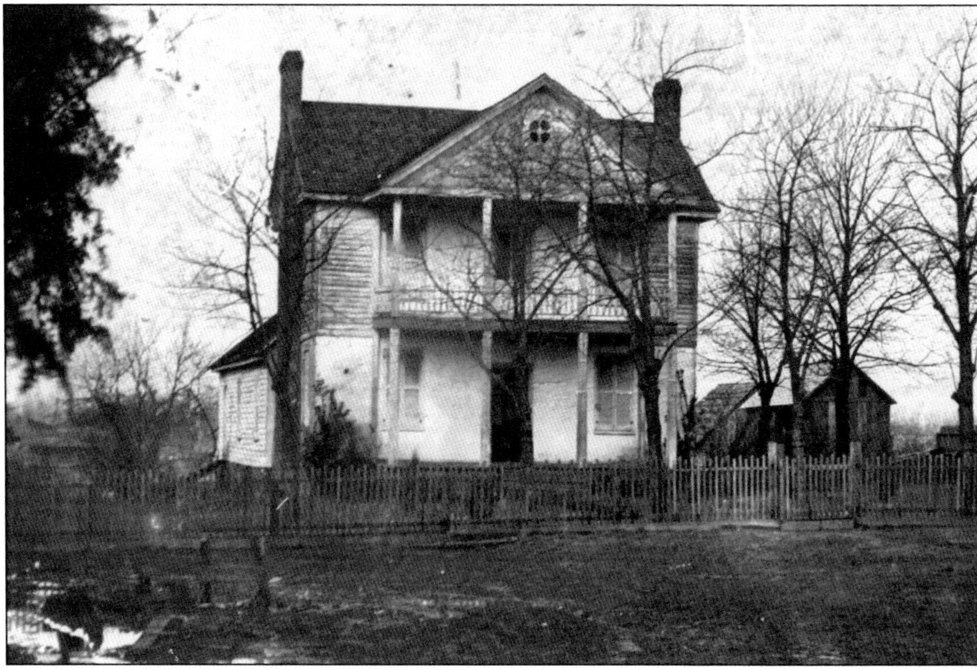

PLUNKETT PLACE. In 1856, this subscription school opened. Sponsored by the Masons and supported by parents paying tuition fees, the institution continued in operation during the Civil War while many other Southern schools closed. (BW.)

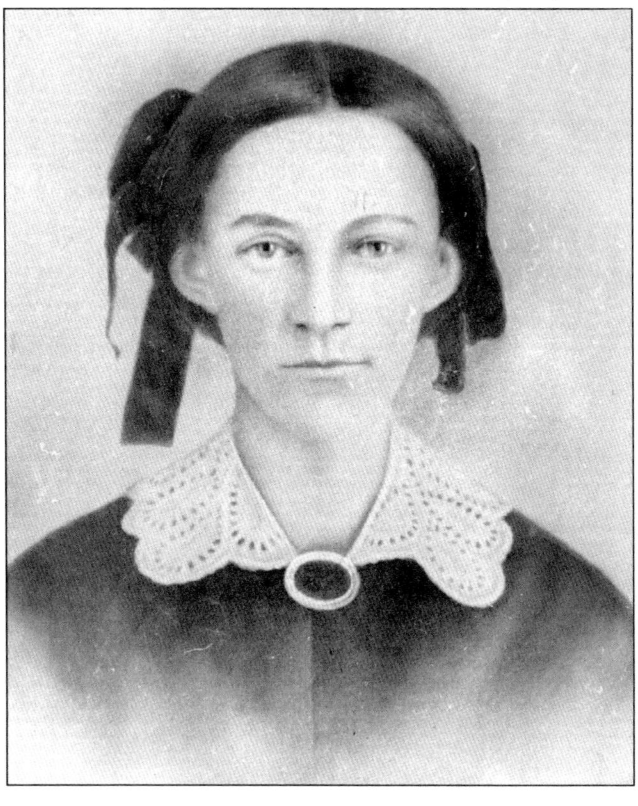

MISS PARTHIA GAISELLE DICKS. When this young woman from Randleman, North Carolina, taught at Plunkett Place, the school consisted of only two rooms in a large house. Miss Dicks later married Dr. Elias Kerner, grandson of the town's founding father. (ES.)

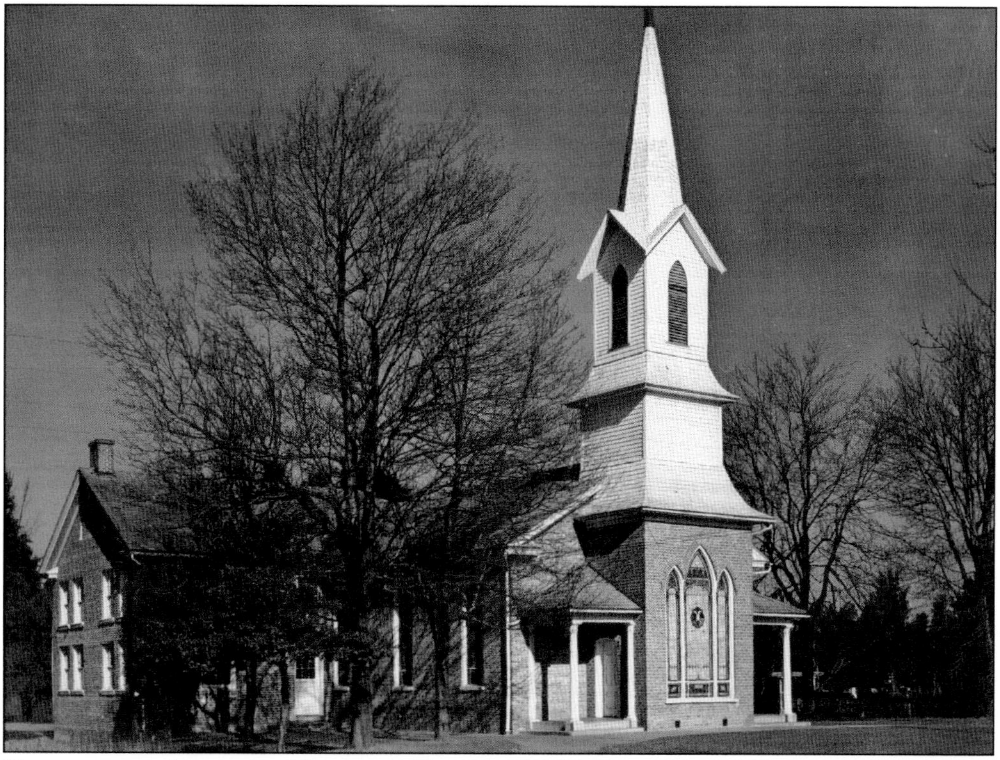

Kernersville Moravian Church. The John Frederick Kerner family donated land for the Kernersville Moravian Church, and Mr. Kerner and his sons personally gathered much of the building materials and supplied clay from their property for the brick used in this 1867 house of worship. Rev. C. Lewis Rights was the pastor. His wife, better known as "Aunt Rights," taught at the Tanyard Lane Free School housed in the church vestry. Known as a disciplinarian, Aunt Rights stressed good manners in addition to "the three Rs." (MKH.)

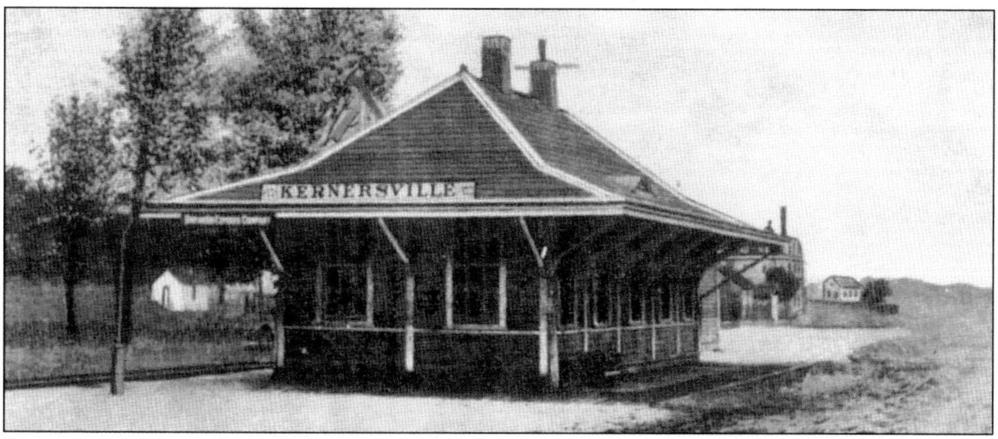

Railroad and Depot. Before the first train ran in 1873, local citizens donated money and personally graded four miles of roadbed and built a depot on the north side of the tracks. The depot, the second oldest in Western North Carolina, included a freight warehouse in addition to an office, ticket window, and passenger waiting room. Huge brick fireplaces and a massive station agent's desk symbolize the importance of the bygone railroad era. This photograph was taken *c.* 1916. (BW.)

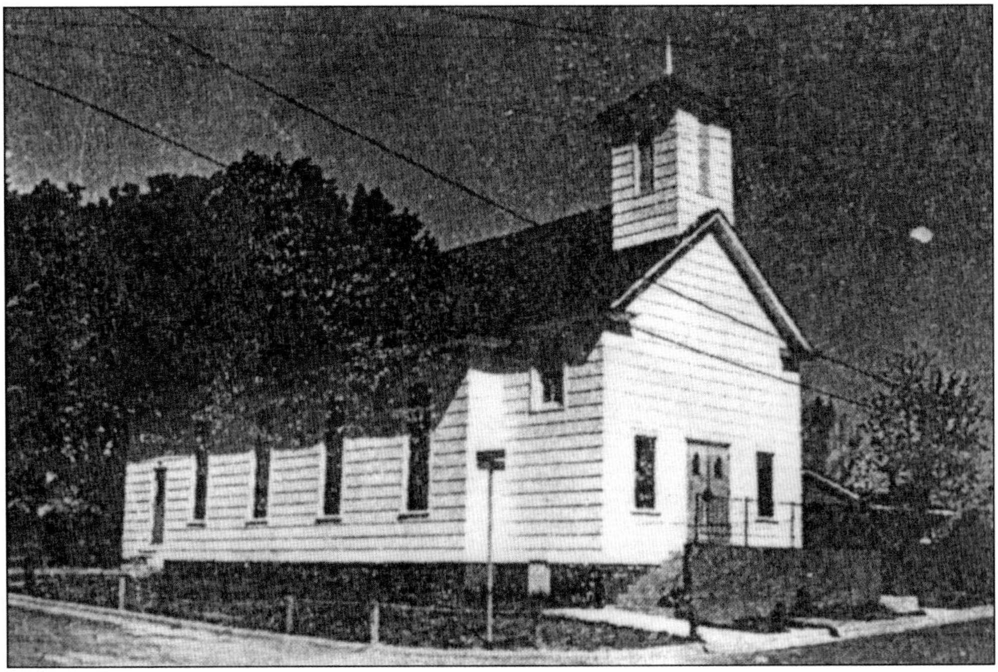

St. Paul's United Methodist Church. St. Paul's originated in the 1870s. The sanctuary, originally occupied by Main Street Methodist Church, was moved to the site occupied by the present St. Paul's Cemetery, the oldest African American cemetery in Kernersville. A community project under the guidance of Sarah Hamlin recently restored the cemetery. (BW.)

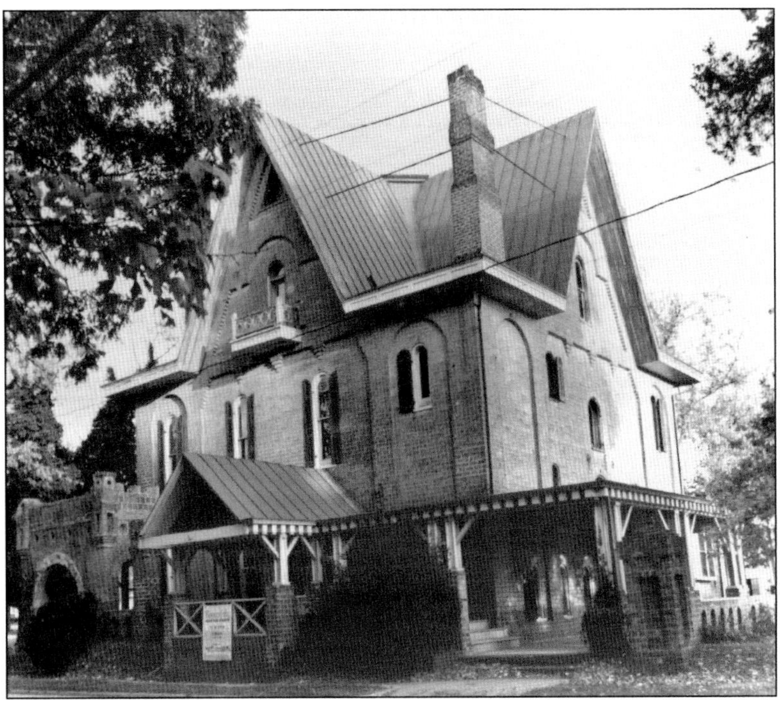

Körner's Folly. Known today as the "Folly," this fabulous house was designed and owned by artist Jule Körner. Completed in 1880, the residence originally contained an inside carriageway and stables, bachelor quarters, and art studios. (MRK.)

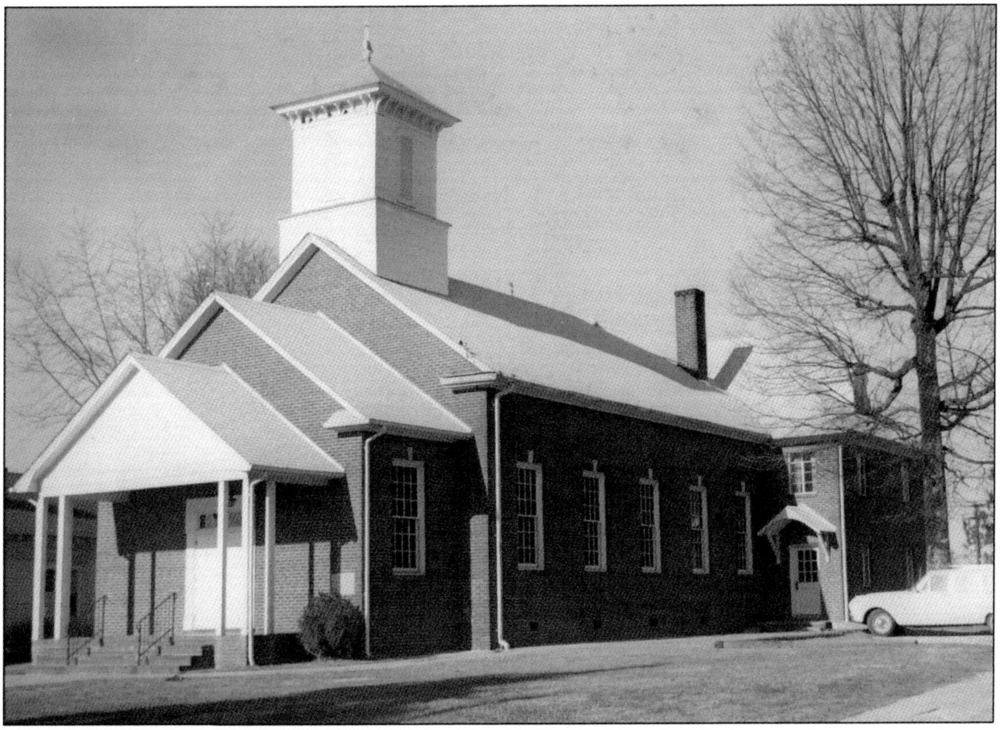

Cherry Street United Methodist Church. With approximately 15 charter members, this church was organized in 1885. Mr. and Mrs. J. C. Roberts, prominent Kernersville citizens, donated the land and $500. Others gave needed materials and provided labor in the building of this church. While this structure was being built, members of the congregation met at the Roberts' home. (MRK.)

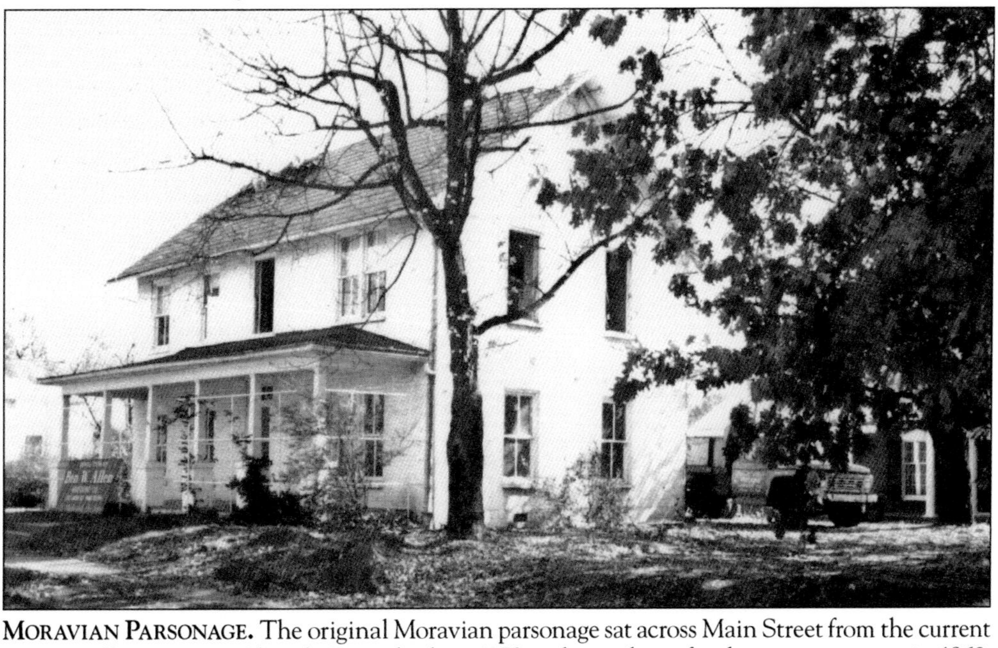

Moravian Parsonage. The original Moravian parsonage sat across Main Street from the current Kernersville Moravian Church. It was built in 1873 and torn down for the new parsonage in 1969. It was the home of the first pastor, Rev. Christian Lewis Rights. (MRK.)

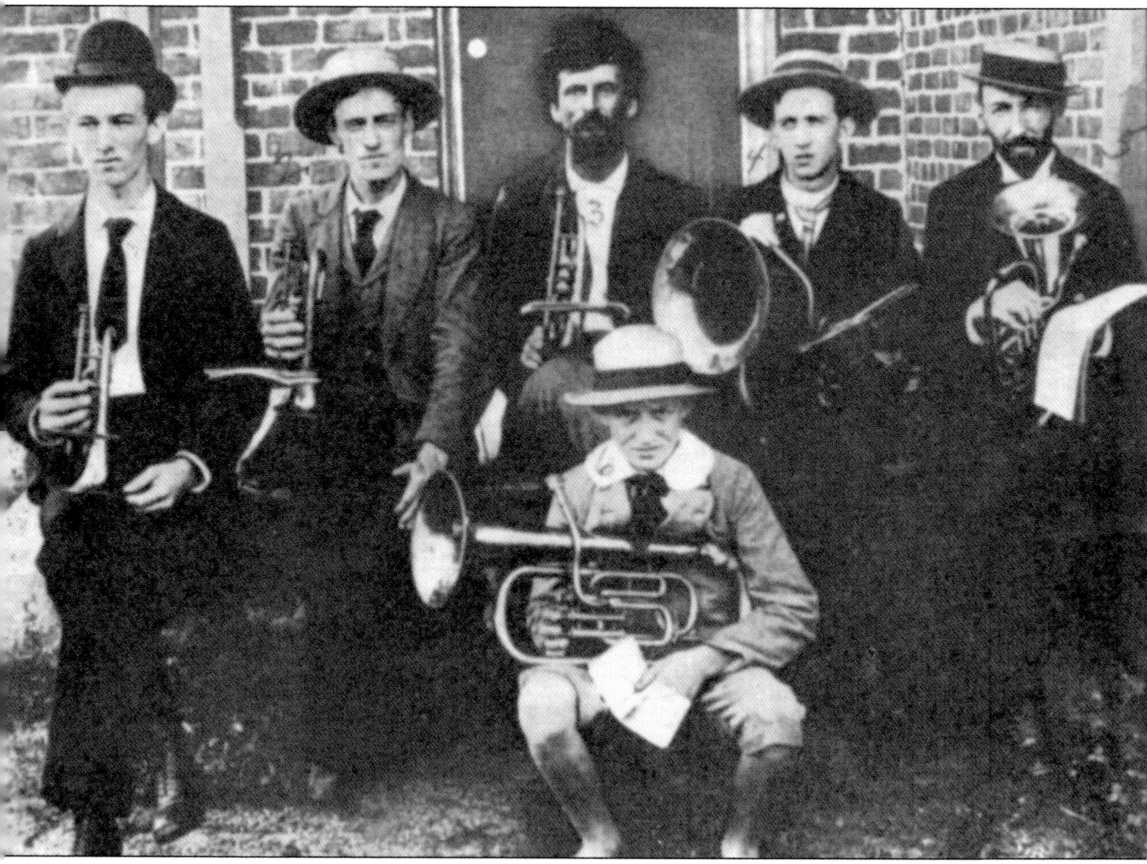

The Original Moravian Church Brass Band. The band, organized about 1890, played in special services. Members moved through the community on foot, playing by lantern light. Original members included, from left to right, Kerr Pepper, James F. Kerner, David Kerner, Carl R. Kerner, H. C. Körner, and Percy Kerner (in front). Different spellings of "Kerner" and "Körner" are pronounced the same. (BW.)

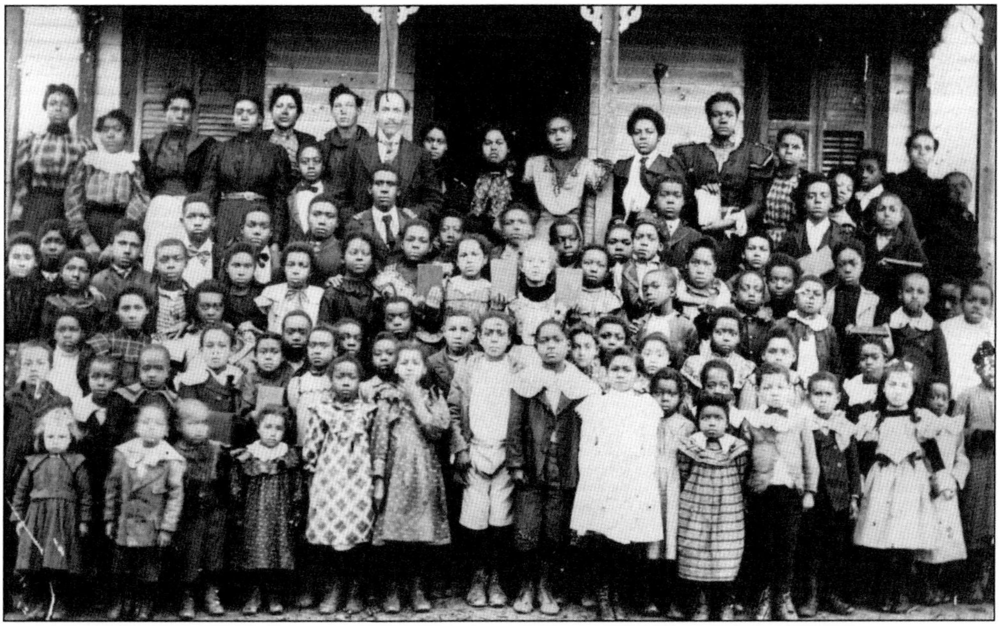

EARLY NEGRO SCHOOL. In the late 1800s, the little Kernersville community had a very small African American population. The Early Negro School, for grades one through seven, was built in 1892 on Nelson Street. Principal Thomas R. Matthews and Mrs. Cornelia Johnson were the only two teachers. When students finished their studies at the Early Negro School, they transferred to High Point Normal for their high school diplomas. Many went on to Bennett College to become certified teachers. (SH.)

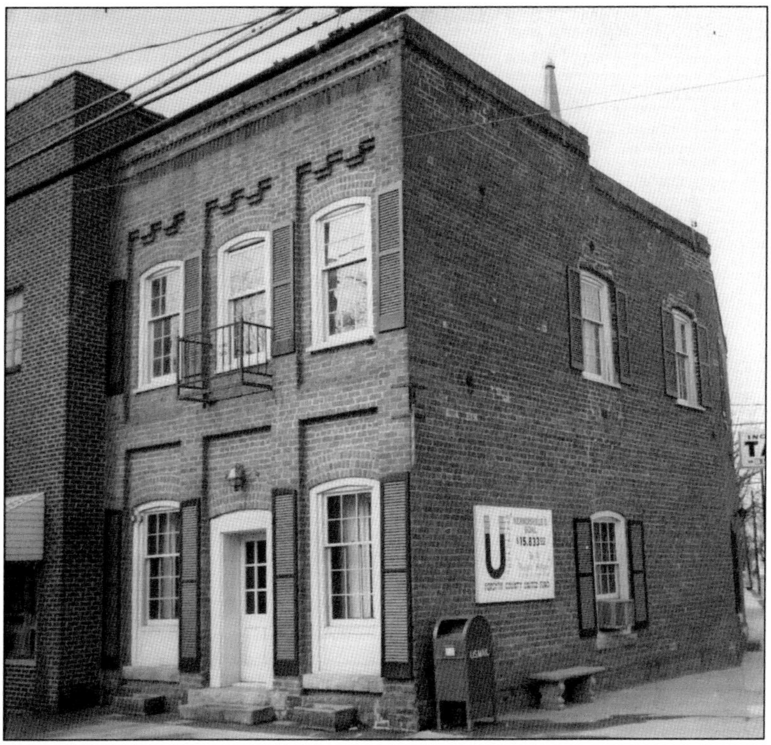

THE OLD BANK BUILDING. Built in 1903 to house the Bank of Kernersville, this establishment had savvy managers in George V. Fulp Sr. and his sons Willard, George, and Paul. It was once called "the best bank in Forsyth County," and normal business continued until all banks were ordered closed in 1933 because of the Depression. This establishment reopened the first day the edict was lifted. (MRK.)

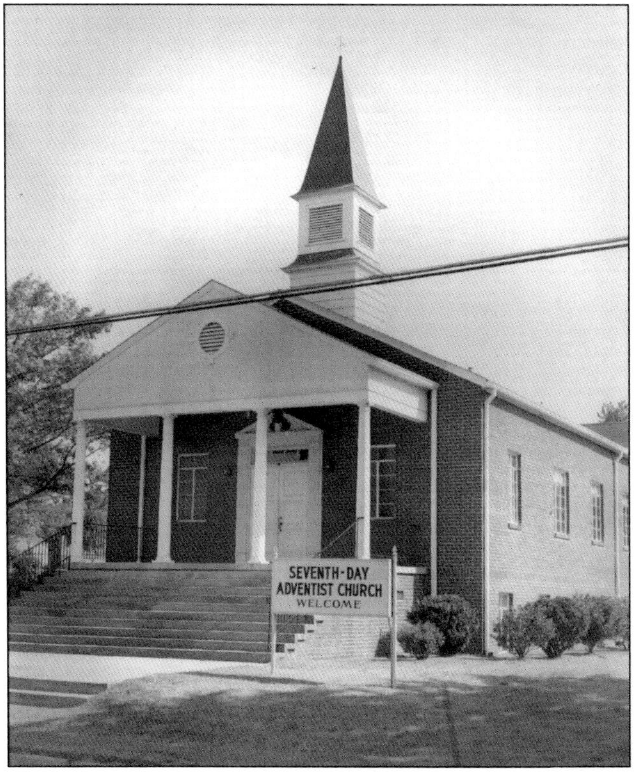

SEVENTH-DAY ADVENTIST CHURCH. The congregation of this church began in 1905 with only three families. Meeting first in private homes and a school building, Pastor G. W. Wells and 13 charter members built this church on Graves Street in 1911. (MRK.)

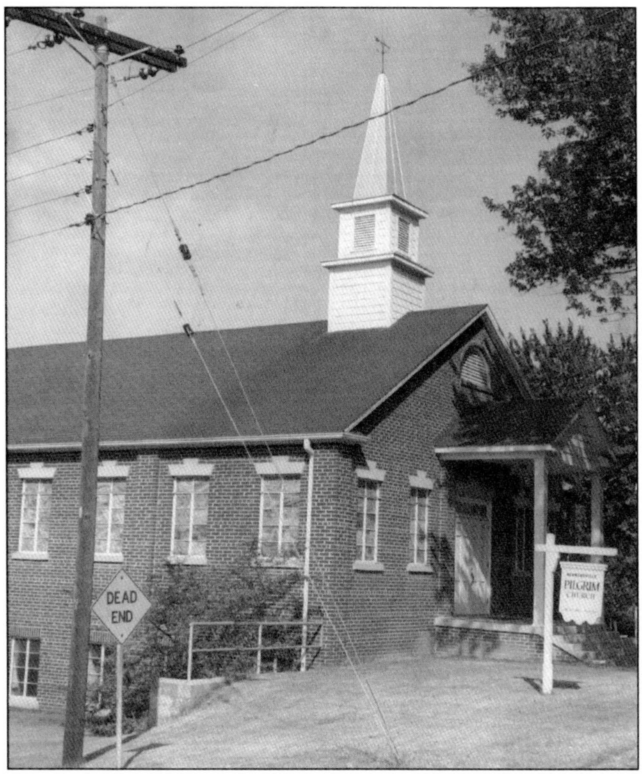

PILGRIM HOLINESS CHURCH. As a result of a 1906 revival led by Reverends Will Allred and W. A. Way, the Pilgrim Holiness Church was founded. Mrs. Louella Teague Gallimore became pastor in 1928. Years later, in 1968, the Pilgrim Holiness Church and the Wesleyan Methodist Church merged and became the Kernersville Wesleyan Church. (MRK.)

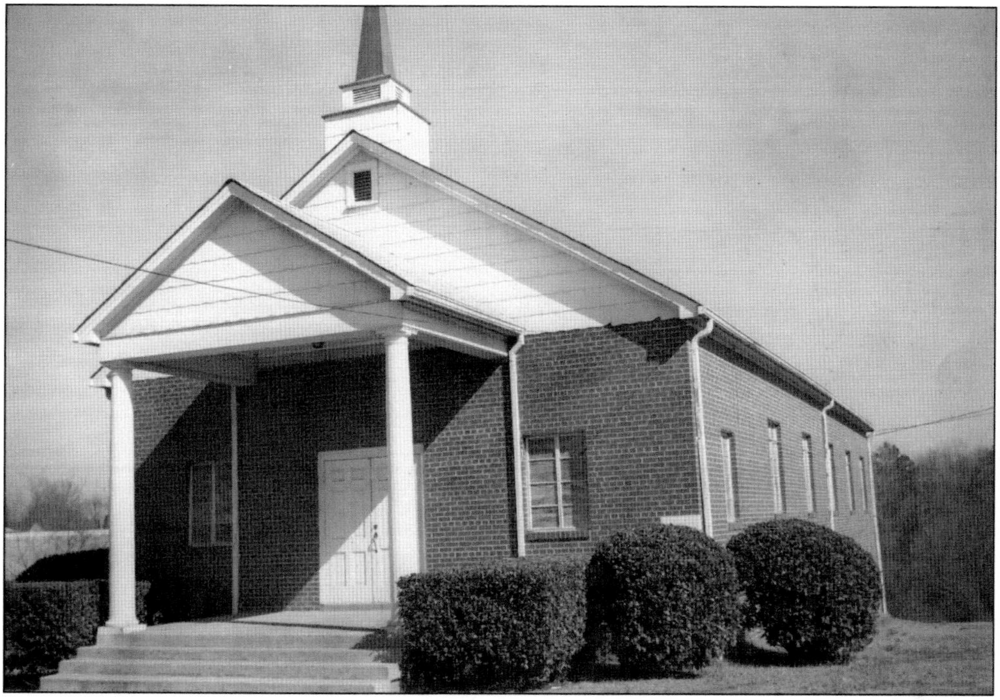

FRIENDS MEETING HOUSE. The Friends Meeting was established in 1906; the first meeting house was built in 1908. This building was constructed in 1953. (MRK.)

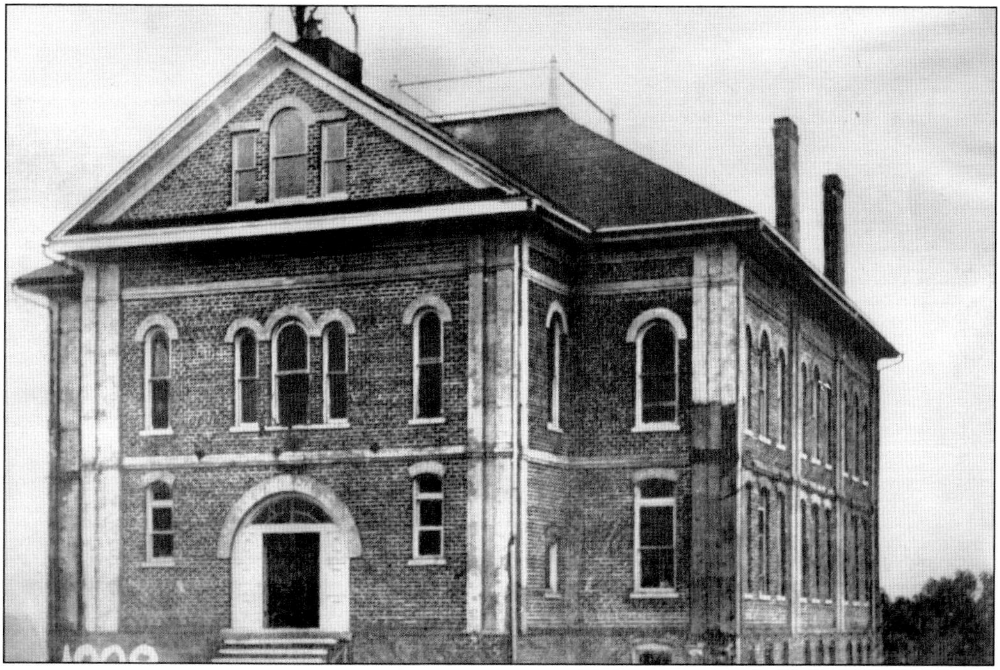

OLD KERNERSVILLE SCHOOL, C. 1906. This graded and high school was built on Mountain Street where the current Chamber of Commerce is located. It burned December 31, 1925. The first principal was the Reverend Henry Wenhold, pastor of the Kernersville Moravian Church. This photograph was taken in 1909. (BW.)

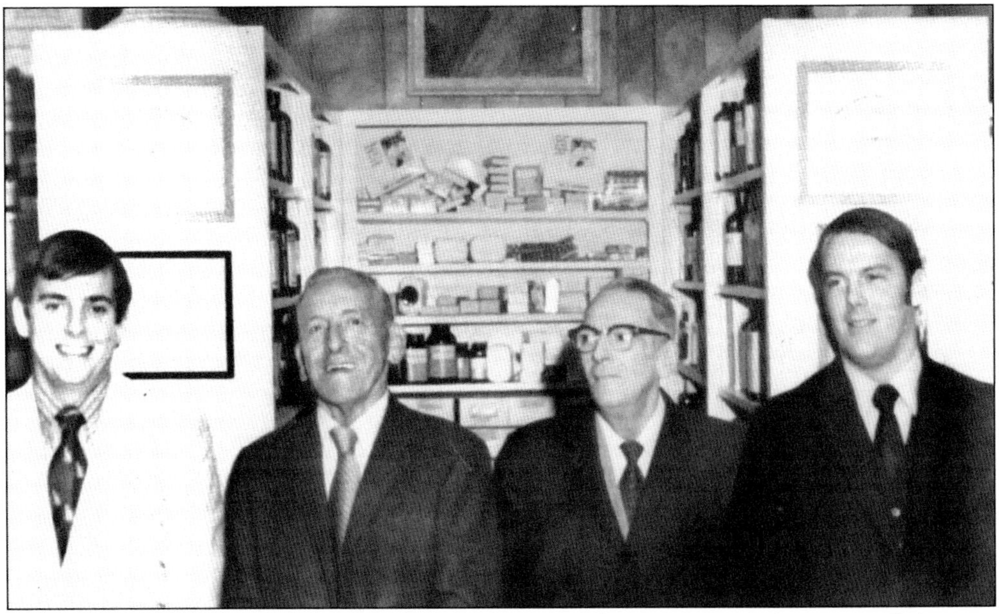

PINNIX DRUG STORE. Established "on the square" in 1904 by J. M. Pinnix, this eventually became the oldest drugstore in North Carolina under the same family ownership in the same location. The business was operated by three generations of Pinnixes. Pictured here from left to right are Joe Pinnix Jr., Joe Pinnix Sr., J. M. Pinnix Jr., and J. M. Pinnix III. (JP.)

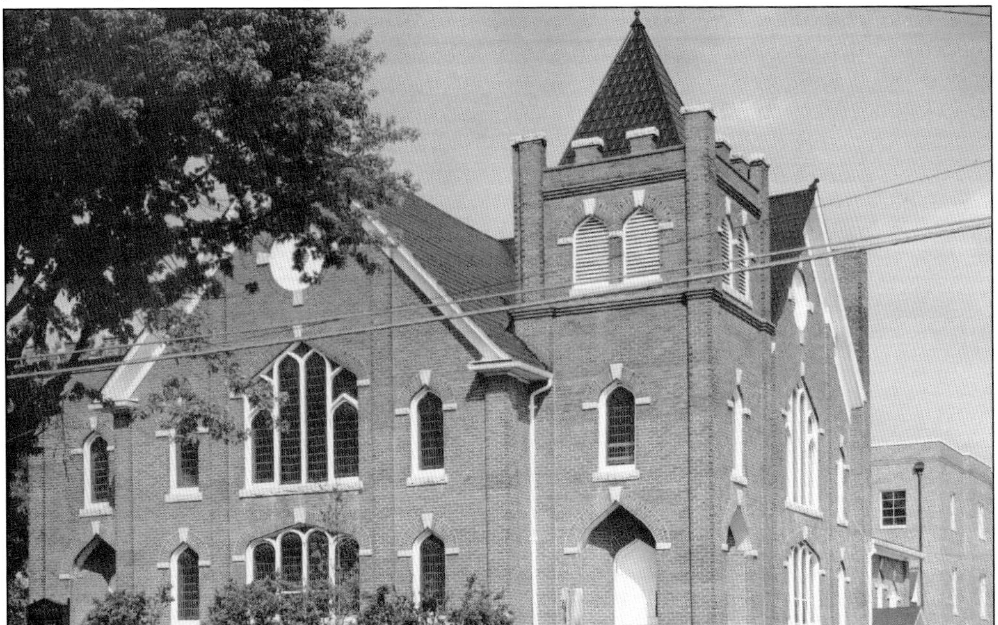

MAIN STREET BAPTIST CHURCH. This structure was originally built for First Baptist Church in 1916; members of that congregation and their pastor, Rev. T. Sloan Guy, held their first service in the new First Baptist Church sanctuary. Membership at this time had reached 128. The building was bought by Main Street Baptist Church in 1960 and continues to be occupied by that church. (MRK.)

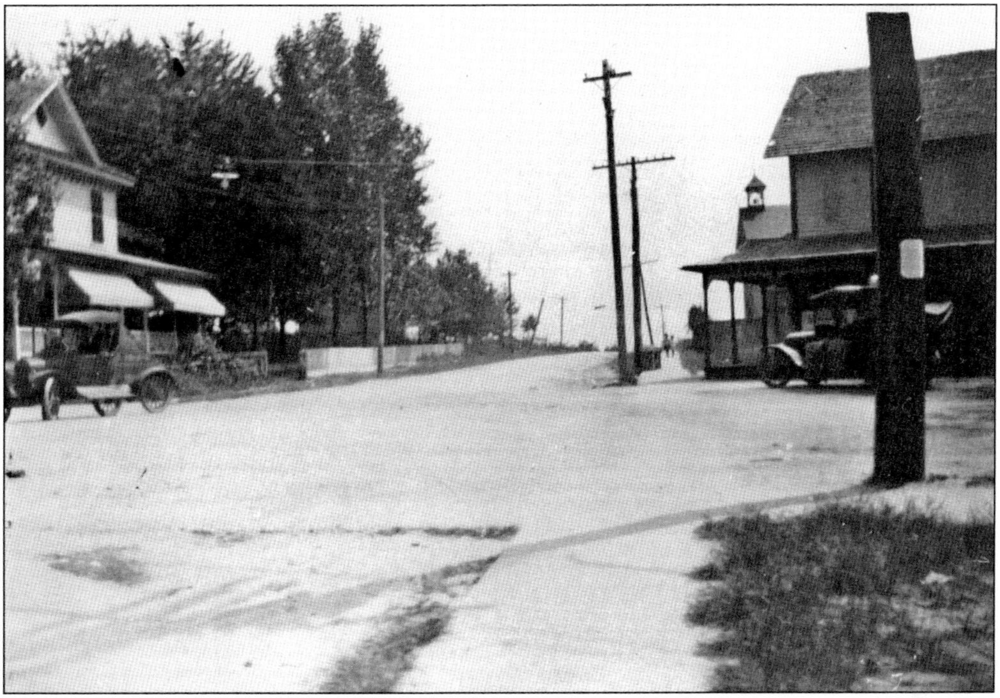

TOWN GROWTH. This photograph depicts town square looking east in 1920. On the right is the Pinnix Building with the old Academy next door. On the left is Dr. C. C. Sapp's hotel, the Auto Inn, touted as the "greatest summer and winter resort in the South." (ES.)

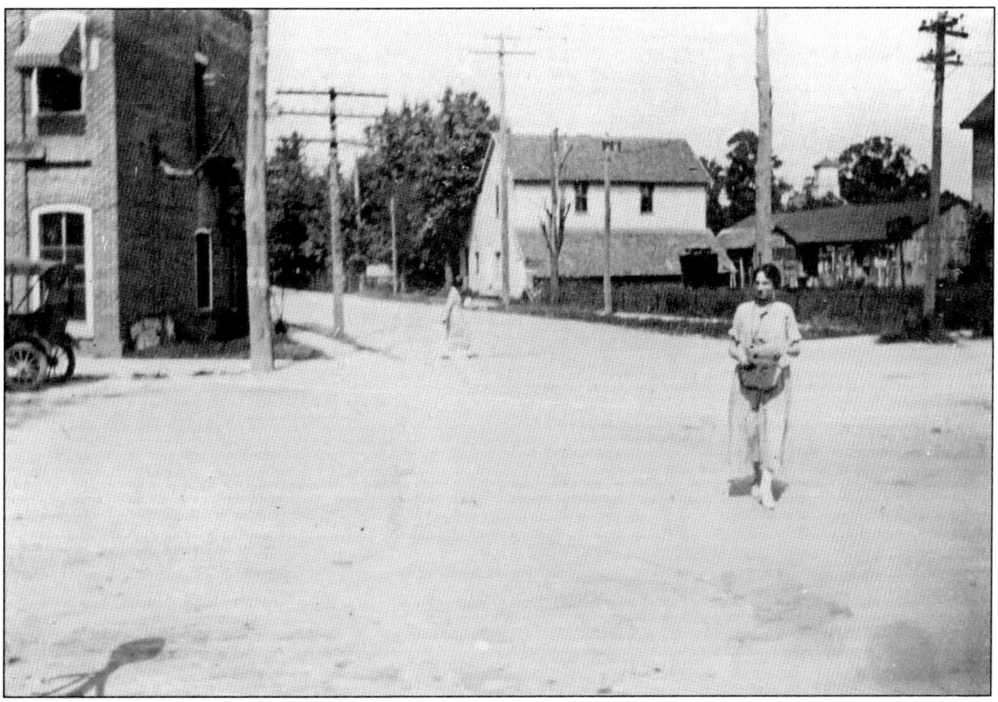

MORE EXPANSION. Another view illustrates Town Square looking west in 1920. The old bank building is on the left. Hellen Shore walks home from market with her basket filled with groceries. (ES.)

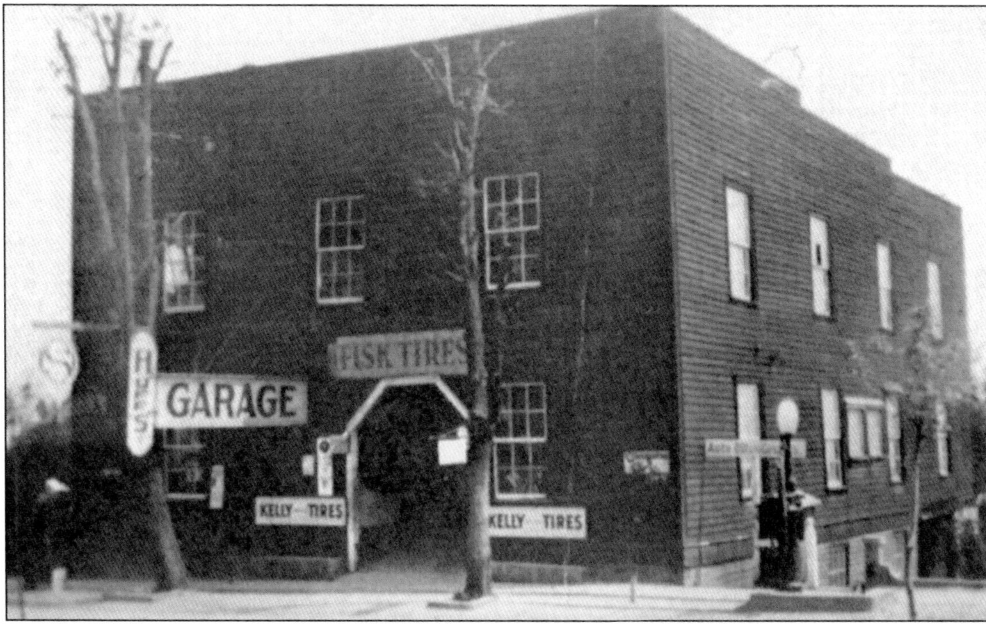

HUFF'S GARAGE. In 1922, Elias Kerner Huff's garage specialized in automobile repair and maintenance. Note the Fisk and Kelly Tire advertisements. At different periods, the building housed a tobacco factory and a hosiery mill. (KBB.)

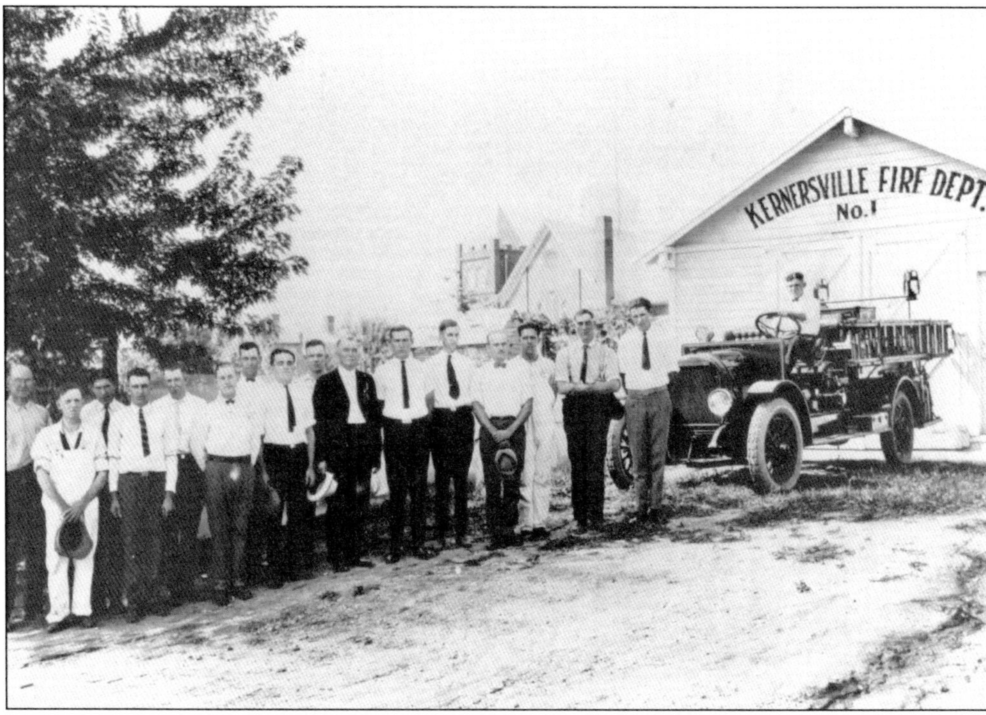

VOLUNTEER FIRE DEPARTMENT. This service was a wonderful addition to the town in 1923. The town bought its first fire truck, a 1923 LaFrance, for $6,500. Prior to this time, there was little hope in saving burning buildings because bucket brigades and water from wells were the only firefighting equipment available. (MRK.)

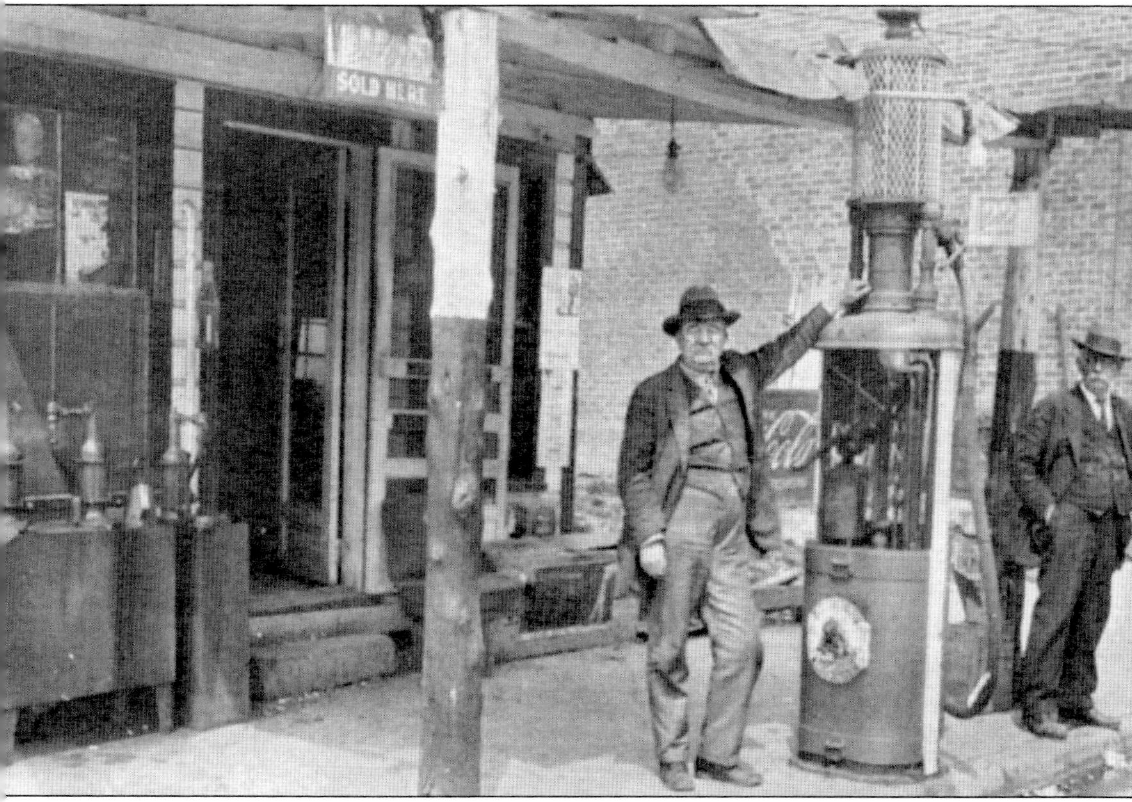

Bodenhamer Store. This business became another favorite spot for friends to gather. Mr. Jake Bodenhamer and Mr. W. C. Stafford visit together in front of the store in the 1920s. In later years, Jake's son, Grover, replaced the wooden structure with brick. (KBB.)

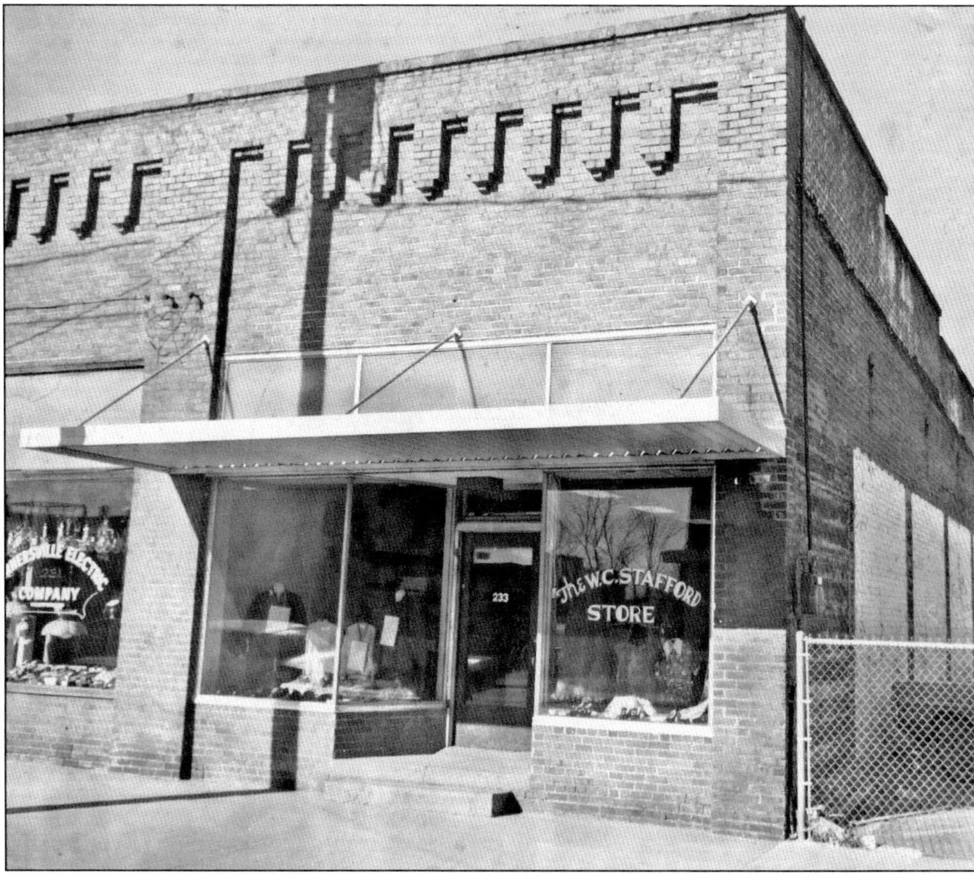

THE L. F. DAVIS & SON STORE. Originally constructed in 1885, this building was gutted by fire in 1919 but rebuilt within the same walls. Until recent years, it operated as a mercantile store under the name W. C. Stafford. (MRK.)

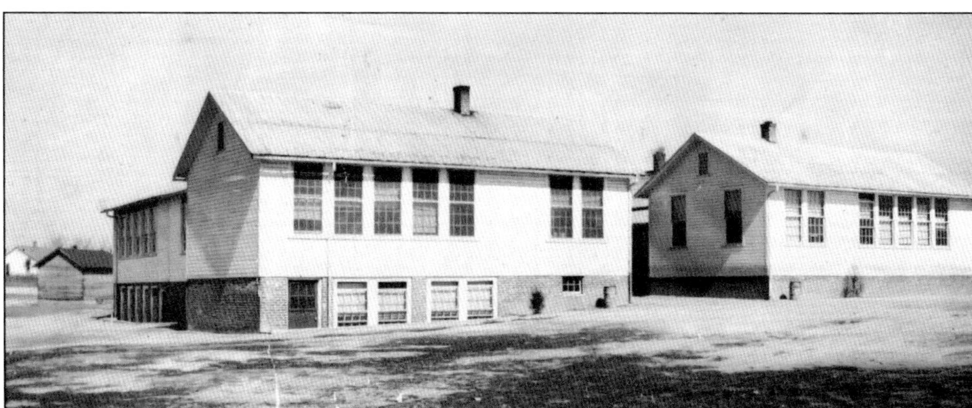

CARVER HIGH SCHOOL. During the 1936–1937 school year, two grades (eighth and ninth) were available for African American students in Forsyth County who lived outside of Winston-Salem. Additional rooms were added the next year. In 1939, Carver High graduated its first class. (SH.)

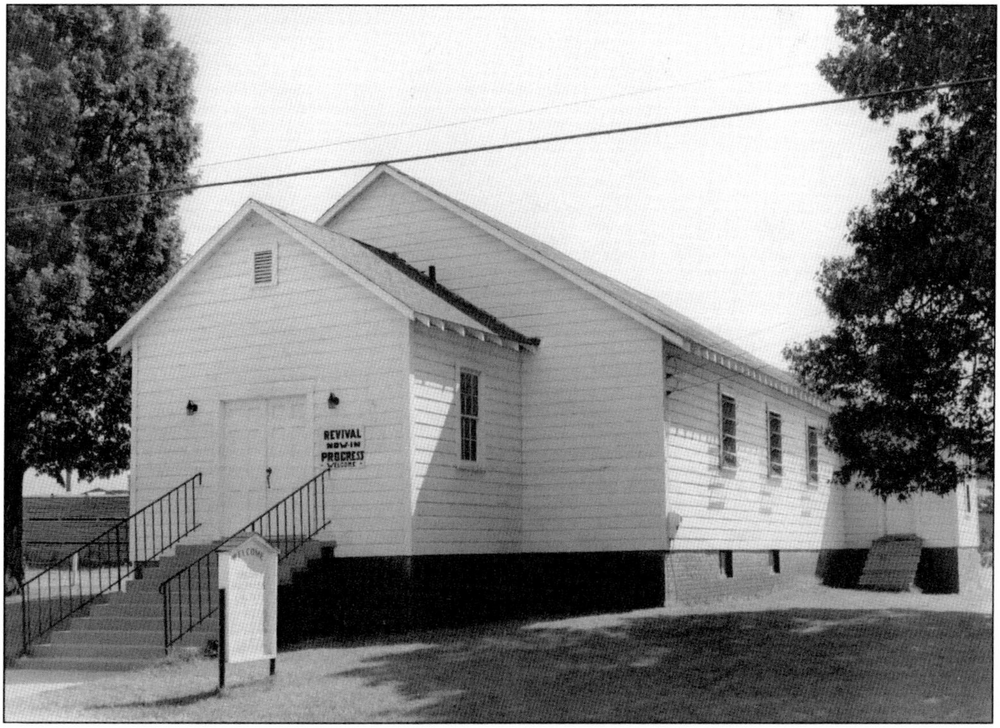

PENTECOSTAL HOLINESS CHURCH. The congregation was organized in 1945, with a church built two years later on Dobson Street. (MRK.)

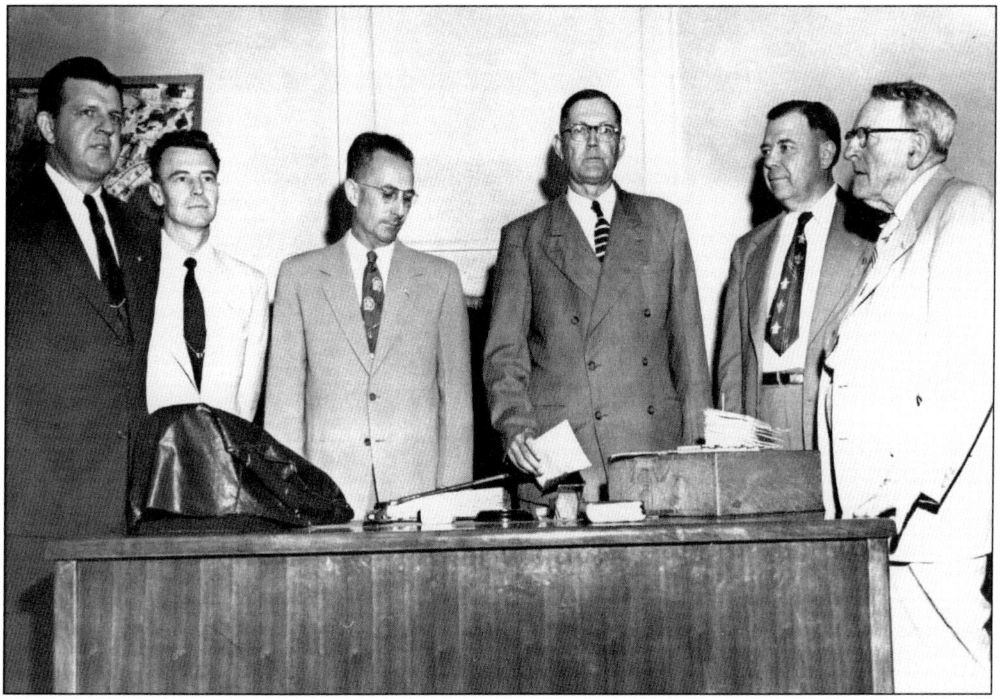

BOARD OF ALDERMEN AND MAYOR, C. 1955. From left to right are Denver Cottingham, Lee Marshall, Conrad Crutchfield, Mayor Bill Morton, D.E. Dunlap, and John M. Pinnix. (JP.)

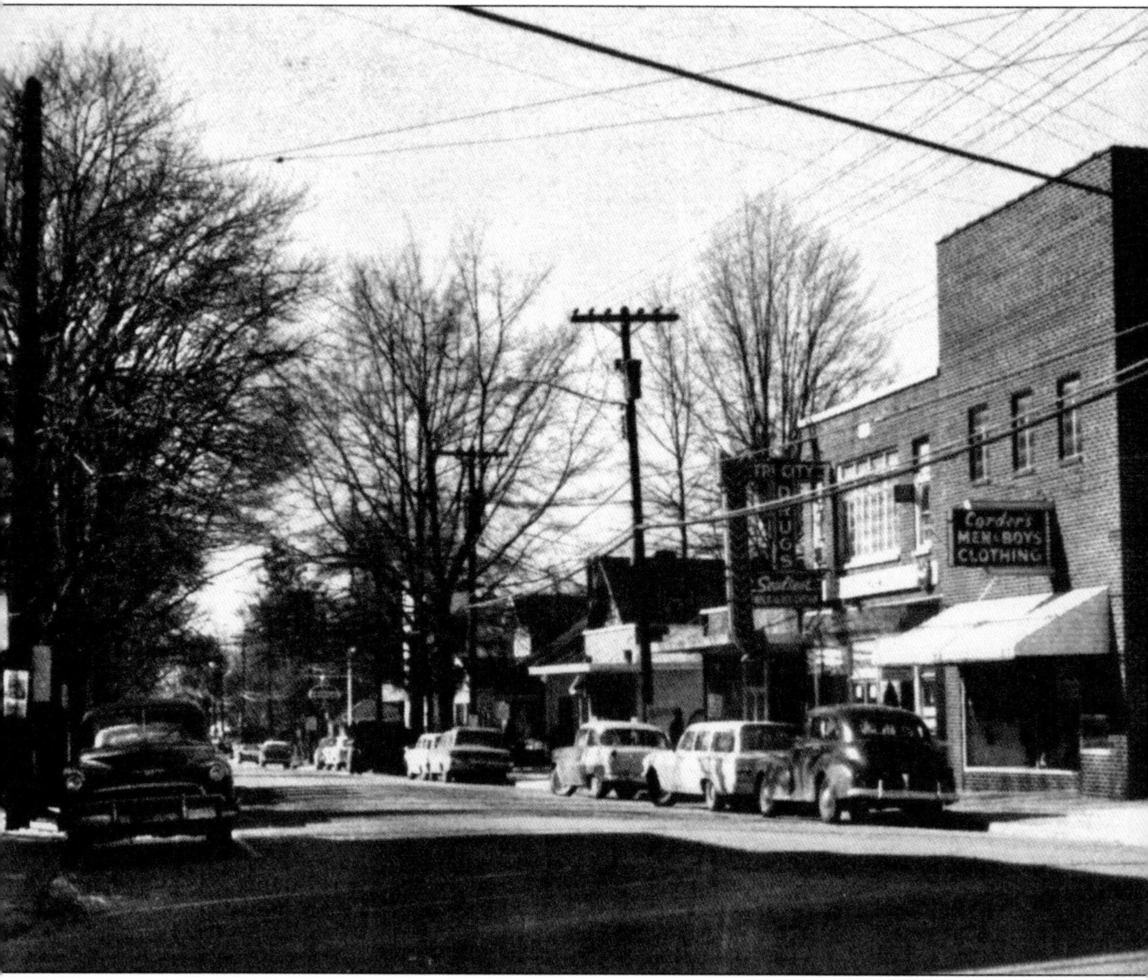

THE CROSSROADS IN THE 1950S. This photograph was taken looking south from the crossroads on Main Street. The businesses and homes shown are Corder's Men-Boys Clothing, the Hedgecock house, the Stafford house, and Kernersville *News* (on the right). In the 1950s, it was not unusual for private homes to be beside stores or shops. (BW.)

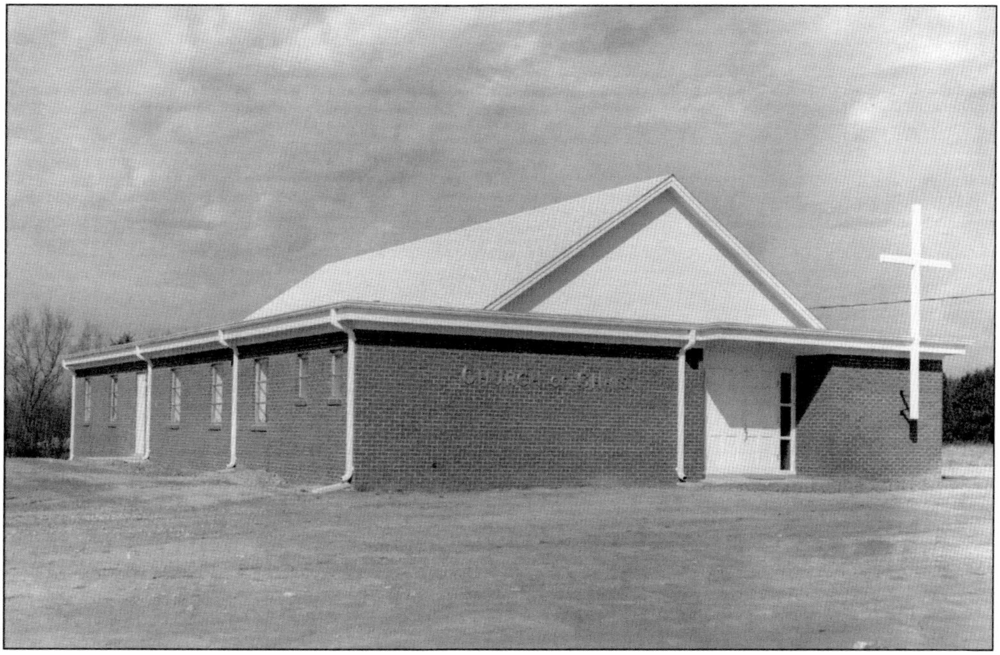

CHURCH OF CHRIST. Established in 1963, the Church of Christ is located on Salisbury Street. (MRK.)

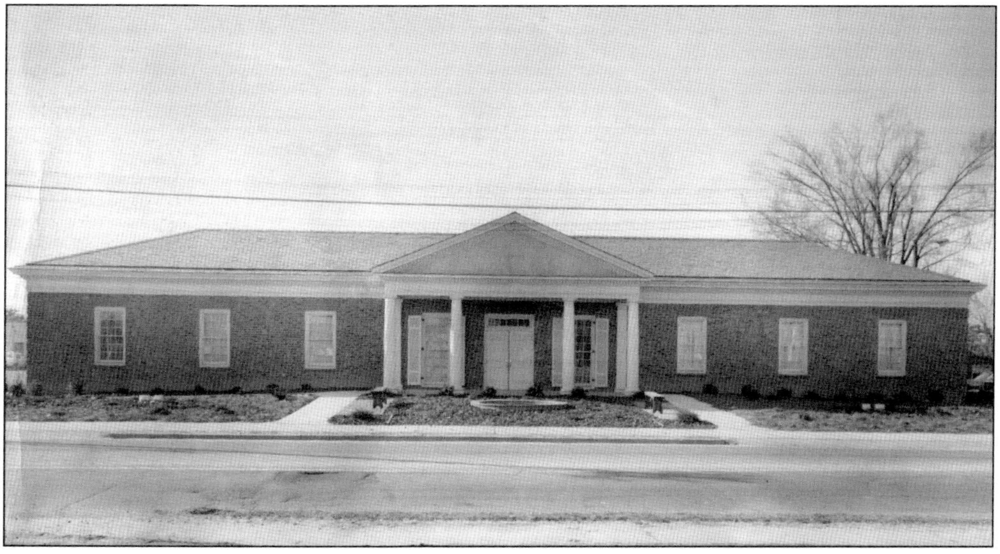

THE PADDISON MEMORIAL LIBRARY. Mrs. Zora Sapp Paddison donated the money and land to build this library in memory of her husband, Dr. John R. Paddison, beloved Kernersville physician. Constructed in traditional Georgian-style architecture, the building, dedicated in 1970, complements historic Kernersville's beautiful old homes and quaint community. (MRK.)

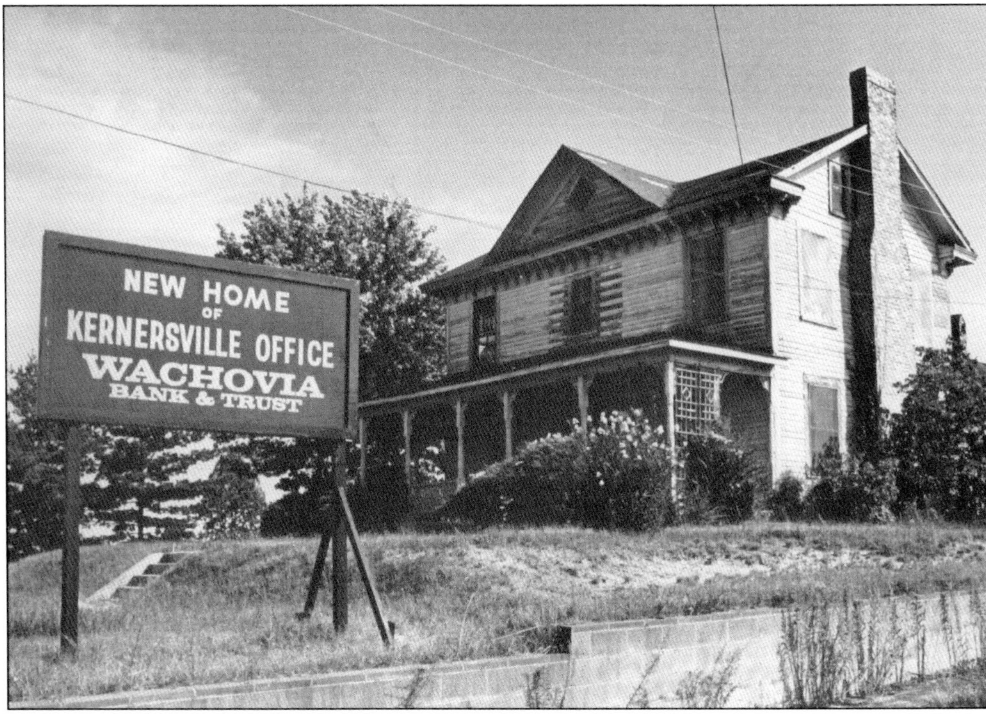

DEMOLITION. In 1966, the last part of Dobson's Tavern was demolished. This building had been moved in 1925 from its original site east on Mountain Street. (MRK.)

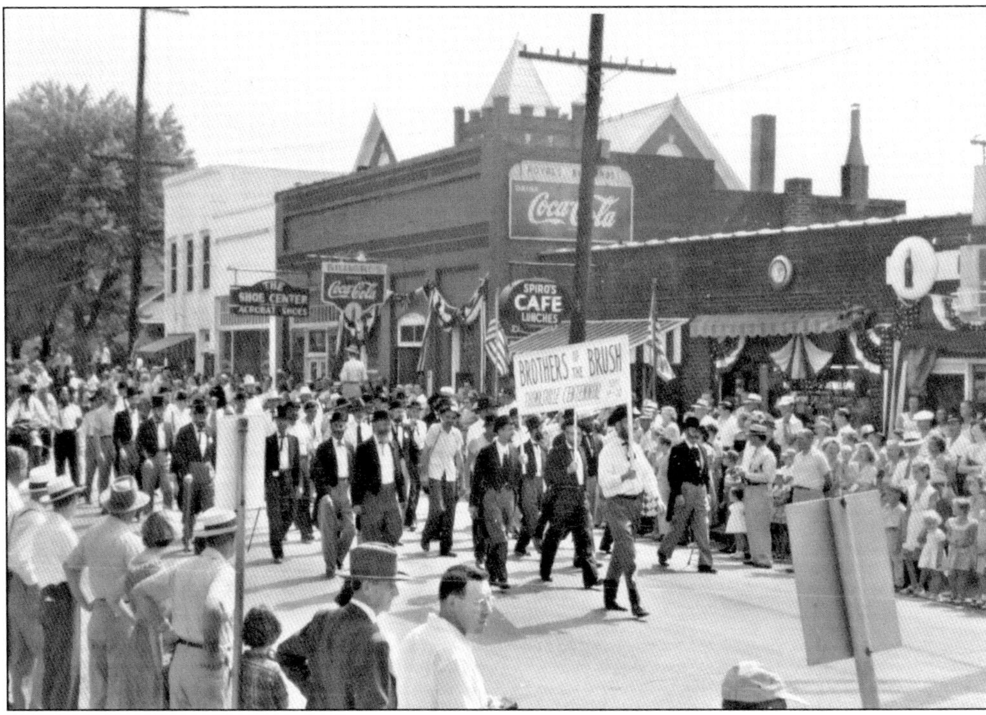

BICENTENNIAL PARADE. In 1971, residents celebrated the 200th birthday of William Dobson's purchase of Dobson's Crossroads. (MVB.)

Two

EARLY HOUSES, FAMILIES, AND ENTREPRENEURSHIPS

What did the first Kernersville homes look like? Who lived where? How were the residents related to Joseph of Kernersville? What interests and talents did these early citizens have? A unique house is an interesting architectural phenomenon, but the families who lived within made a structure their home.

Both the homes and their families have wonderful stories to tell. From little clapboard cottages to log cabins to elegant dwellings, if these walls (some 14 inches thick) could talk, they would reminisce about their different owners. From hand-hewn plank ceilings to heart-of-pine floors to bricks made from basement dirt and fired in backyard kilns, these residences were built with hard work, pride, and dedication. Men and women did not stop there. They continued to contribute their time, talents, and energy into developing a little crossroads into a charming town.

The people who lived in these earliest homes were doctors, teachers, pastors, entrepreneurs, politicians, and public servants. They tended the sick; taught the children of the community; ministered to various congregations; built stores, mills, and manufacturing companies; served as elected town officials; and engaged in public service occupations. Busy and productive, these homeowners diligently tended to every aspect of Kernersville's growth and development, and today the town is known as "The Heart of the Triad."

Some of the houses have had only a few owners. Others have seen many families. Renovations and restorations have preserved many of these stately dwellings, and today visitors are invited to enjoy a walking tour sponsored by the Kernersville Historic Preservation Society.

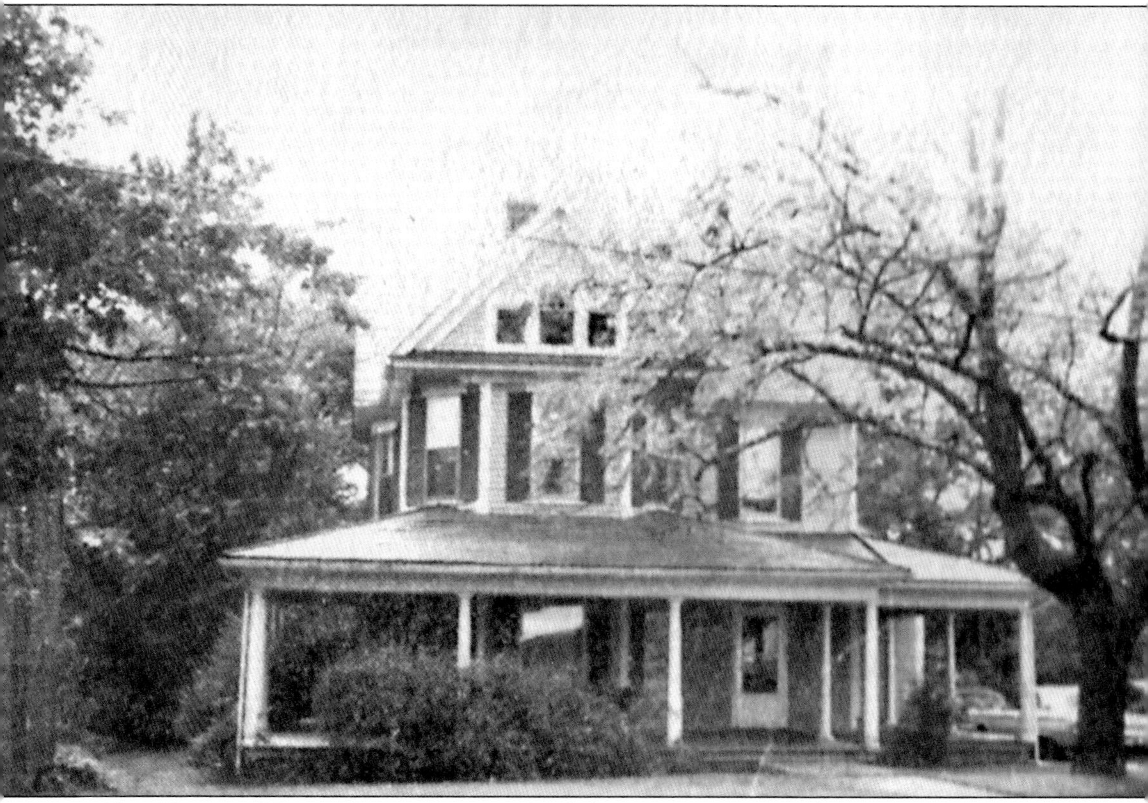

THE HARMON-VANCE HOUSE, C. 1900. Built by D. W. Harmon and lived in for many years by the Fred Vance family, this Queen Anne–Colonial revival style house stood at 117 West Mountain Street until its demolition to make room for town parking.

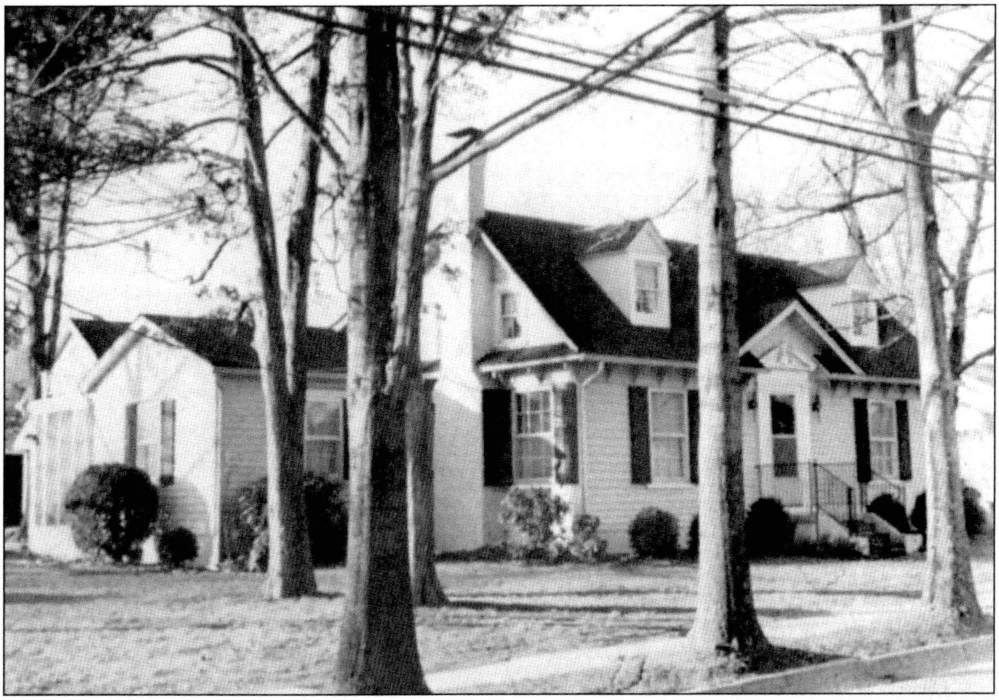

THE HESTER-VANCE HOUSE, ALSO KNOWN AS THE SAM F. VANCE HOUSE. This 412 Salisbury Street house was built in 1834 on what was originally part of the property that Joseph J. Körner bought from John Jester. It features hand-hewn wide plank ceilings in the two front rooms. Mr. and Mrs. Sam Vance bought and remodeled the house in 1942. (MVB.)

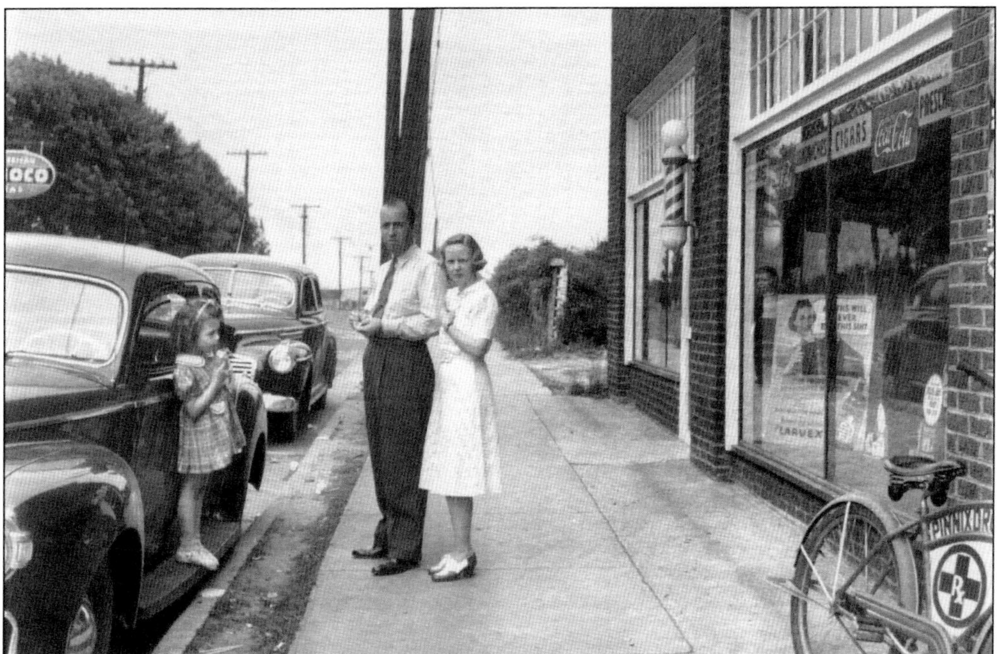

FRED AND ILA VANCE. In this 1940s shot, Fred and Ila Vance pose on East Mountain Street beside Pinnix Drug Store. Notice the drug store delivery bicycle. The little girl is unidentified. (SC.)

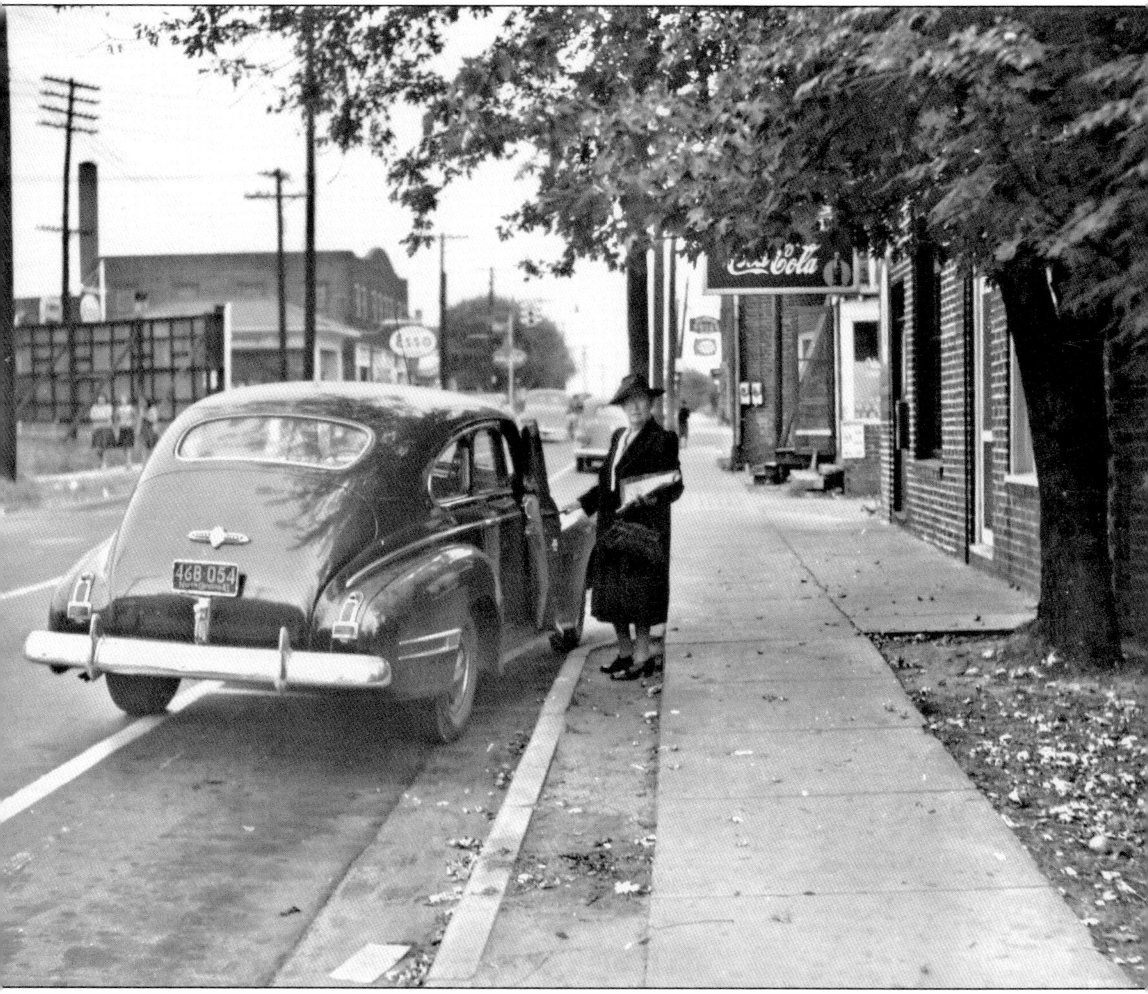

GRANDMOTHER VANCE. Respected Kernersville citizen Sallie Fulton Vance, known to many as "Grandmother Vance," gets in a car in front of the Vance house—no longer standing—on Main Street. Her two-story home had a wraparound porch where family and friends gathered to chat in the white rocking chairs or on the porch swing. A huge walnut tree shaded the residence. (MVB.)

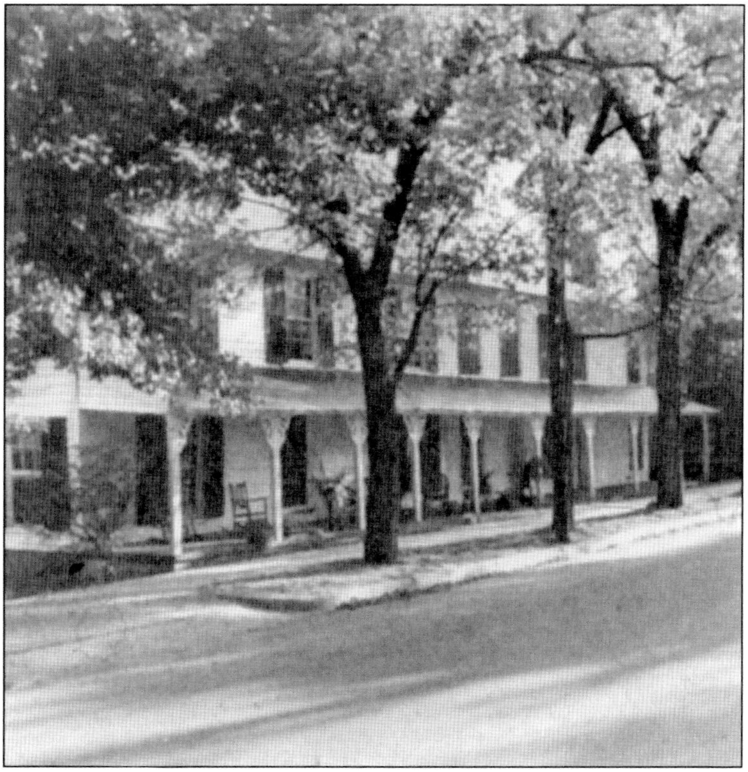

THE LEAK HOUSE, C. 1840. One of the oldest structures in town, this long, low, white brick and frame house on South Main Street was once a combination store and residence. When P. J. Nash resided here, he had a printing company in a portion of the house. The log structure beneath the siding of this home dates back to 1840. Original logs are exposed in the attic room. Ivy around the house came from Mount Vernon in 1921. (KBB.)

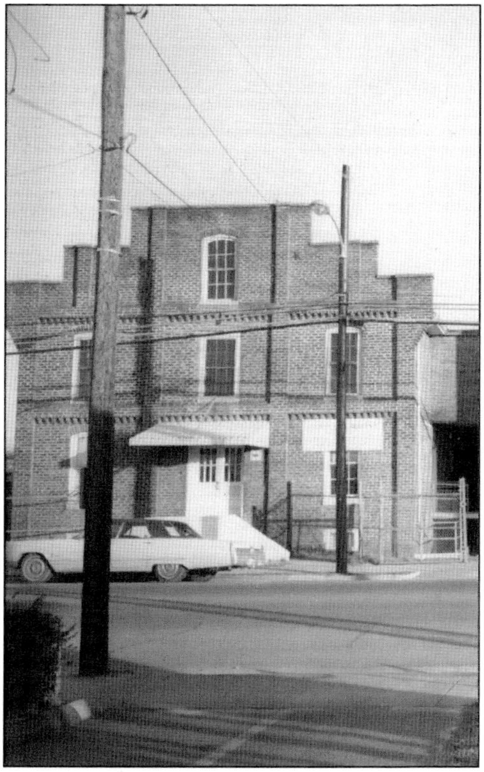

LEAK TOBACCO COMPANY. This building was originally the W. H. Leak and Company Tobacco Factory of 1884. It was later converted into a knitting mill and eventually bought by Hooker Furniture Corporation as a manufacturing plant. (MRK.)

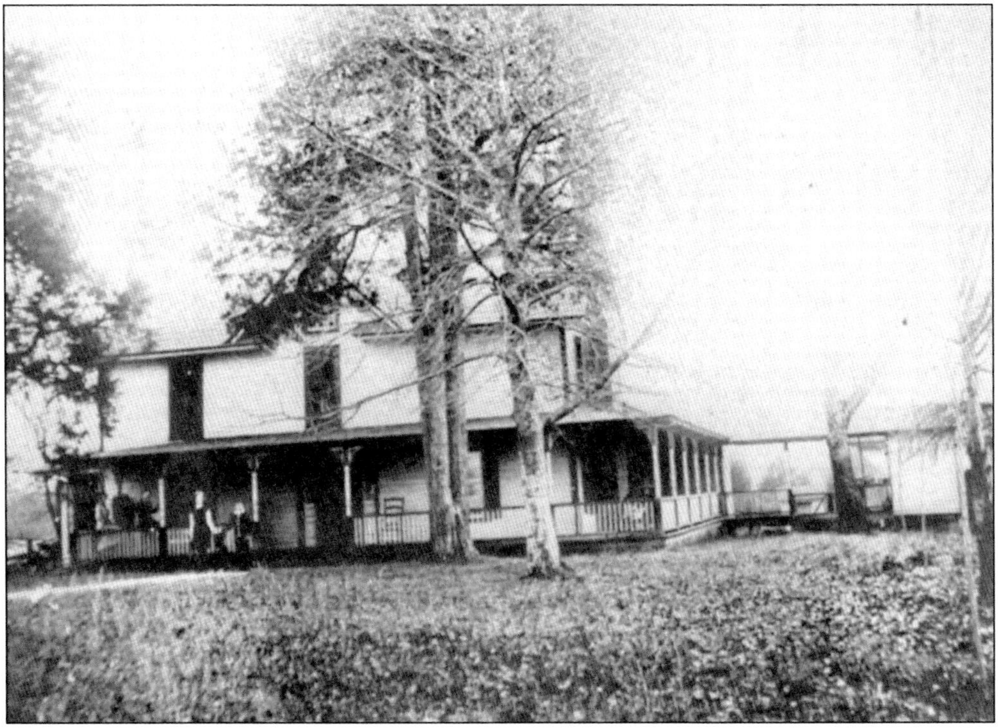

THE FRANCIS MARION STAFFORD HOUSE, C. 1840. This home was originally a two-story log cabin. In 1856, Francis Stafford added a living room and a bedroom. William Cornelius Stafford bought the house from his father's estate and turned the front stairs around. Some of the log walls are originals, as are the floors and beaded ceilings. Sallie Greenfield, the great-granddaughter of Francis Marion Stafford, moved and restored the house in 1987–1988. (KBB.)

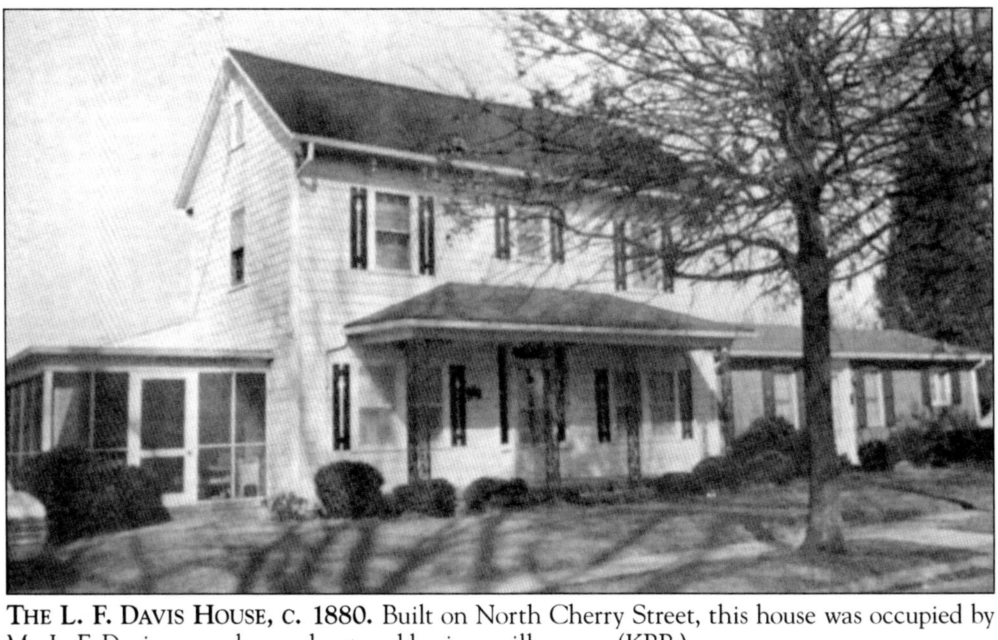

THE L. F. DAVIS HOUSE, C. 1880. Built on North Cherry Street, this house was occupied by Mr. L. F. Davis, an early merchant and hosiery mill owner. (KBB.)

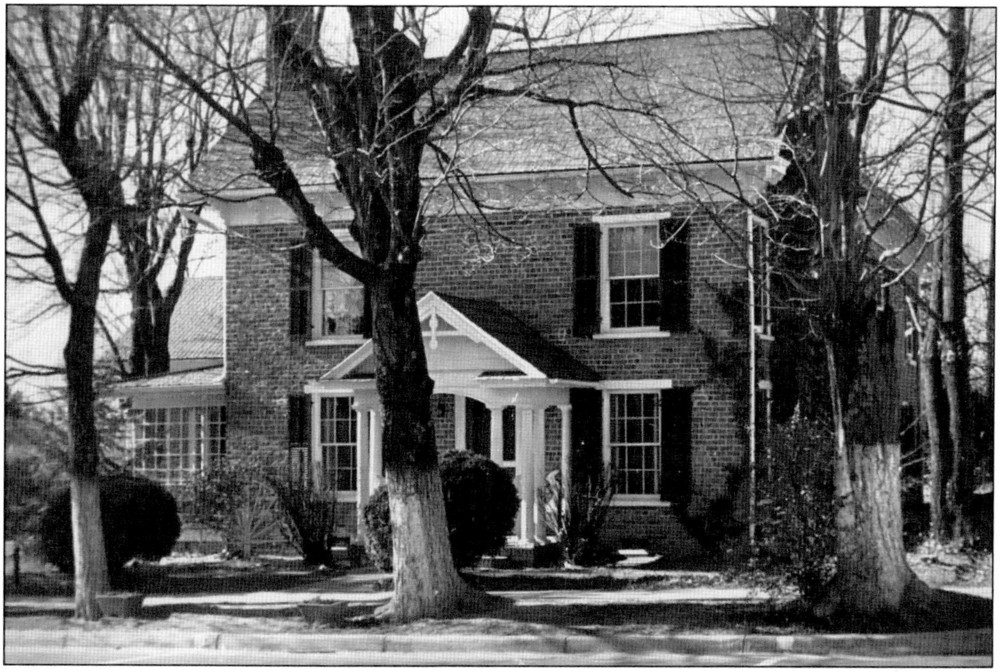

THE NATHANIEL MACON KERNER HOUSE, 1857. Made with common bond brick from local clay, this two-story Greek Revival residence on Main Street stands on part of the original Joseph Kerner estate. Nathaniel, grandson of "Joseph of Kernersville," took his bride, Martha Stockton, to live here in October 1857. Only three families have lived in the house including present residents Mr. and Mrs. John Wolfe III—all Körner/Kerners. (BW.)

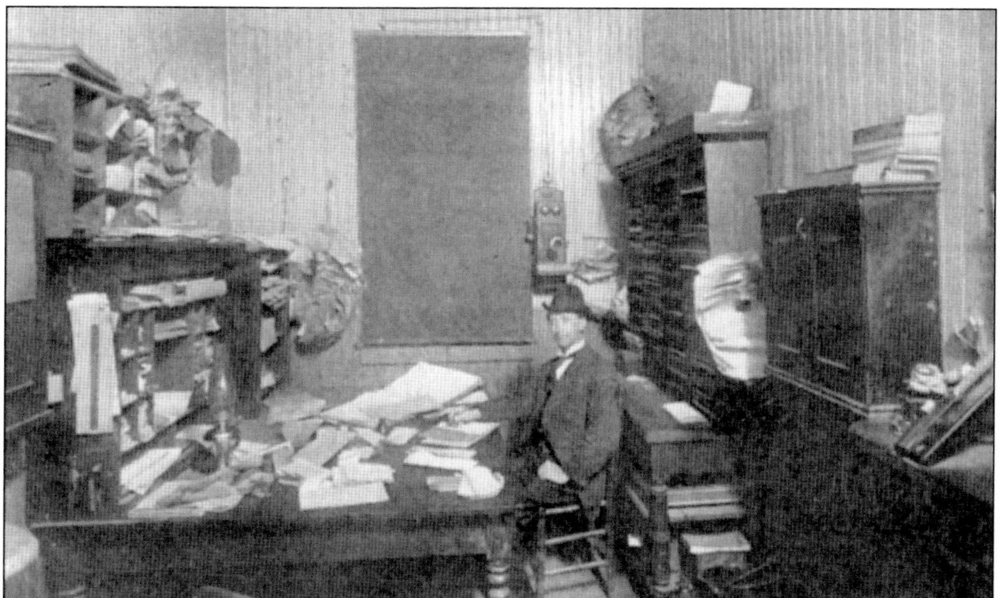

CARL R. KERNER. Son of Nathaniel Macon Kerner and grandson of John Frederick Kerner, Carl was born in the Nathaniel Macon Kerner house. Carl followed Richard P. Kerner as railroad agent until his retirement. (KBB.)

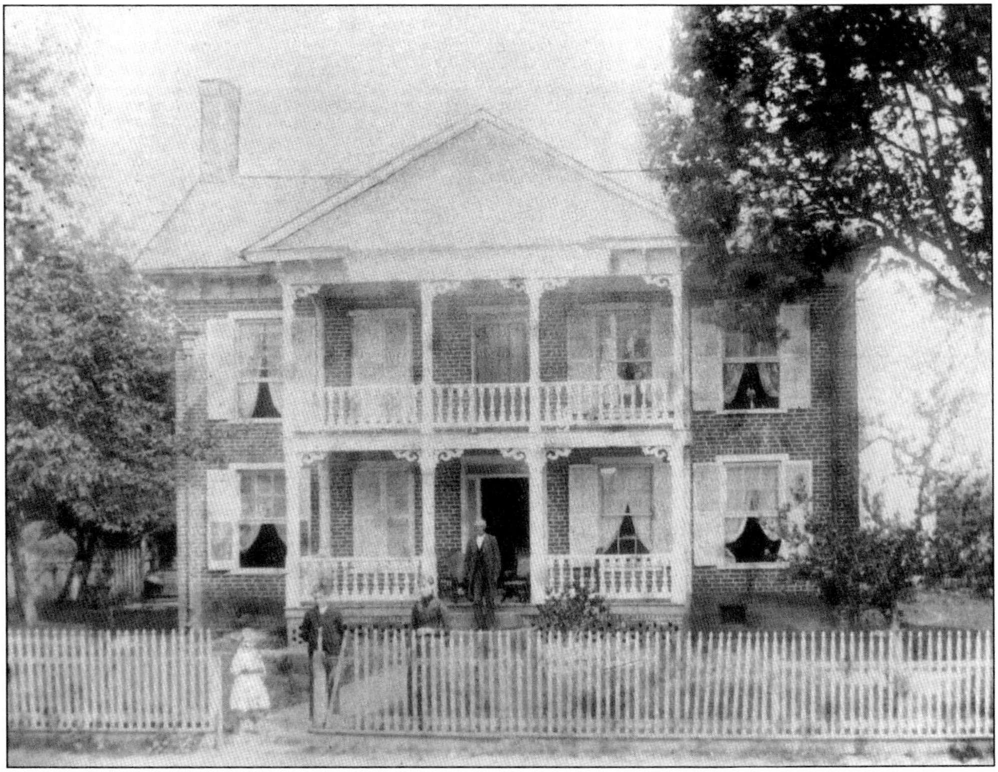

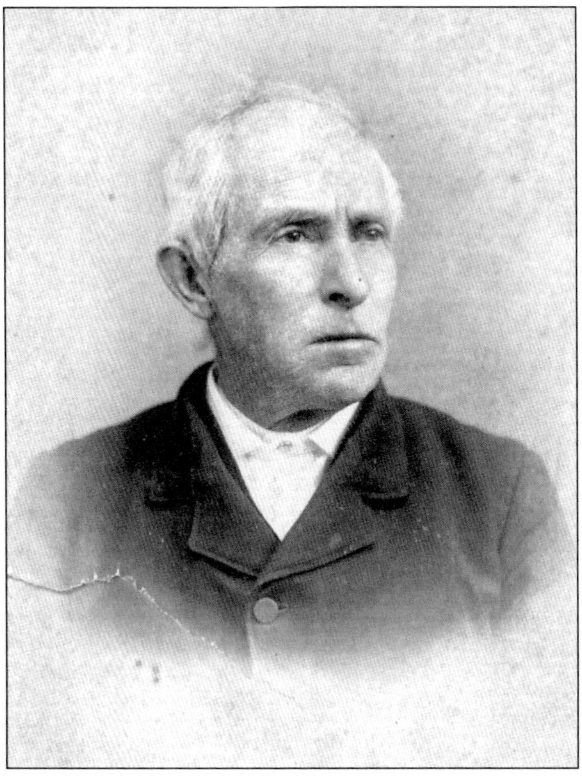

THE DR. ELIAS KERNER HOUSE, 1857. This house was built among oak and magnolia trees on South Main Street. The bricks were manufactured in a kiln located in a nearby hollow. Timber on the property provided necessary wood. Dr. Kerner stands on the porch while his grandchildren play in the yard. A multi-talented individual, Dr. Kerner actively involved himself in church affairs, operated a water power mill, and manufactured brick. (ES.)

DR. ELIAS KERNER. Dr. Elias Kerner, son of John Frederick and third generation of Joseph Kerner, was Kernersville's first full-time doctor. In the 1880s, he, J. Calvin Roberts, and W. C. Stafford went to Raleigh to petition Kernersville as a county seat. The request was denied. Dr. Kerner served as a member of Kernersville's first board of aldermen and then became fifth mayor of the town. (ES.)

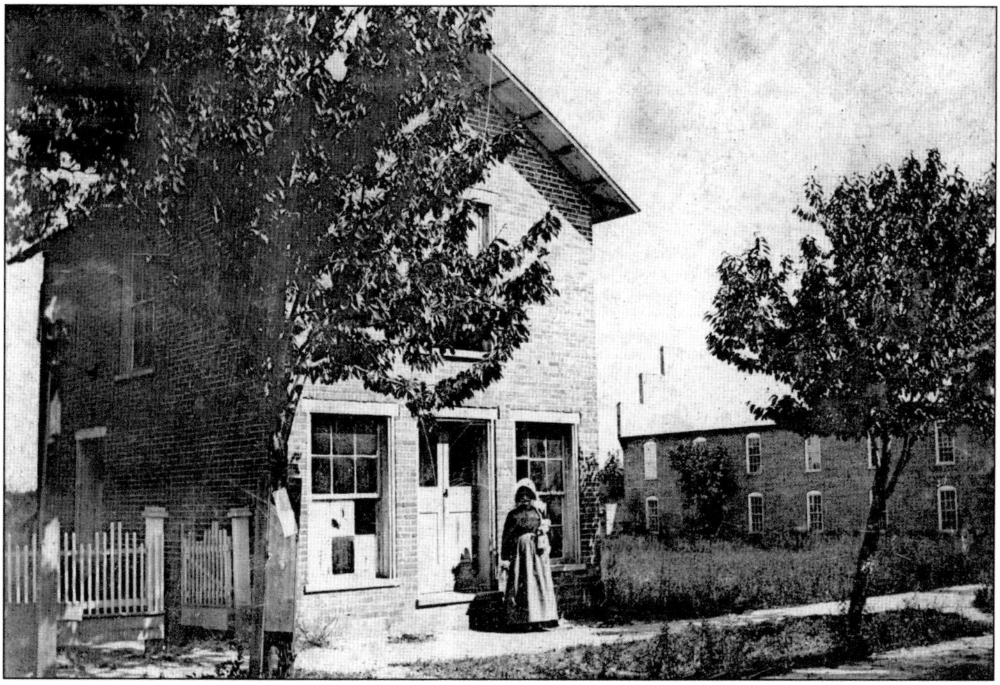

DR. ELIAS KERNER'S OFFICE. A separate building in the side yard housed the doctor's medical office. Cherry trees lined the sidewalk. This photograph, taken about 1909, shows a tobacco factory on the right. (ES.)

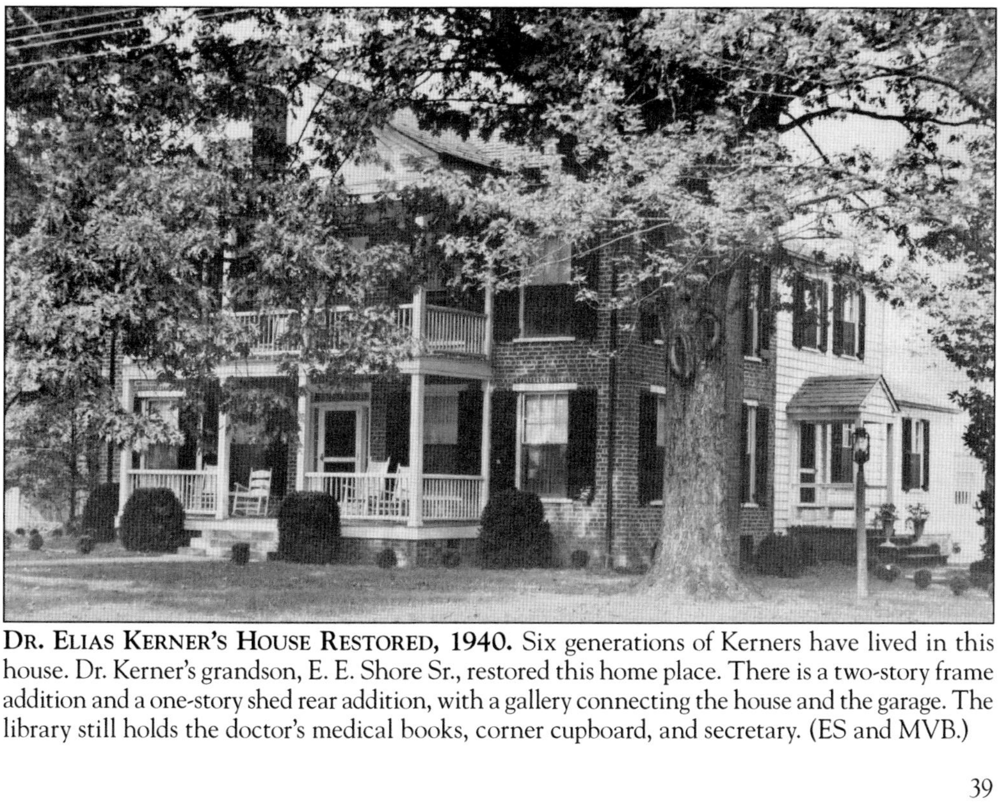

DR. ELIAS KERNER'S HOUSE RESTORED, 1940. Six generations of Kerners have lived in this house. Dr. Kerner's grandson, E. E. Shore Sr., restored this home place. There is a two-story frame addition and a one-story shed rear addition, with a gallery connecting the house and the garage. The library still holds the doctor's medical books, corner cupboard, and secretary. (ES and MVB.)

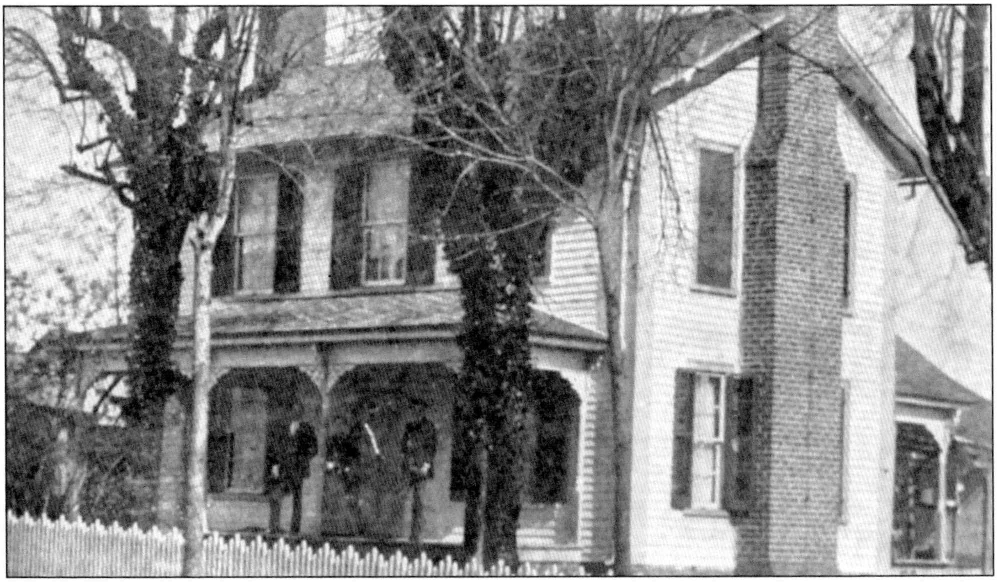

The Julius S. Harmon House, 1858. Julius S. Harmon and his wife, Marie Antoinette Körner, both third-generation descendants of Joseph Kerner, lived in this South Main Street house. Fine boxwoods and a rose garden enhanced its beauty. Julius was a millwright, farmer, carpenter, builder, and gristmill operator. (MRK and ES.)

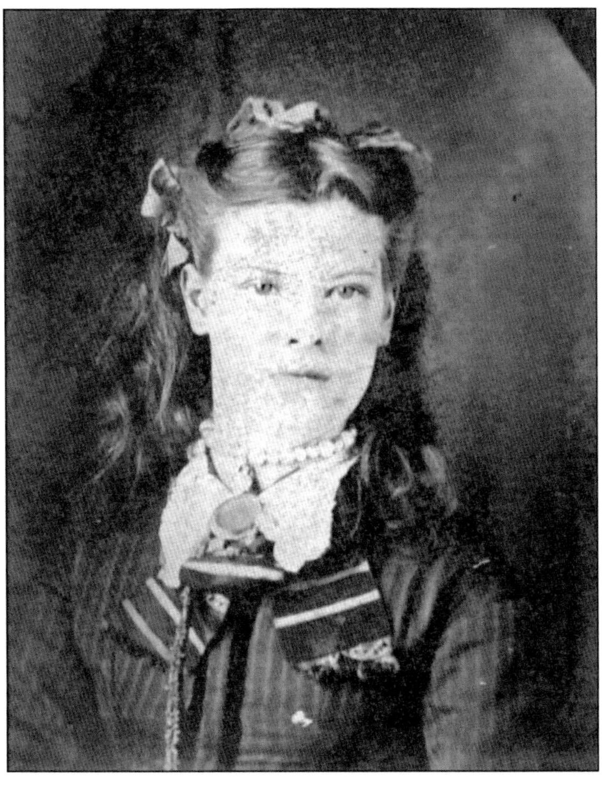

Cora Harmon. Pictured here is Cora Harmon (1857–1873), daughter of Julius and Marie Antoinette Harmon. (JW.)

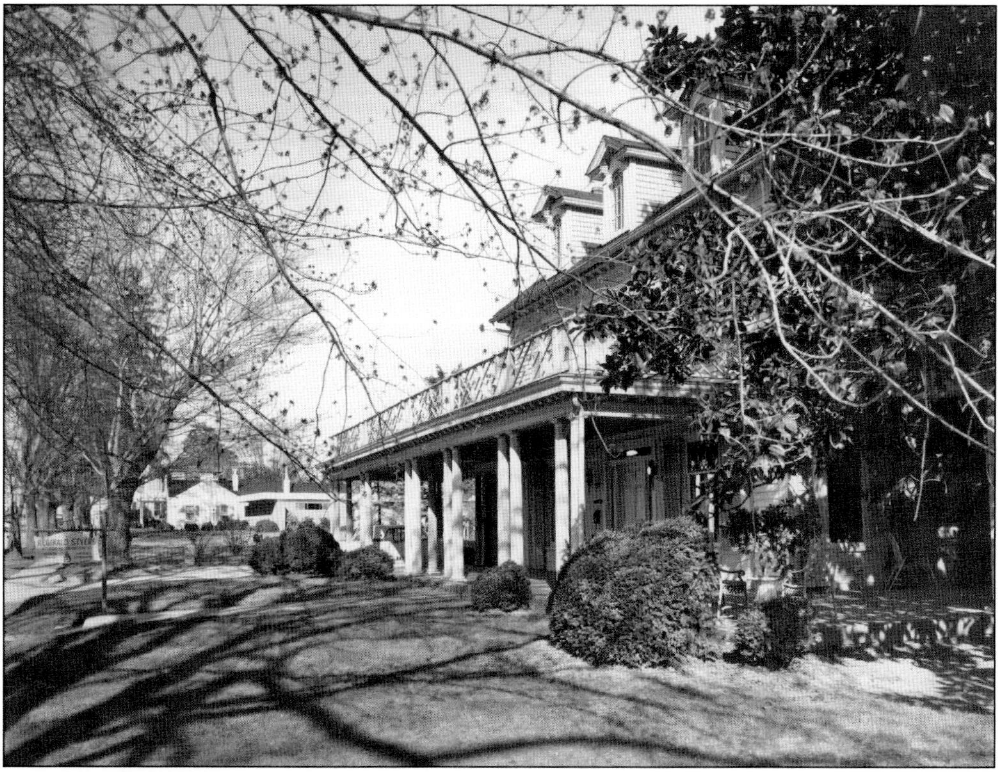

Julius S. Harmon House Remodeled. Julius's son DeWitt Harmon remodeled the Julius Harmon house in the 1890s and again in the late 1920s to resemble the Colonial Revival style. DeWitt, who was a professional surveyor, also served as town clerk, a Forsyth County commissioner, and county engineer. This house has served as private home, antique shop, interior decorating office, and herb shop. (KBB.)

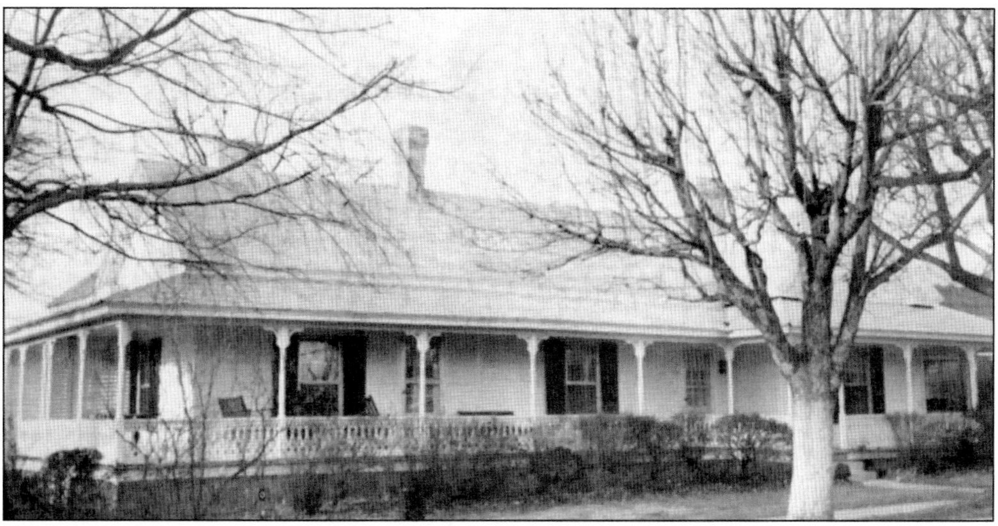

The Robah Kerner House, 1886. This South Cherry Street house was built by Gid F. Kerner, great-grandson of Joseph. In 1922, Robah Kerner remodeled the family home. (KBB.)

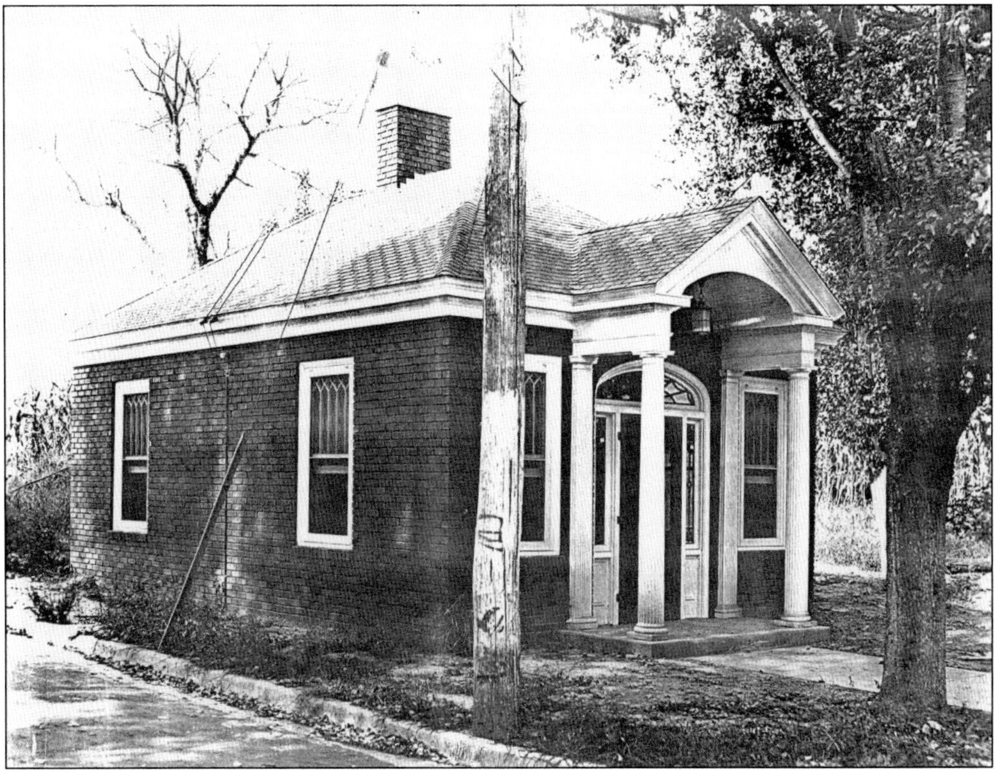

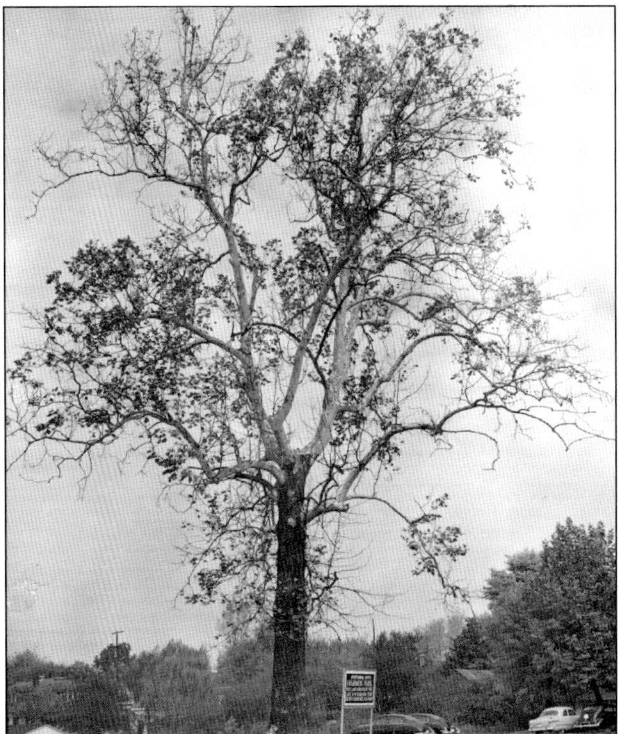

D. W. HARMON OFFICE. In the late 1920s, DeWitt Harmon built a two-room brick Neoclassical Revival office. This small building has, through the years, served as a town hall, library, license bureau, and Kernersville Historic Preservation Society office. Currently the office houses Little Theatre headquarters. (MRK.)

FUTURE HARMON PARK, 1950. The land for Harmon Park was given by DeWitt Harmon, son of Julius and Marie Antoinette Kerner Harmon. His office still stands on the corner of the park. (MRK.)

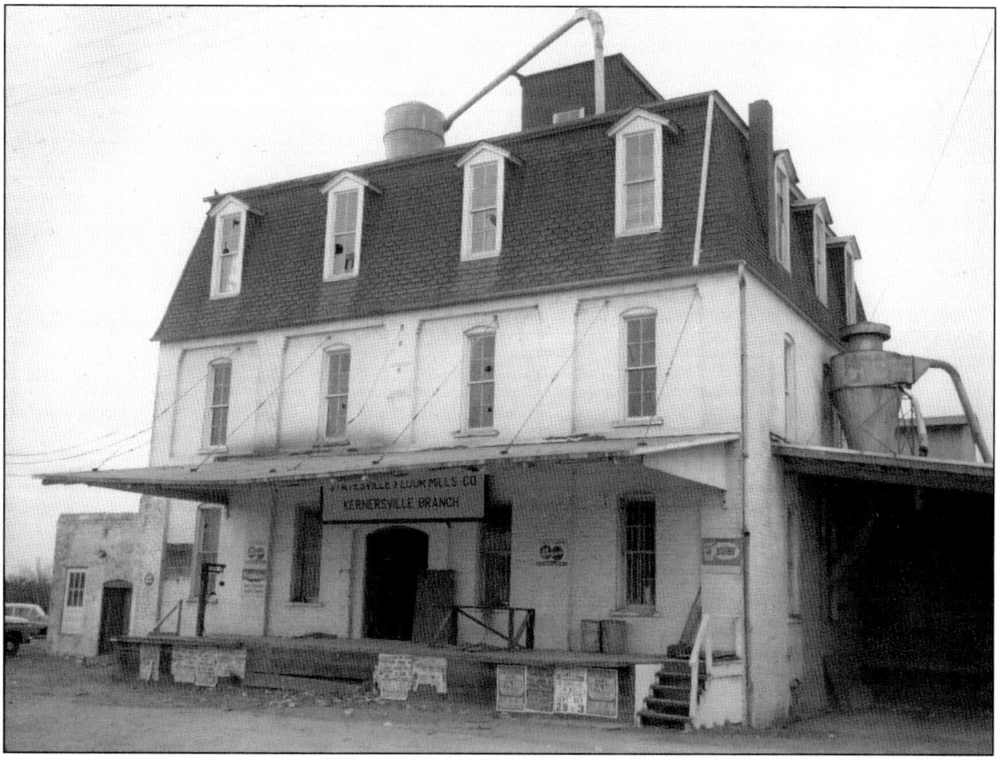

HARMON AND REID MILL, 1897. Located on Bodenhamer Street, the Harmon and Reid Mill was built by D. W. Harmon and John Reid. In recent years, it has been restored and occupied by Caudill Electric Company. (MRK and MVB.)

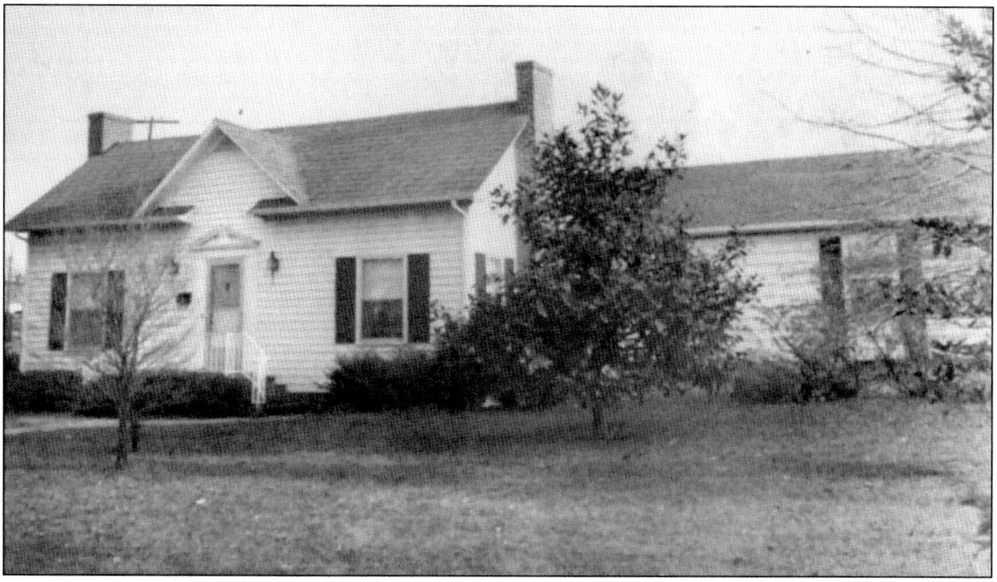

THE RUFUS HARMON HOUSE, C. 1860S. Rufus Harmon, grandson of "Joseph of Kernersville," originally built this residence on the east side of Main Street. Rufus was a coach maker, and he and his brother Julius also owned two water-powered mills called "The Big Mill" and "The Little Mill." (KBB.)

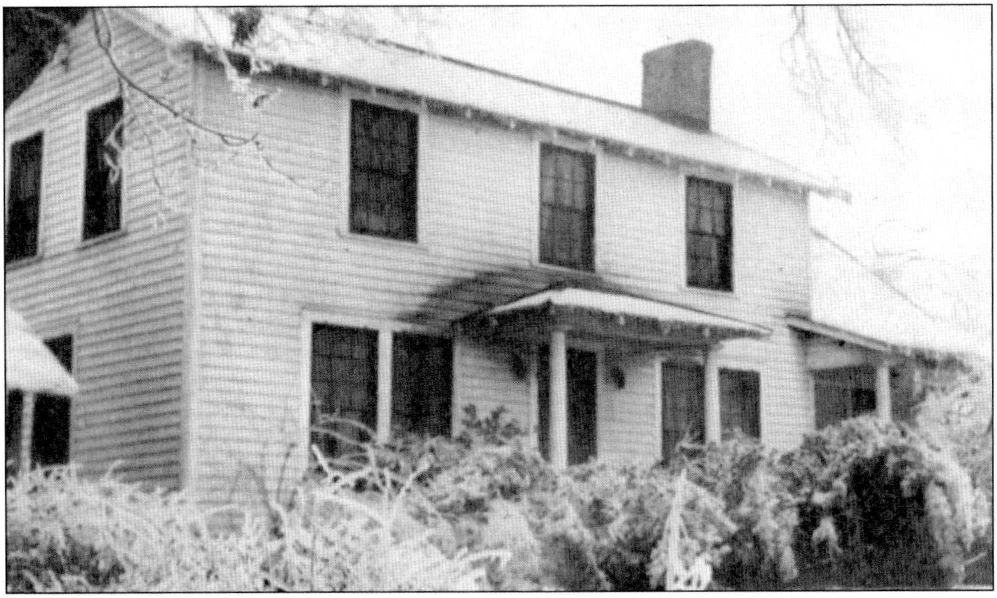

THE GENTRY-GREENFIELD HOUSE, C. 1861. John W. Gentry built this house in the 1860s for himself and his wife, Parmelia Kerner Gentry, daughter of John Frederick Kerner. Gentry, a local merchant, sold the property to John Mabry Greenfield, who came to Kernersville to engage in the tobacco business with his brother-in-law, Theodore E. Kerner. In 1881, the house was remodeled in the Colonial Revival style, and in 1987, it was moved from its original site to South Main Street. (KBB.)

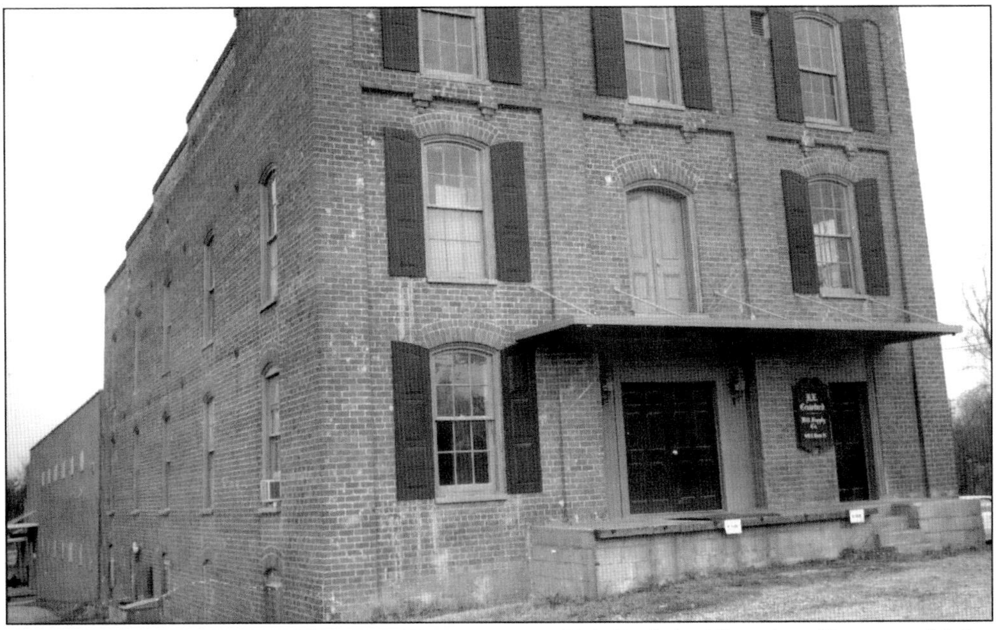

KERNER AND GREENFIELD TOBACCO FACTORY, C. 1884. Built by Theodore Kerner and John Greenfield, this is the oldest remaining tobacco factory building in Forsyth County. In the 1880s, tobacco was the principal manufacturing industry in Kernersville with its prime product being plug tobacco. The structure was later converted into a hosiery mill, and in 1986, it became three luxury condominiums. (ES.)

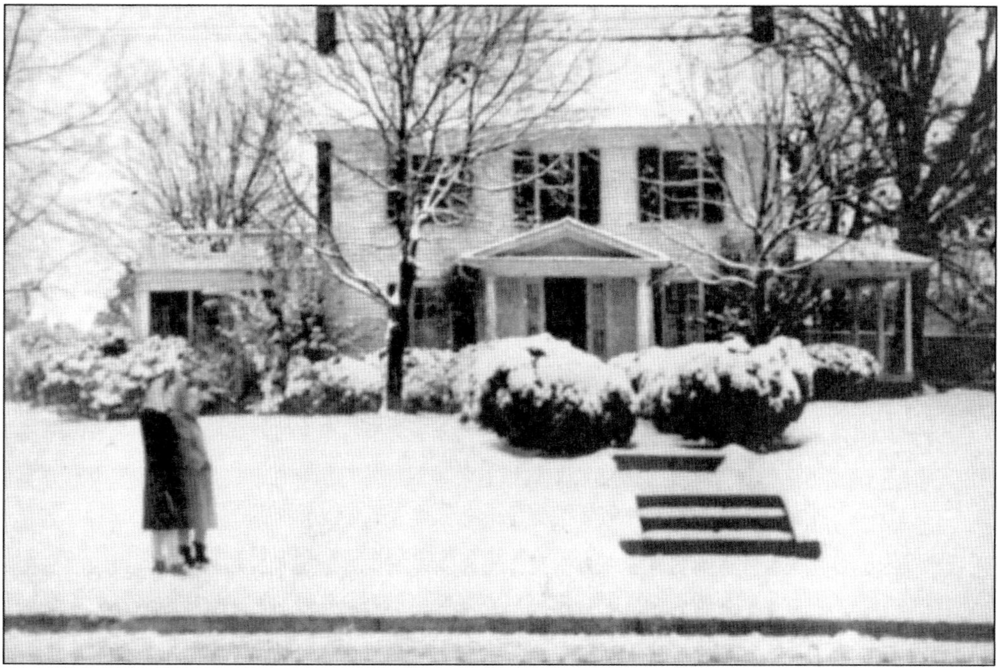

THE W. S. LINVILLE HOUSE, C. 1865. The main part of this West Mountain Street home was constructed in 1865 or 1866. Walter Linville was co-owner and operator of Fulp and Linville Store, which sold general merchandise for business and farm trade. (KBB.)

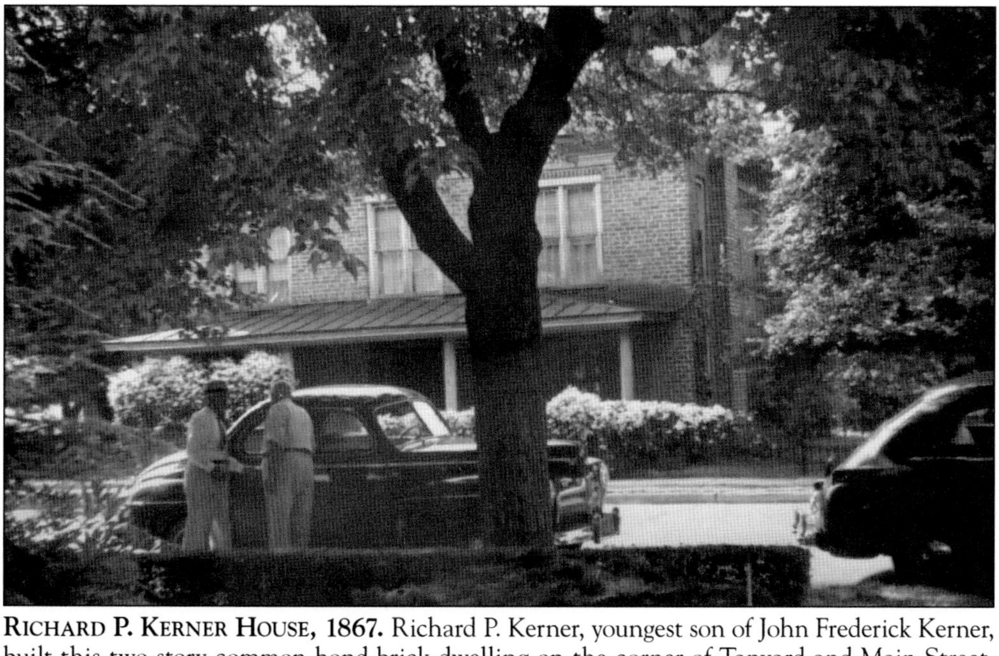

RICHARD P. KERNER HOUSE, 1867. Richard P. Kerner, youngest son of John Frederick Kerner, built this two-story common bond brick dwelling on the corner of Tanyard and Main Street. Richard served as the first principal of Kernersville Academy. For more than 50 years, he was the local agent for the Northwestern North Carolina Railroad. In addition to being freight, passenger, and express agent, he was also the telegrapher. (MRK.)

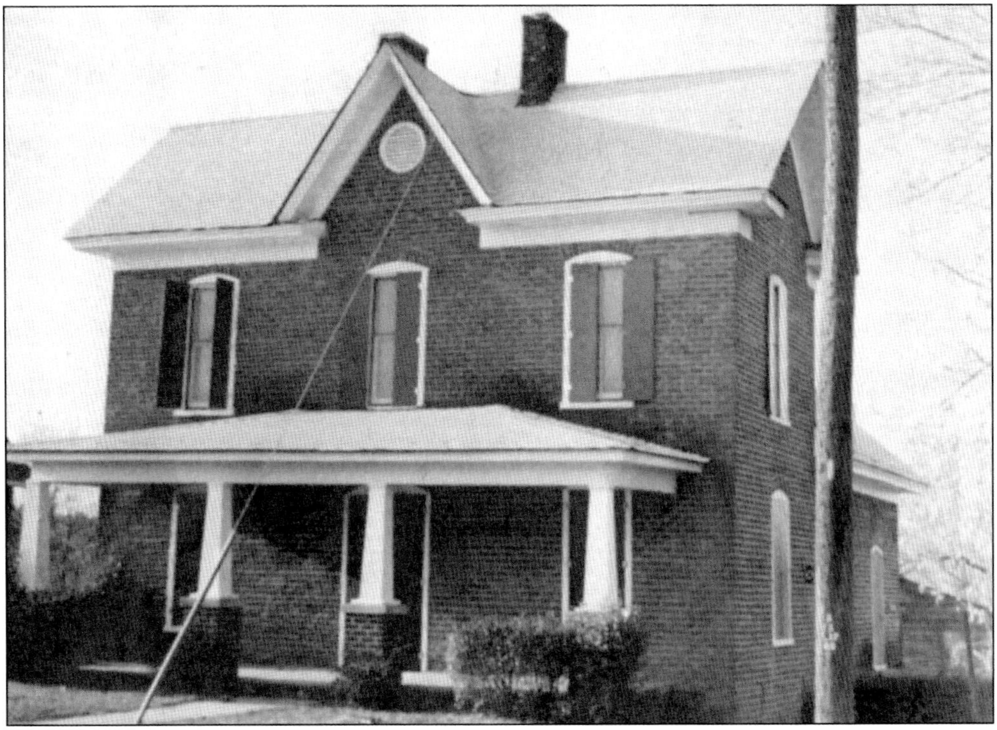

THE DR. KERR PEPPER HOUSE, C. 1870. Also called the Tom Fleshman house, this was the South Cherry Street home of Dr. Kerr Pepper and his daughter, Mina Pepper, who married Tom Fleshman. (KBB.)

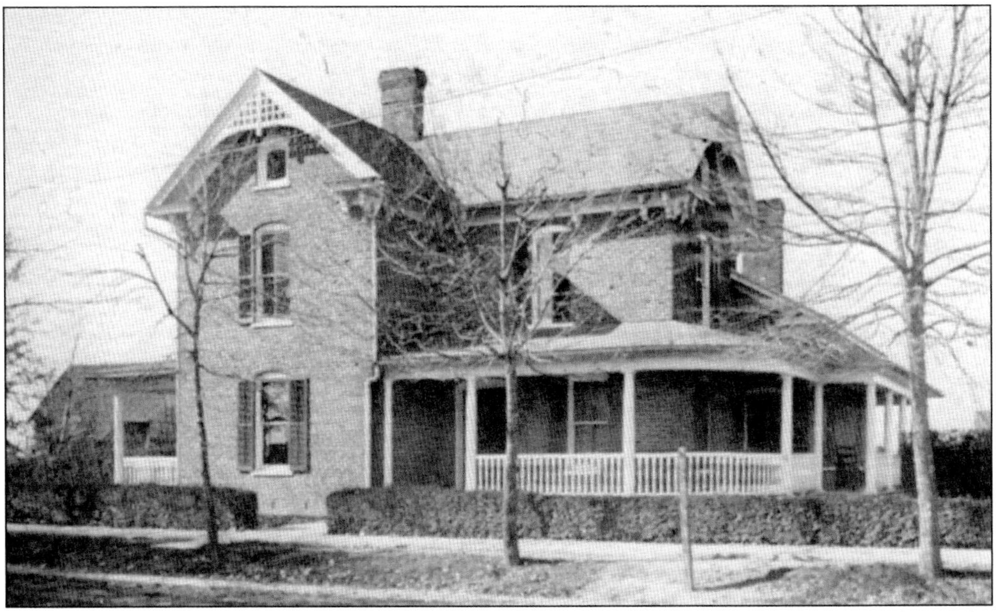

THE GID RING HOUSE, C. 1870S. John Frederick Kerner built this South Main Street home for his son Dr. Cornelius Kerner, known as "Little Doc." Mr. and Mrs. S. G. (Gid) Ring bought the house in 1892 for $550. From the early 1900s through the 1920s, Gid Ring was part owner of Kernersville Furniture Manufacturing Company, which supplied jobs for many workers. (KBB.)

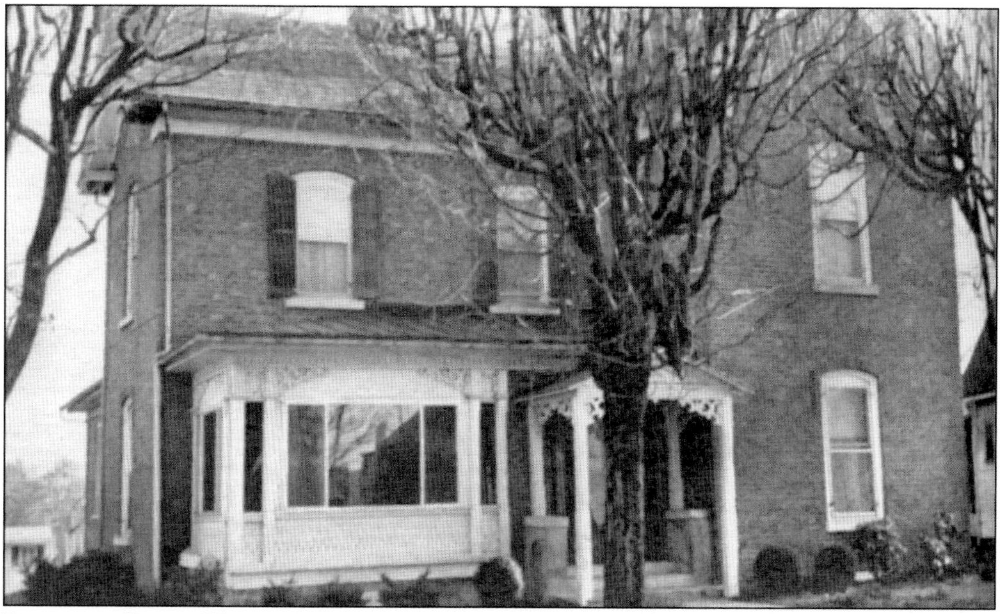

REPHELIUS BYRON KERNER HOUSE, C. 1870. R. B. Kerner Sr. constructed this South Main Street two-story, L-shaped Italianate residence of handmade brick. During Kerner's tenure as mayor in 1925, the ladies of Kernersville decreed "owners of vacant property move the rubbish, mow the grass, and clean up and keep such lots in sanitary condition." Rephelius Byron Kerner Jr. built S & R Motor Company about 1928. This commercial building, which is seven bays deep, still stands on South Main Street. (KBB.)

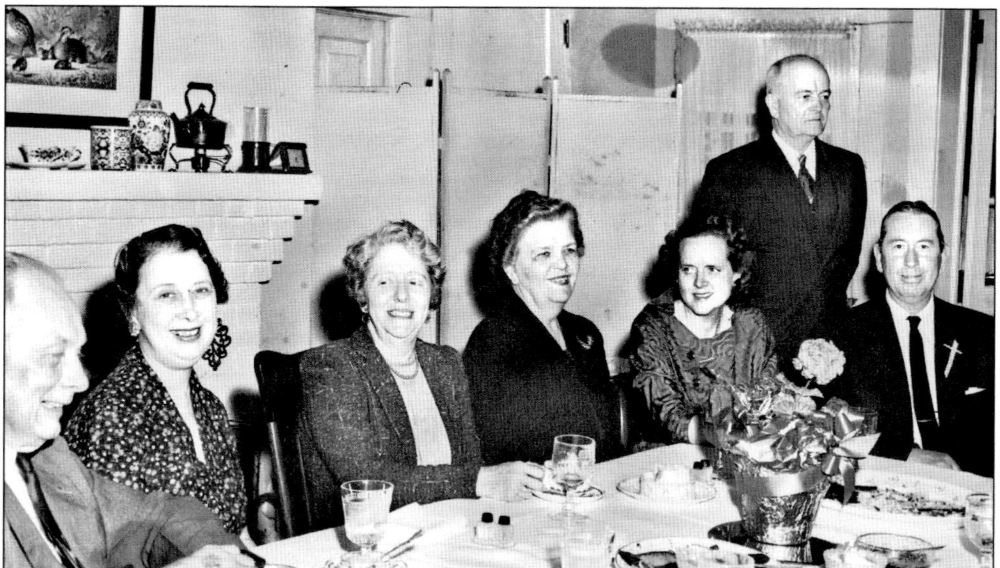

THE BETH TARTAN HOUSE. The R. B. Kerner house was later owned by Rephelius's granddaughter, Elizabeth Stuart Sparks, whose pen name was Beth Tartan. She was a famous regional cooking author and food editor for the *Winston-Salem Journal*. This photograph shows, from left to right, Kenneth Greenfield, Bea Vance, Anna Lee Greenfield, Erie Hedgecock (the first grade teacher at Kernersville School), Elizabeth Stuart Sparks (Erie's daughter, also known as Beth Tartan), Ned Stuart (Beth's father), and Coy Sparks (Beth's husband). (MVB.)

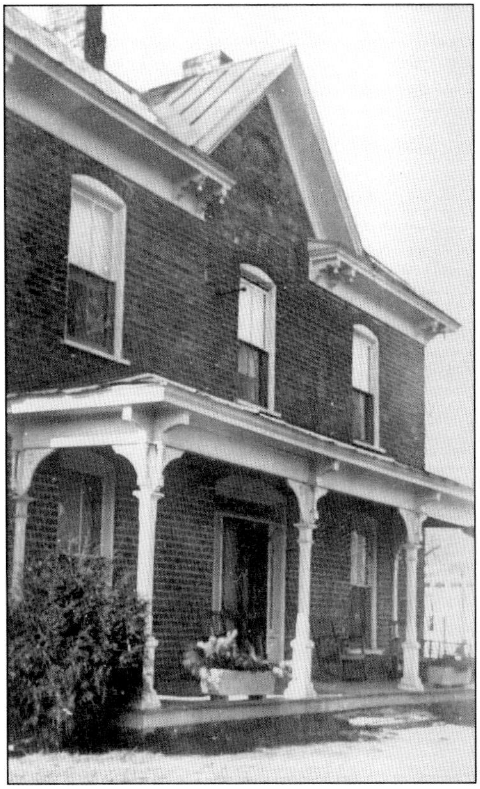

THE ISAAC HARRISON MCKAUGHAN HOUSE, 1875. This two-story, handmade brick structure on Salisbury Street features Italianate-style eaves, brackets, and segmental arched windows and doors. Ceilings are 10 feet high, floors are original heart of pine, and the roof is the original standing-seam tin. The bricks were made from dirt dug in the basement. This homestead is also called the White Horse Clan because the McKaughans chose the horse as their symbol. (AT.)

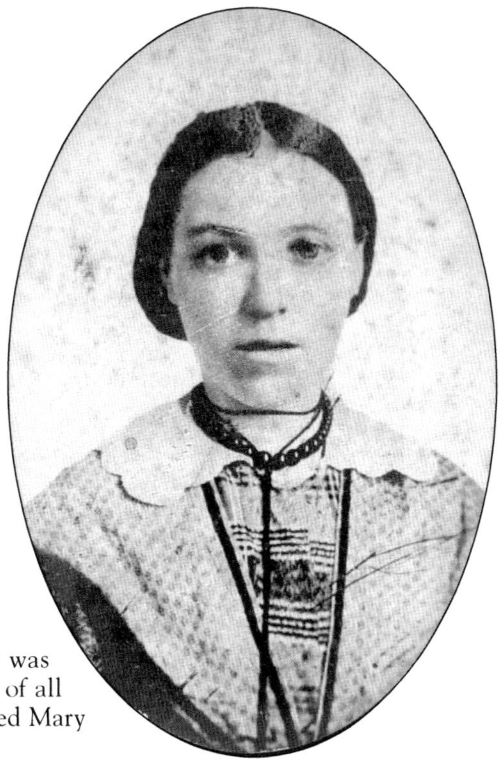

ESTHER CATHERINE MCKAUGHAN. Esther was Isaac McKaughan's first wife and the mother of all his children. After Esther's death, Isaac married Mary Pegram *c.* 1900. (AT.)

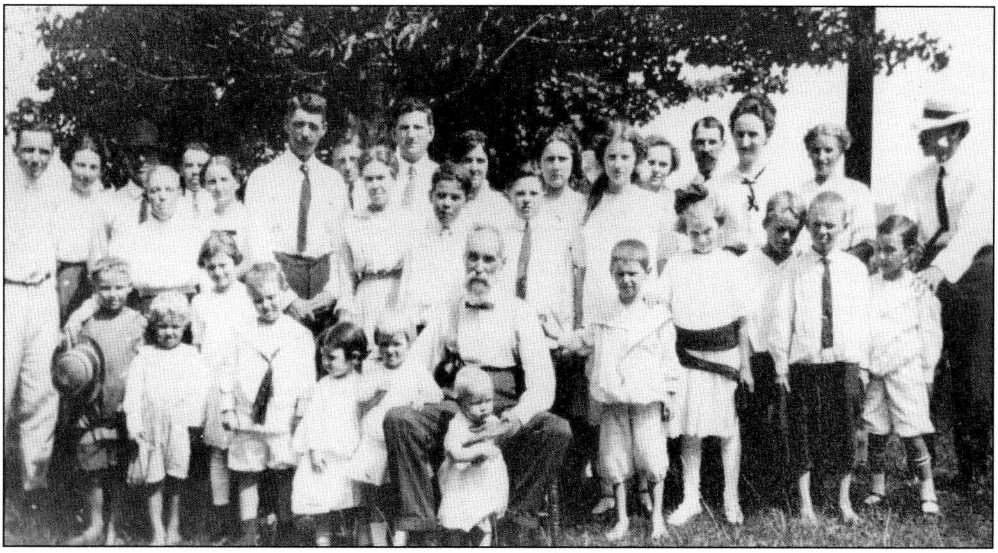

CELEBRATION, 1912. Isaac Harrison McKaughan's 75th birthday party is pictured in front of his house. Isaac was a well-to-do farmer who owned much of the land from this house to Beeson's Crossroads, a distance of about two miles. (AT.)

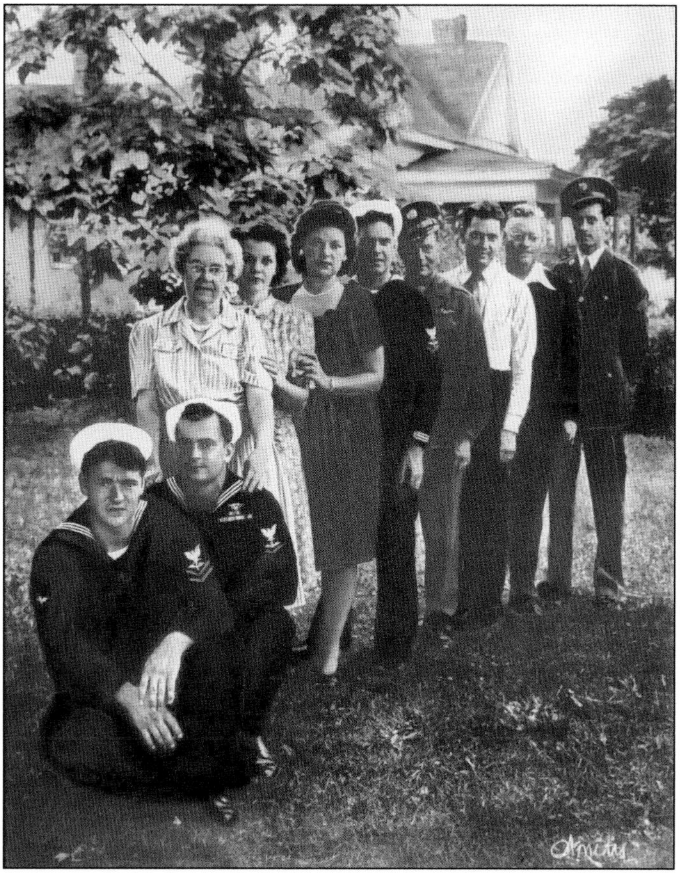

THE SMITH FAMILY. Ora and Maggie Smith bought the Isaac Harrison McKaughan house in 1931. Pictured here from left to right are Donald (navy), Jack (navy), Miss Maggie, Zora, Mary Alice, Tom (navy), Ora Lee (army), Richard, Ora, and William Edward (army). (AT.)

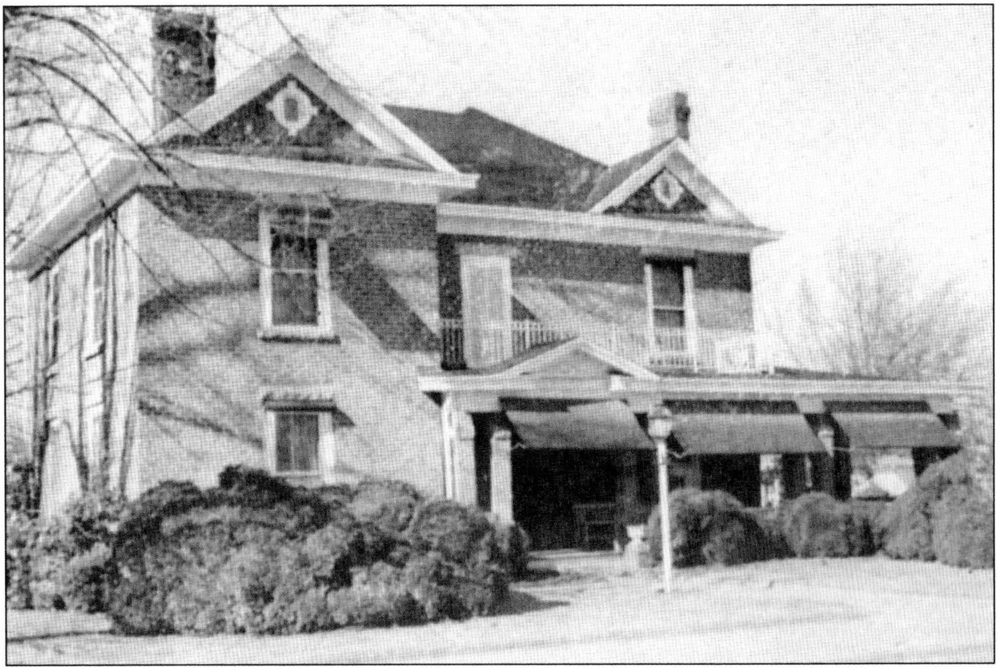

THE DR. JUSTICE HOUSE, 1877. This elegant brick residence on North Main Street was built by J. C. Roberts, one of the founders of Cherry Street Methodist Church. Mr. Roberts operated a produce store, specializing in dried berries and fruits. Later Dr. James T. Justice Sr. and his family bought the home. In addition to being a physician, Dr. Justice was town commissioner, school board member, and active businessman. (KBB.)

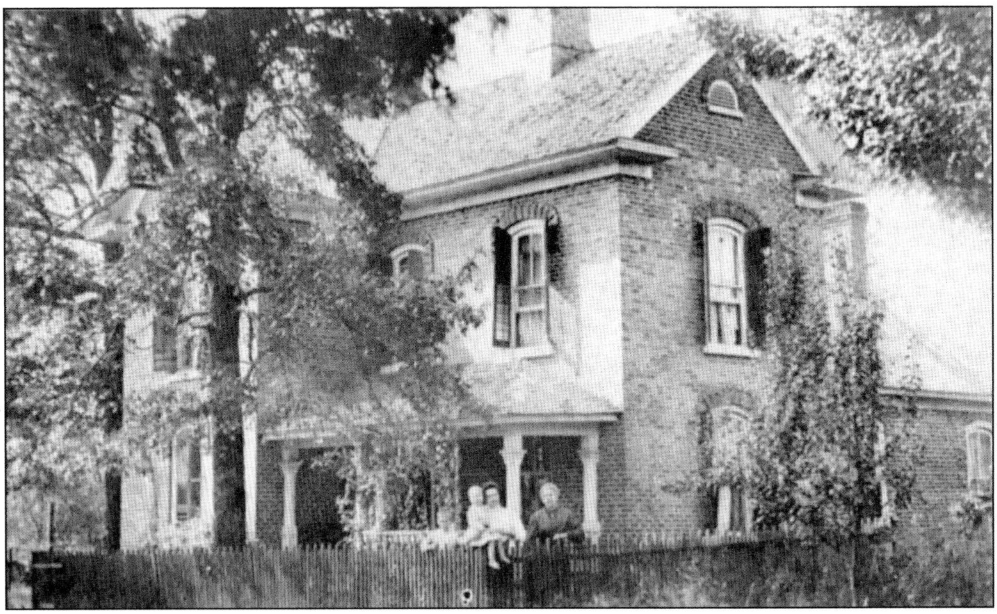

THE THEODORE E. KERNER HOUSE, C. 1877. The home of Theodore and Elizabeth Kerner on South Main Street is one of Kernersville's oldest landmarks. Theodore's father, Israel Kerner, gave him the land. The house has 14-inch-thick brick walls. This brick was made in a kiln about 600 feet behind the house. Four generations of Kerners have lived in the house. (KBB.)

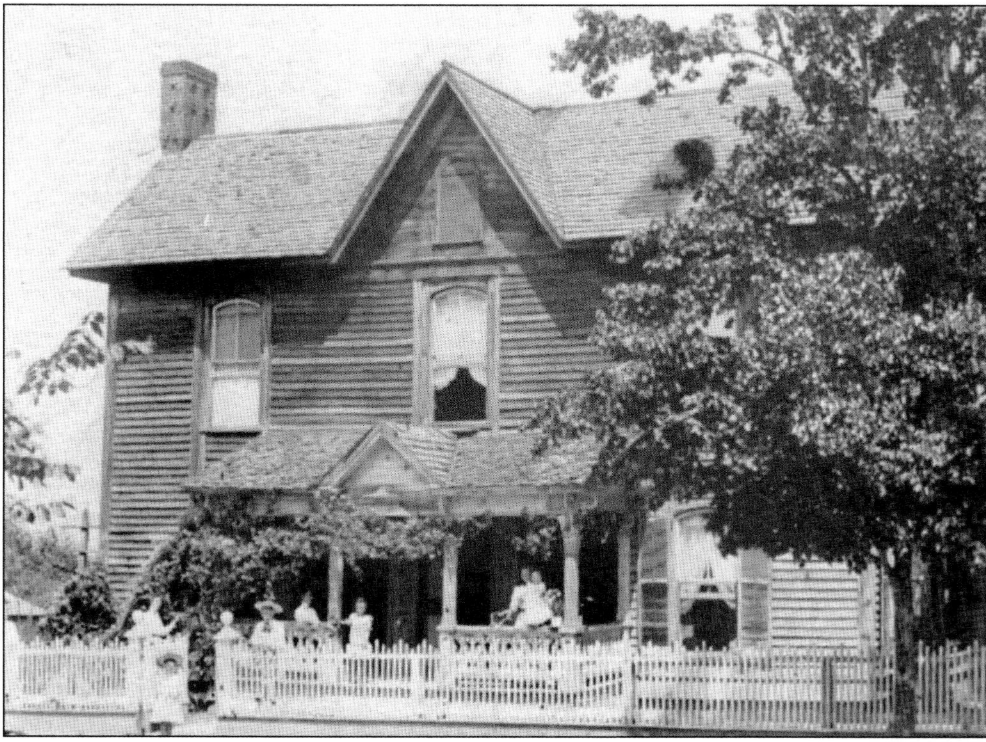

THE ALEXANDER HASTINGS HOUSE. This house on South Main Street stood on the site of the current Moravian church parking lot. The residence was built by Robert and Paulina Kerner Fulton for their daughter Cornelia, who married Alexander Hastings. (KBB.)

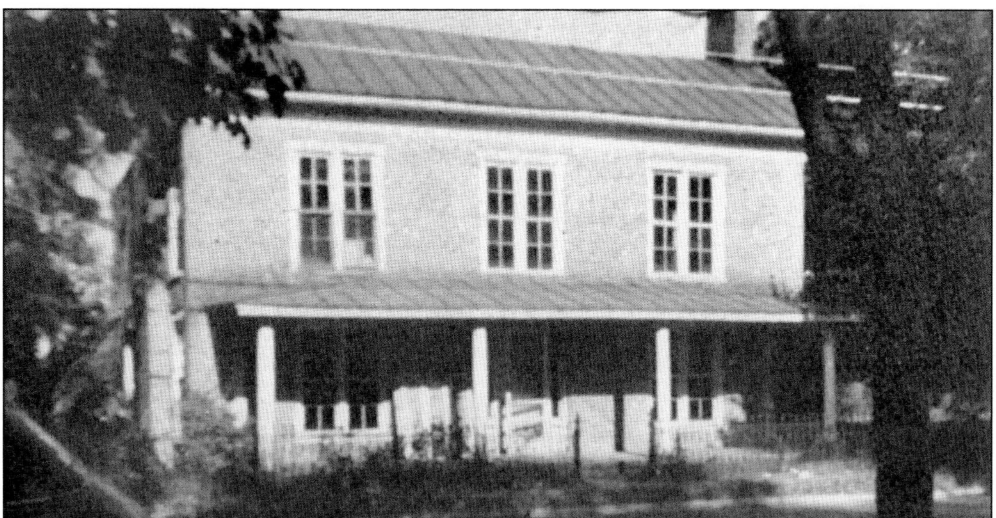

THE L. F. DAVIS HOUSE, C. 1880. This residence was built on North Cherry Street by L. F. Davis, owner of a general merchandise store. He and his son also established the first knitting mill on Bodenhamer Street. (KBB.)

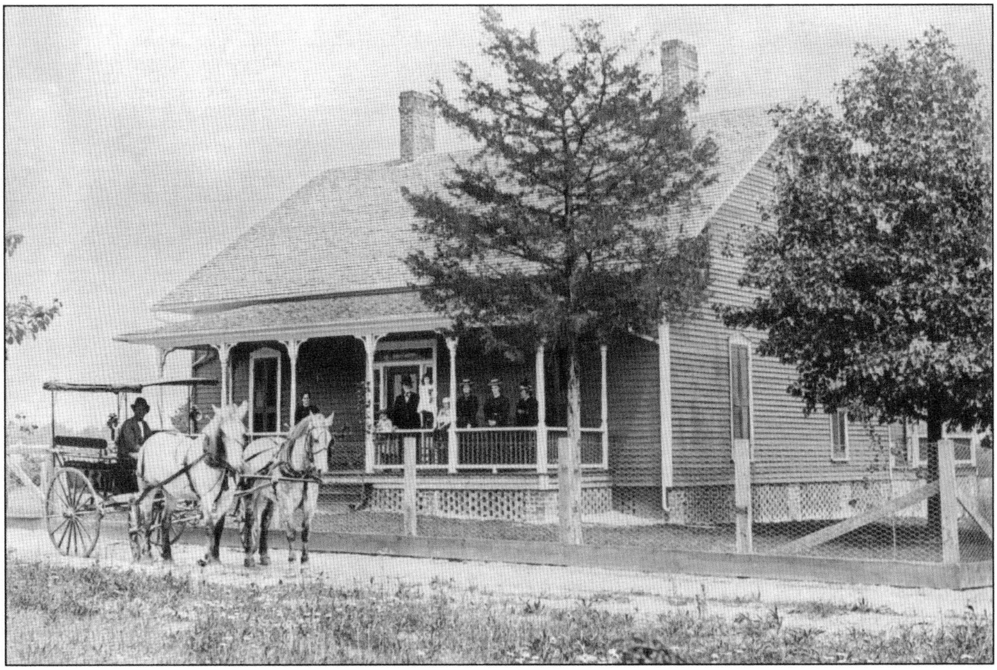

THE JONES HOUSE, 1884. The Jones House was built on Beard Street (now on Church Street) for the John L. Jones family. It has been remodeled and continues to be occupied today. This picture includes John and Emma Jones, their daughters—Mattie, Jenny, and Jesse (Jinx)—and Jesse's children—Kathleen, Philip Sr., and Mattie Lee Körner. (MRK.)

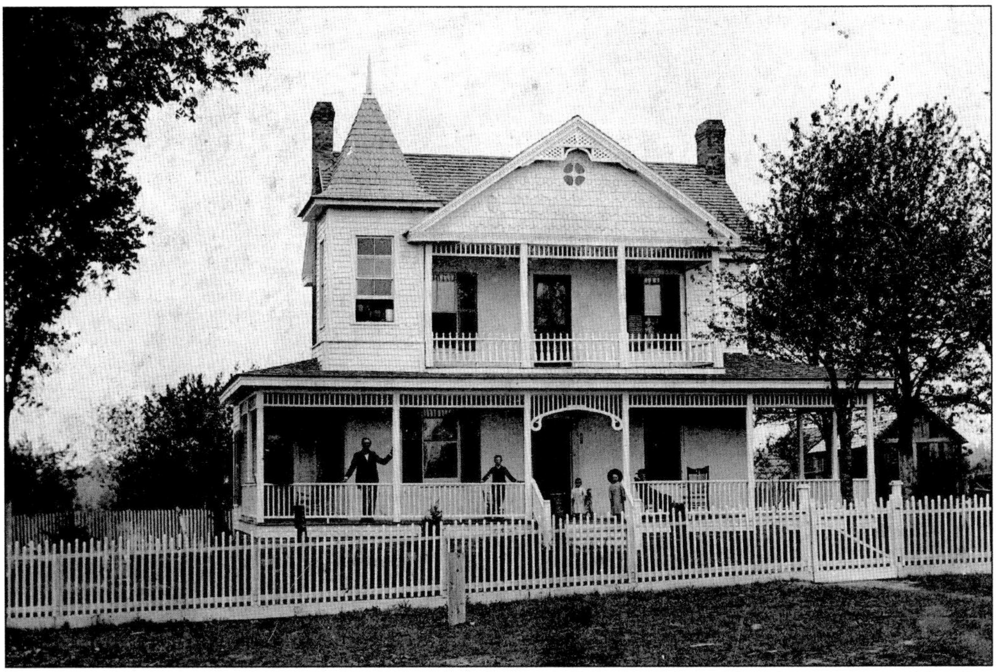

THE HENRY SHORE HOUSE, 1890. Formerly Plunkett Place, the first school in Kernersville, this house was later occupied by the Henry Shore family. Edgar Shore, Henry's son, was born here. The same house is now Pierce-Jefferson Funeral Service on West Mountain Street. (ES.)

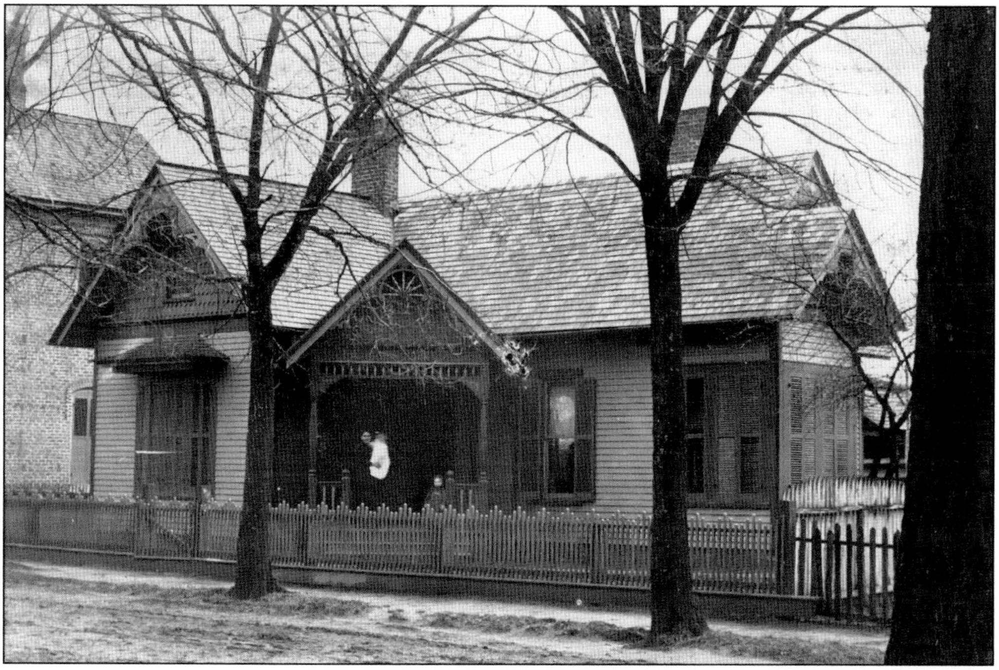

HENRY CLAY KÖRNER HOUSE, 1892. Henry built this house on South Main Street for his mother, fondly called "Aunt Sallie" by the townspeople. The southern front room features a three-part bay projection and a late-Victorian mantel with mirrored over-mantel. The wainscot in the house consisted of tooled leather and Caesar Milch murals; however, the murals have been painted over. The residence was restored in 1986 by Mary Ruth Körner, fifth-generation descendant of Joseph Kerner, and continues to be occupied by descendants today. (MKH.)

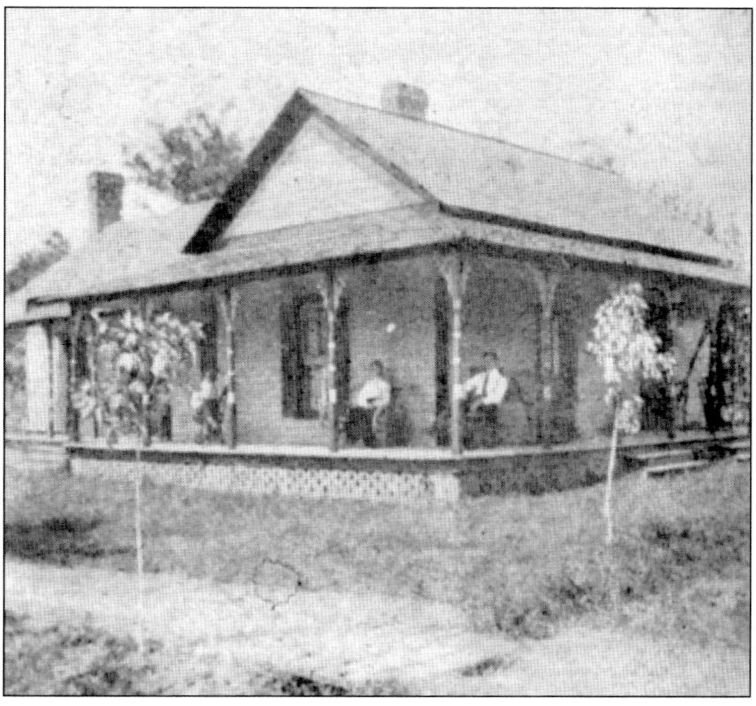

THE R. E. STEELE HOUSE, LATE 1800S. This West Mountain Street house, built by R. E. Steele, was purchased by Mr. and Mrs. Will Cooke in 1911 and occupied by Cooke family members for many years. (KBB.)

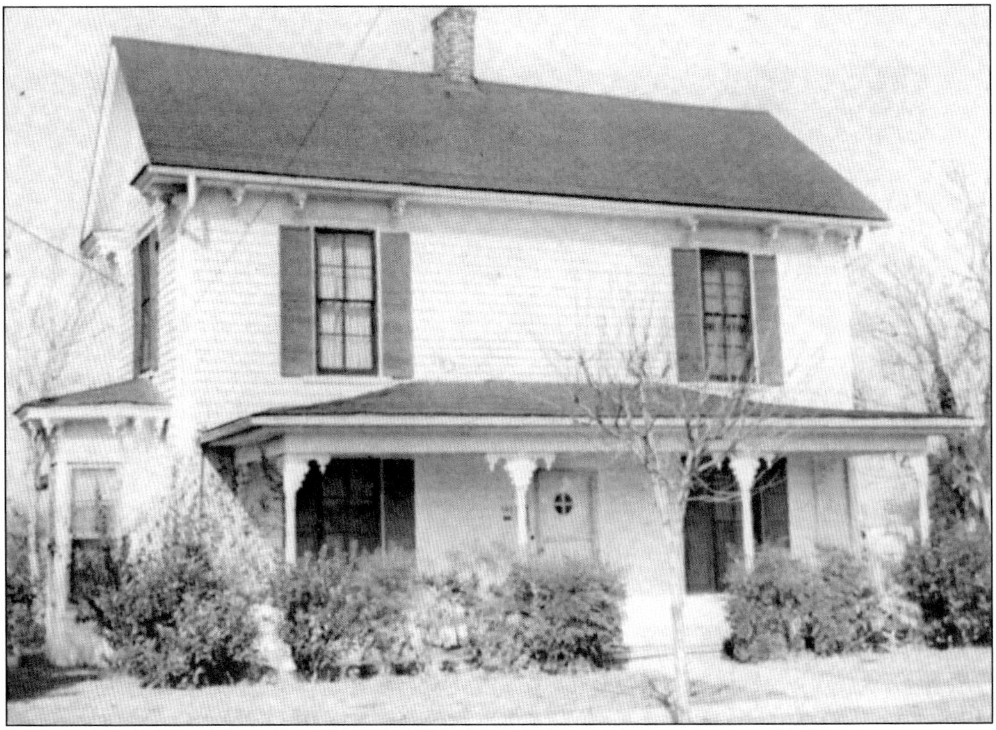

THE TOTTEN/GOSLEN HOME. Rev. J. H. Totten, one of the charter members of Mt. Gur Cemetery (organized in 1894), owned this house. Totten's son-in-law was the first person to be buried in Mt. Gur. Through the years, this has been home to Mr. and Mrs. C. L. Linville and Mr. and Mrs. Henry Goslen. (KBB.)

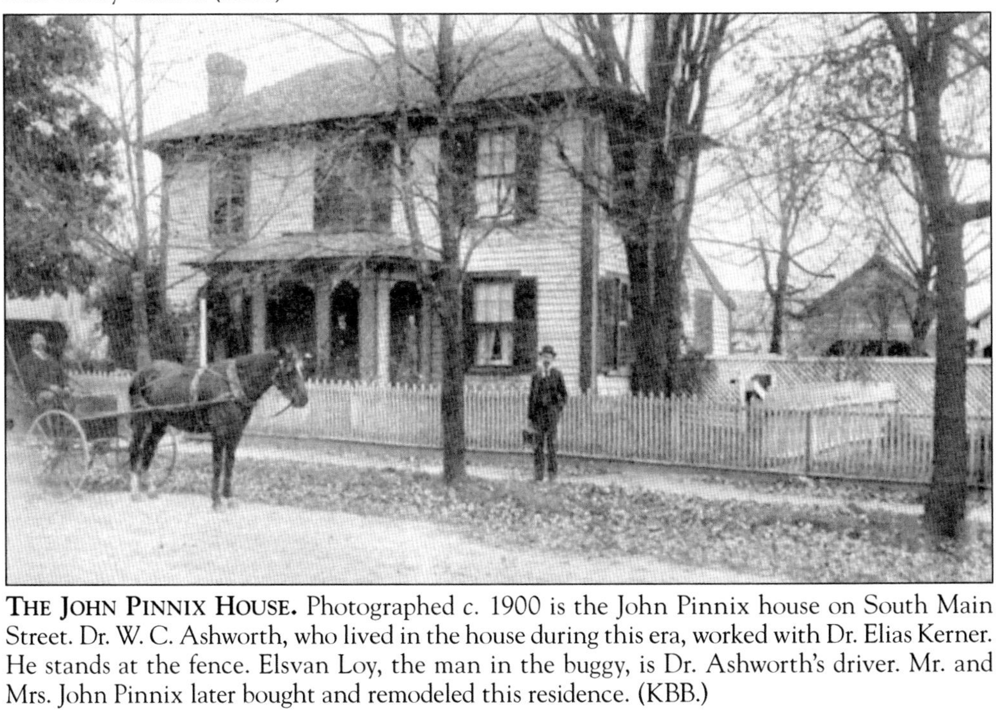

THE JOHN PINNIX HOUSE. Photographed *c.* 1900 is the John Pinnix house on South Main Street. Dr. W. C. Ashworth, who lived in the house during this era, worked with Dr. Elias Kerner. He stands at the fence. Elsvan Loy, the man in the buggy, is Dr. Ashworth's driver. Mr. and Mrs. John Pinnix later bought and remodeled this residence. (KBB.)

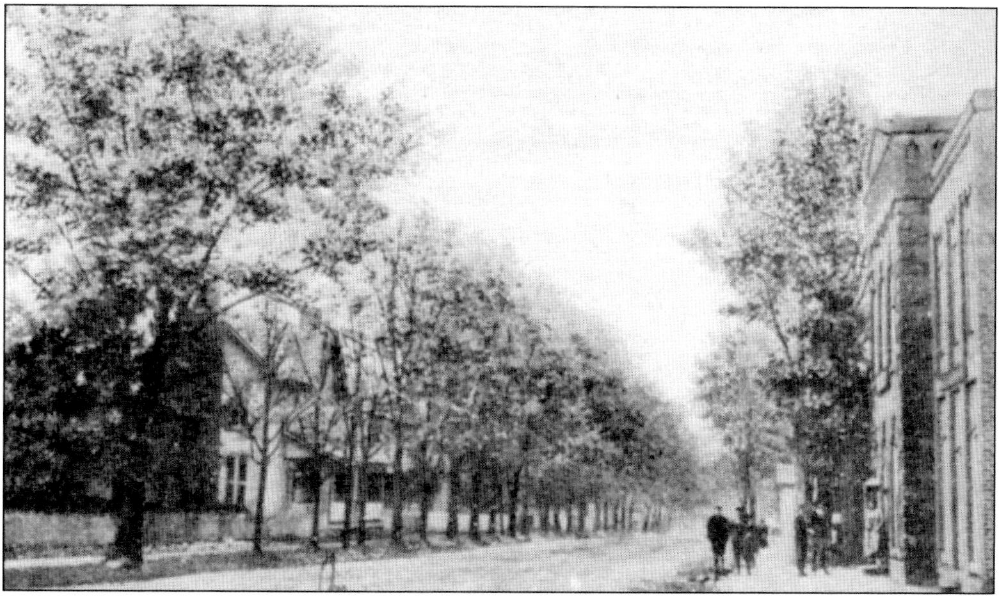

SOUTH MAIN STREET VIEW, 1893. The John R. Paddison house is shown on the left side of South Main Street. On the opposite side of the street are the old bank building and the W. S. Linville Store. (KBB.)

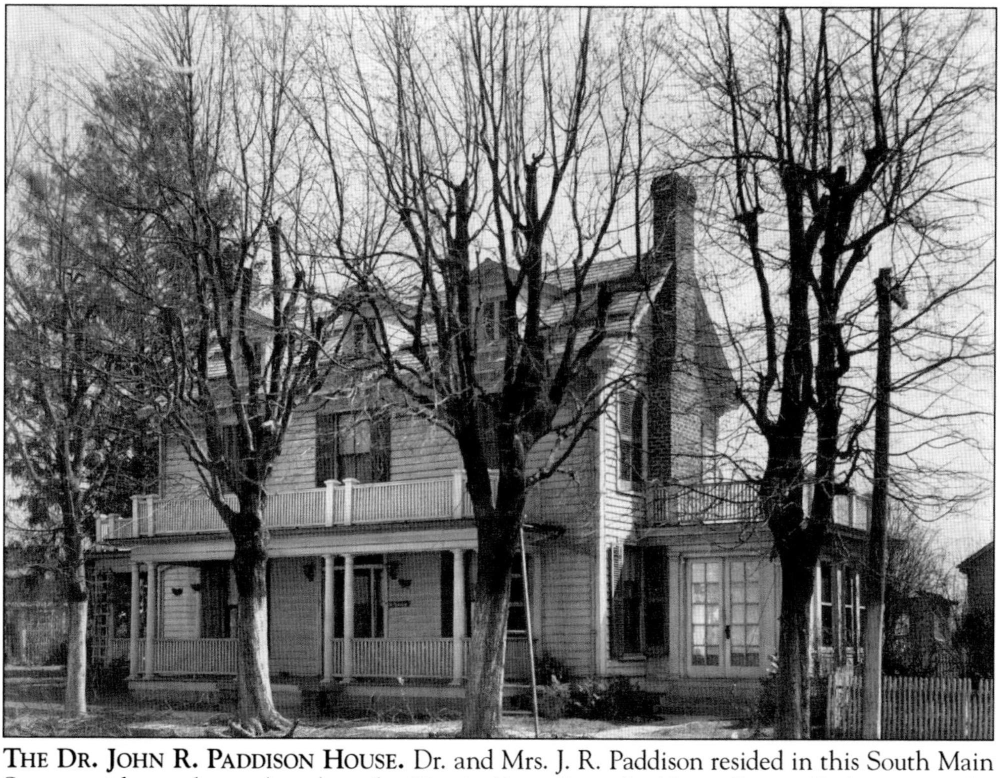

THE DR. JOHN R. PADDISON HOUSE. Dr. and Mrs. J. R. Paddison resided in this South Main Street residence, located next to the Pinnix Drug Store building. Originally known as the N. W. Sapp home place, this home was the birthplace of Mrs. Zora Sapp Paddison, wife of Dr. Paddison. (BW.)

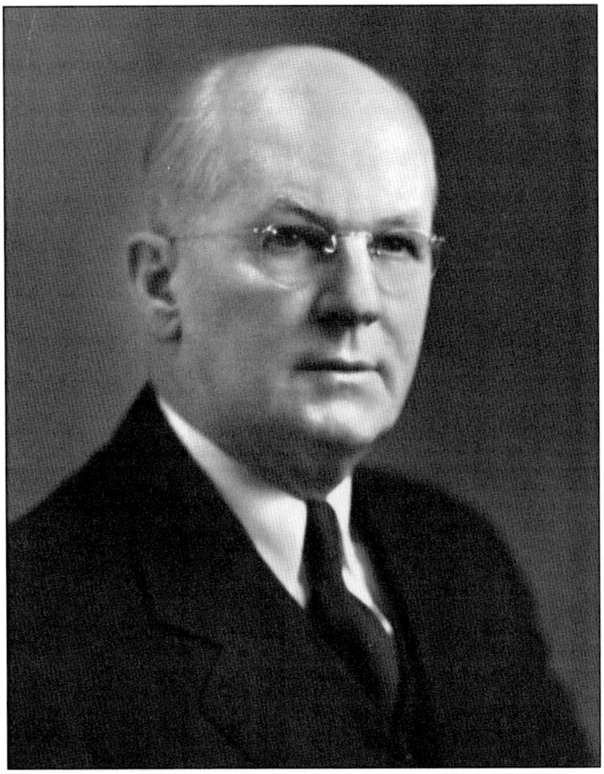

Dr. J. R. Paddison. In addition to practicing medicine in Kernersville from 1910 until 1936, Dr. Paddison was the physician for Southern Railway and served as president of the Forsyth County Medical Association. (BW.)

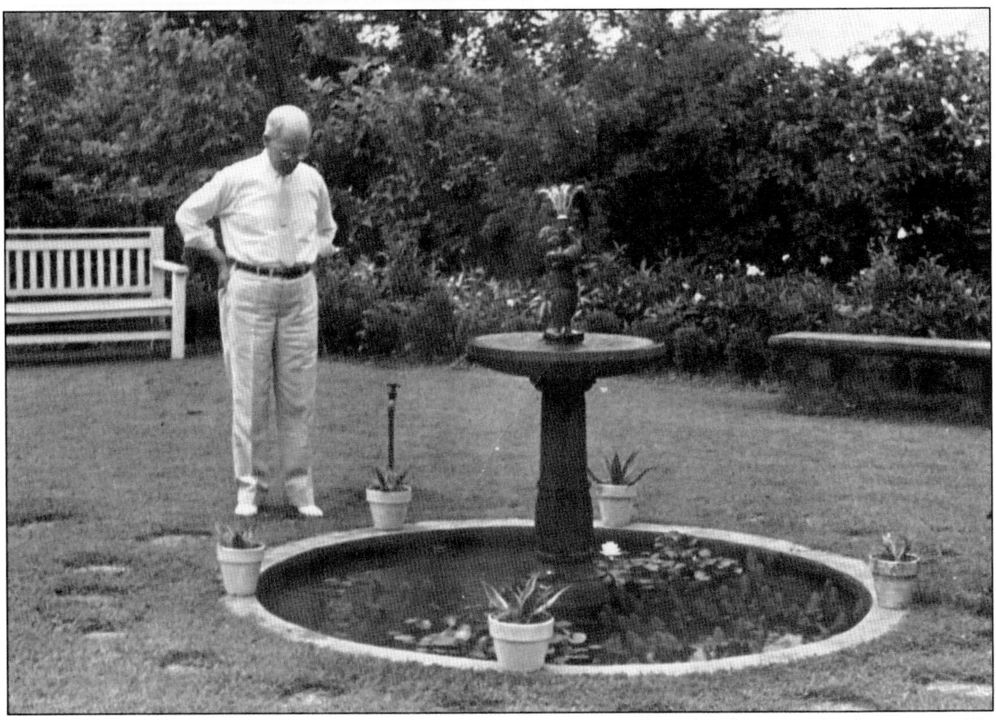

Dr. Paddison in Garden. The good doctor enjoys a respite from his busy medical practice. He delivered many babies in Kernersville. (BW.)

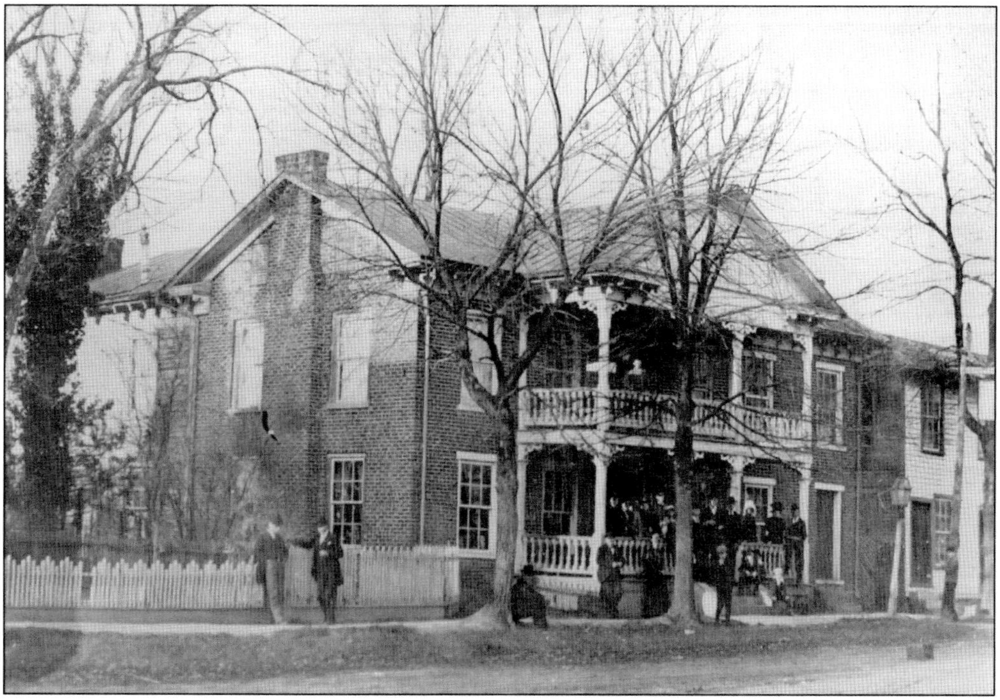

THE ISRAEL KERNER HOUSE. Built before the Civil War, this residence at Salisbury and Main Streets was destroyed by fire in 1912. Israel Kerner operated a tannery, where leather was made from animal skins. He also farmed, managed a hotel, and ran a community store. The Kerners boarded students who attended the Kernersville Academy. (MRK and ES.)

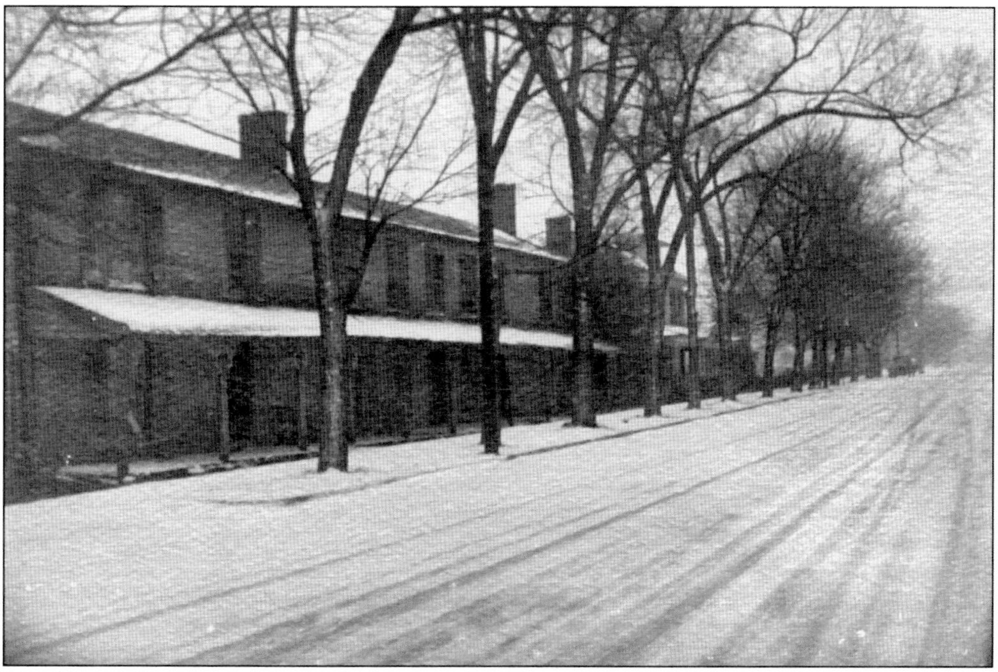

THE NASH HOUSE. In this view looking south of Main Street on a winter day, Pete Nash's house is on the left. It stood at the corner of Harmon and South Main Streets. (MRK.)

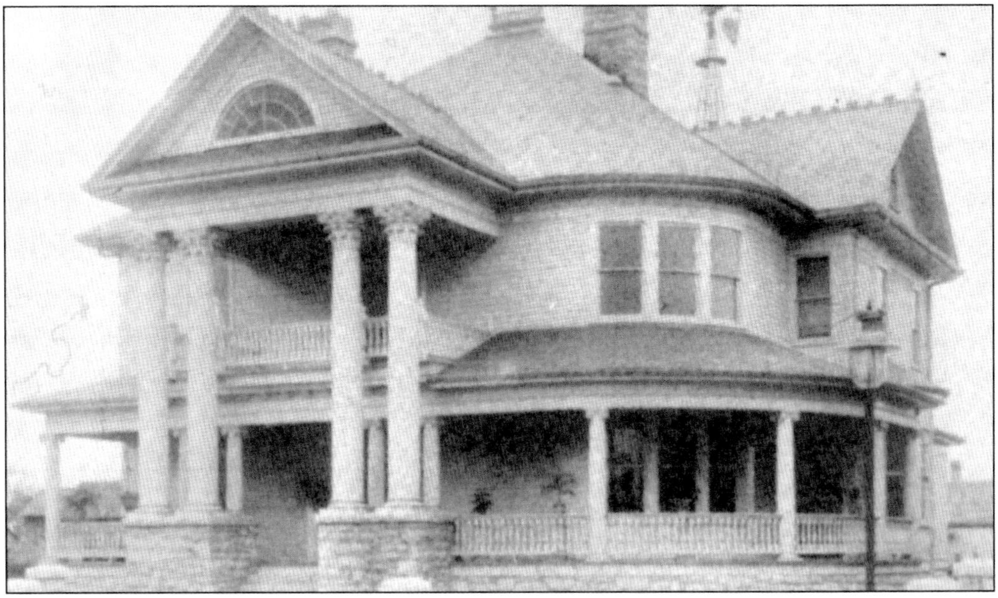

The Tom C. McCuiston House, c. 1908. This house, built about 1908 on North Main Street, has been demolished. In 1896, Tom began repairing and selling bicycles. (KBB.)

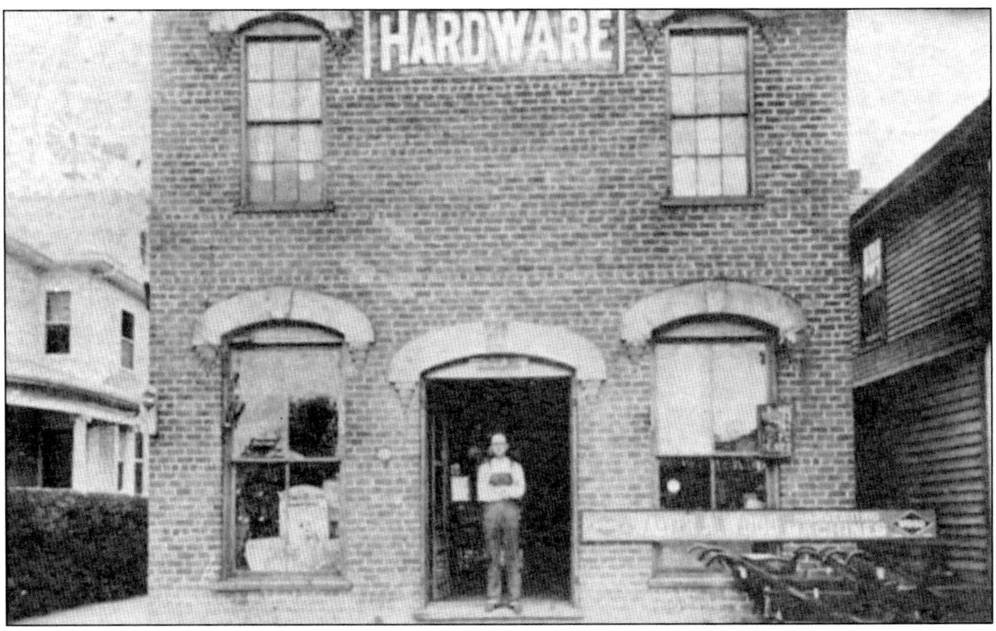

Tom McCuiston's Hardware Store. In 1903, Tom built and opened a hardware store. This multi-talented man also specialized in making tobacco barn flues. This photograph was taken of Tom and his store in 1915. (KBB.)

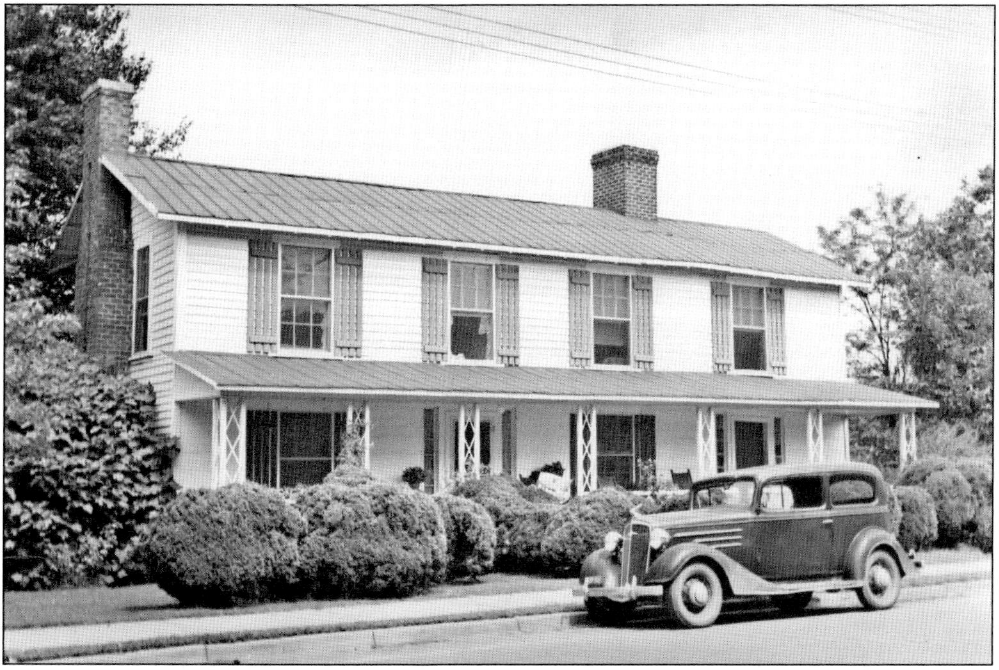

MAMIE GUIRE'S MAIN STREET BOARDING HOUSE. By the late 1930s, North Carolina had begun recovering from the Great Depression. Mills and factories re-opened, so men looking for work migrated from rural areas. They needed a place to live. Mamie Guire offered room and board in her home (beside the Dr. James T. Justice house) at a nominal cost per week. (MVB.)

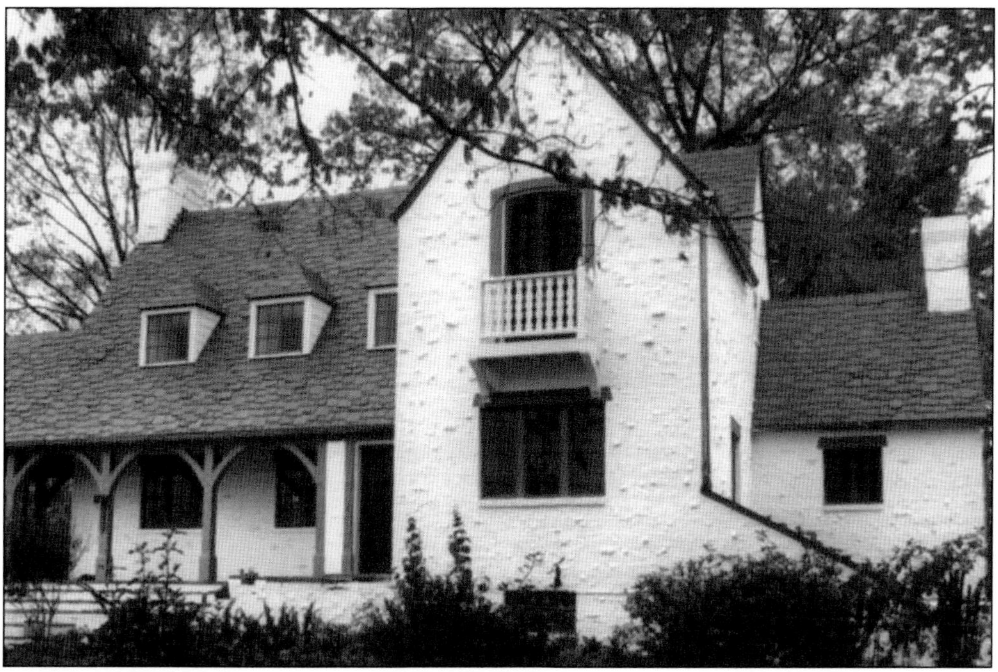

THE FAGG HOUSE, 1938. A Kernersville landmark, this Classic Norman French–style home place on South Main Street was constructed for Ralph Fagg and his wife, India McCuiston Fagg, who lived there until their deaths. The residence has recently been restored for continued use. (BW.)

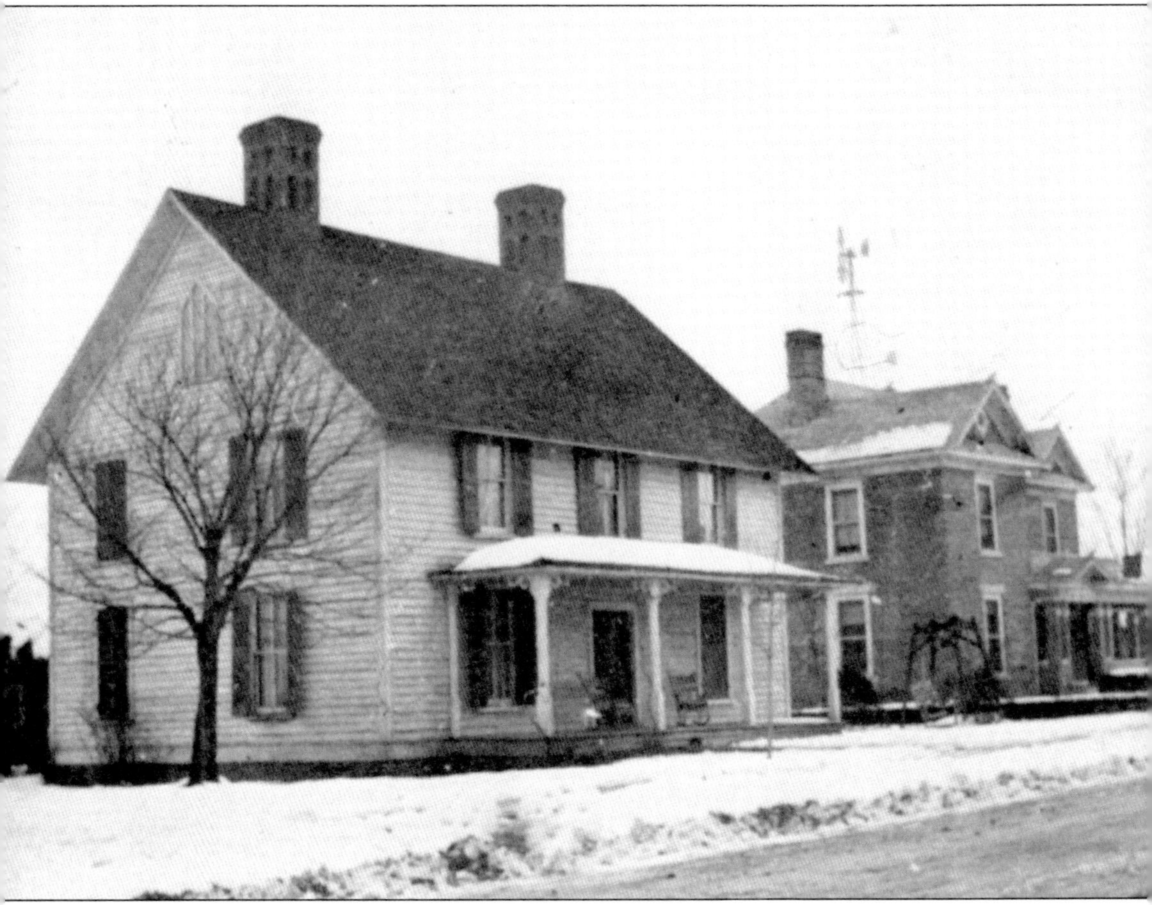

THE AUGUSTUS H. BEARD HOUSE. Shown here are the North Main Street homes of Augustus H. Beard, Dr. J. T. Justice, and Mamie Guire. The site of the Beard home is where Christinia (Kastner) Kerner, widow of Joseph of Kernersville, moved after her husband's death in 1830. (KBB.)

Three

KÖRNER'S FOLLY

In 1878, Jule Körner, grandson of Joseph of Kernersville, designed and built an eclectic bachelor home in the heart of Kernersville. The brick for the exterior, handmade on the premises, consisted of eight different shapes and sizes. Jule, a 27-year old artist, wanted multi-purpose quarters, so he positioned stables on the right lower floors, a carriage way with high arches through the center of the house, and living quarters on the left lower floors. His art studios went upstairs.

When completed, Jule's residence had 22 rooms on 3 (some reports say 4) floors—with 7 different levels, which included trapdoors and cubbyholes. Some ceilings ranged from under 6 feet to more than 25 feet. He built his 15 fireplaces with different designs of American Encaustic tiles. No two doors were alike. Pivoting windows produced a unique air distribution system; natural air currents cooled the entire house during summer months.

After Jule married Polly Alice Masten in 1886, the layout of the house changed significantly. Former bachelor's quarters became the couple's living area. The horses went to a nearby barn, and the old stables were transformed into a sewing room. In the center of the house, a vestibule, breakfast room, and dining room replaced the old carriageway. Jule hired Caesar Milch, a graduate of Boston's Royal School of Arts, to paint murals and ceiling frescoes to complement the damask wall coverings and fine furnishings.

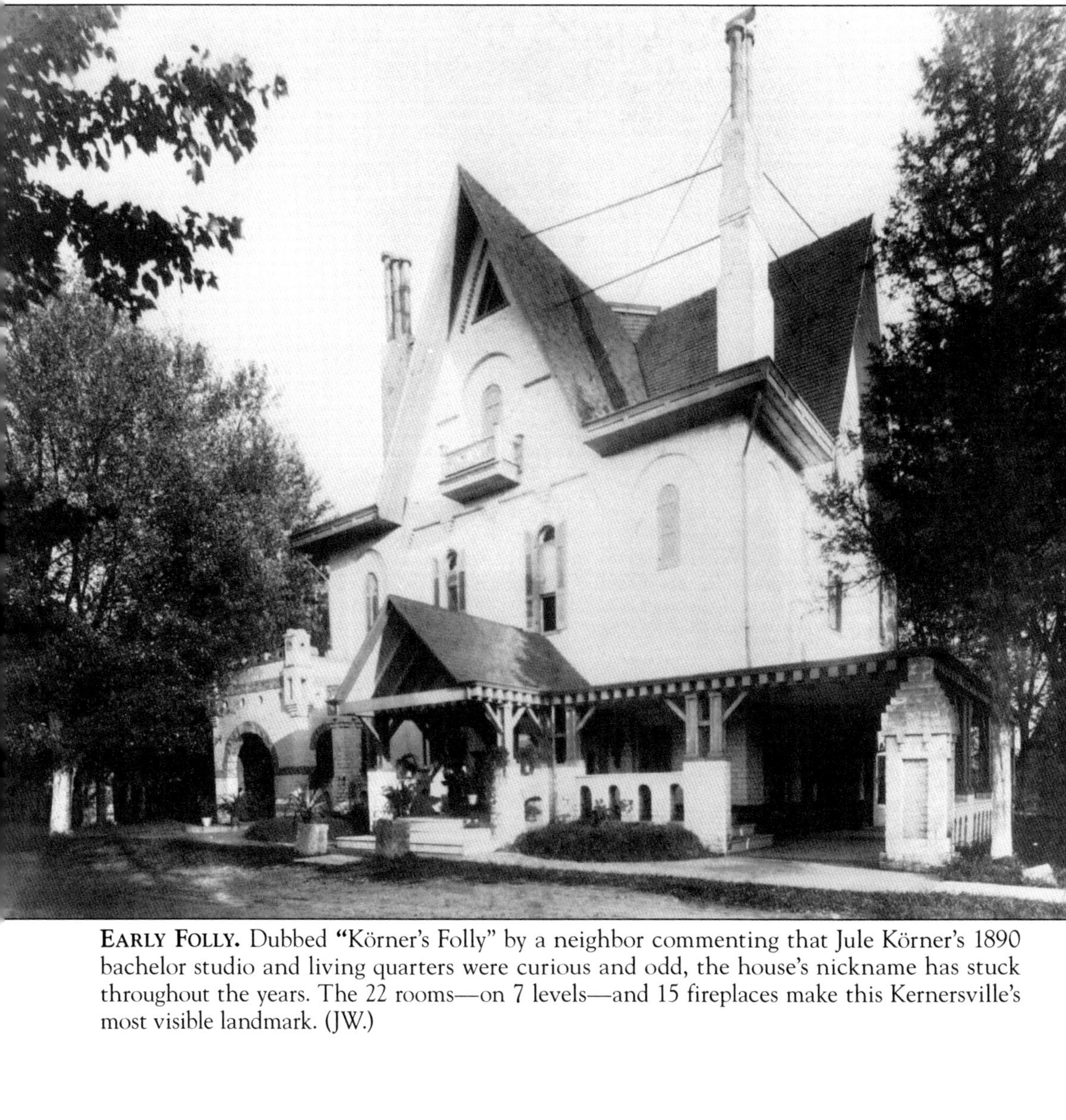

EARLY FOLLY. Dubbed "Körner's Folly" by a neighbor commenting that Jule Körner's 1890 bachelor studio and living quarters were curious and odd, the house's nickname has stuck throughout the years. The 22 rooms—on 7 levels—and 15 fireplaces make this Kernersville's most visible landmark. (JW.)

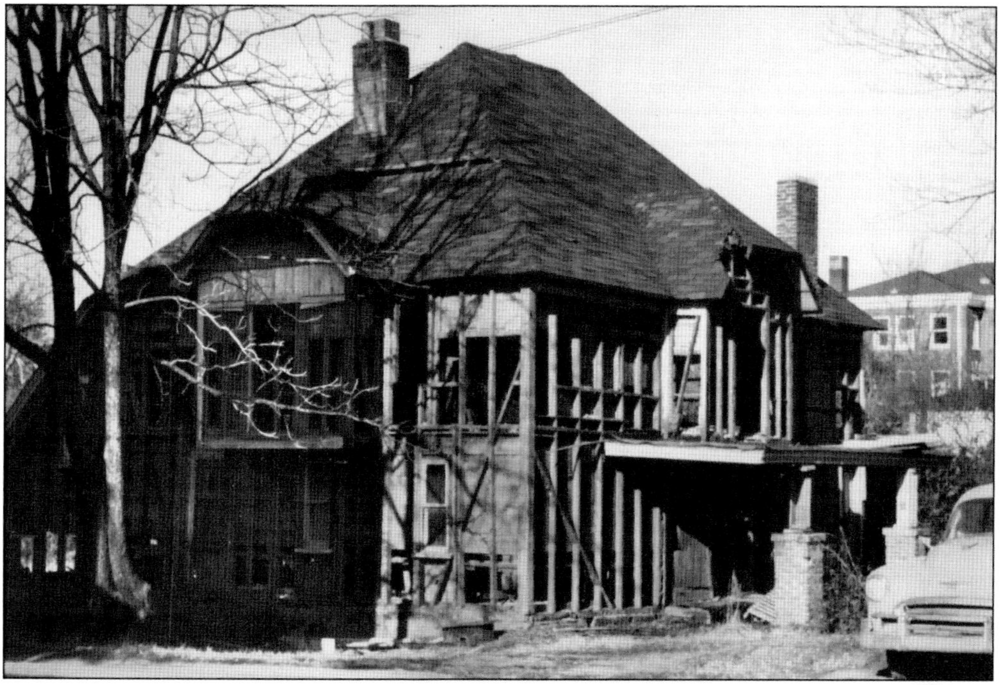

Carriage House Demolition. After Jule married Polly Alice Masten in 1886, the house began to take on a new look. In 1990, the stables originally built inside the Folly were removed. Jule built a carriage house for the horses one block north. This served as a Folly guesthouse and was later converted into apartments before being torn down in 1962. (JW.)

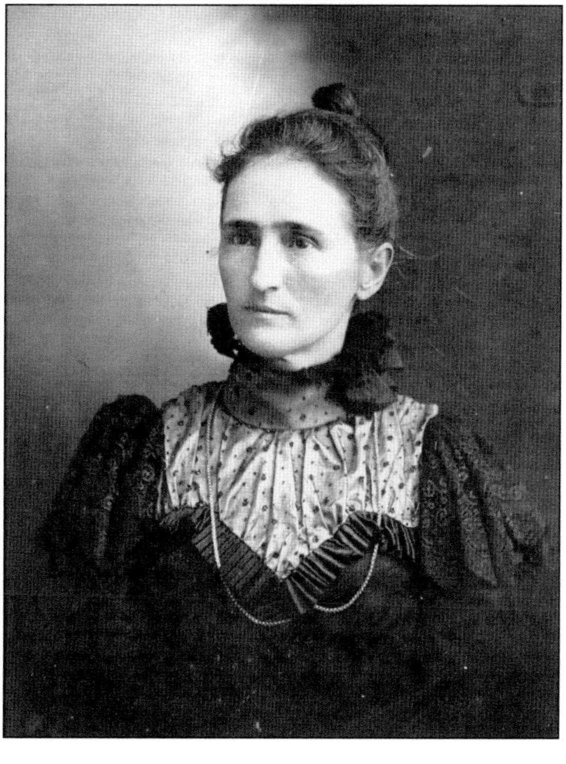

Polly Alice Körner. With the arrival of Alice Körner, bachelor quarters became living quarters with a breakfast room and kitchen later added to the rear of the house. The old stables became a library and sewing room. (JW.)

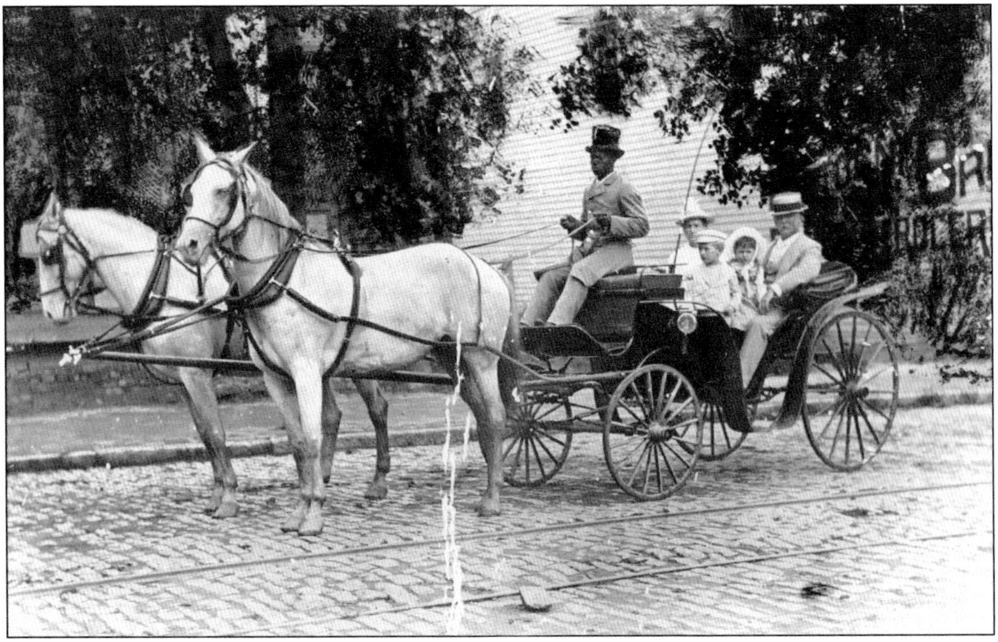

FAMILY CARRIAGE. This 1893 photograph presents Jule with his children, Dore and Gilmer, in the family carriage. (JW.)

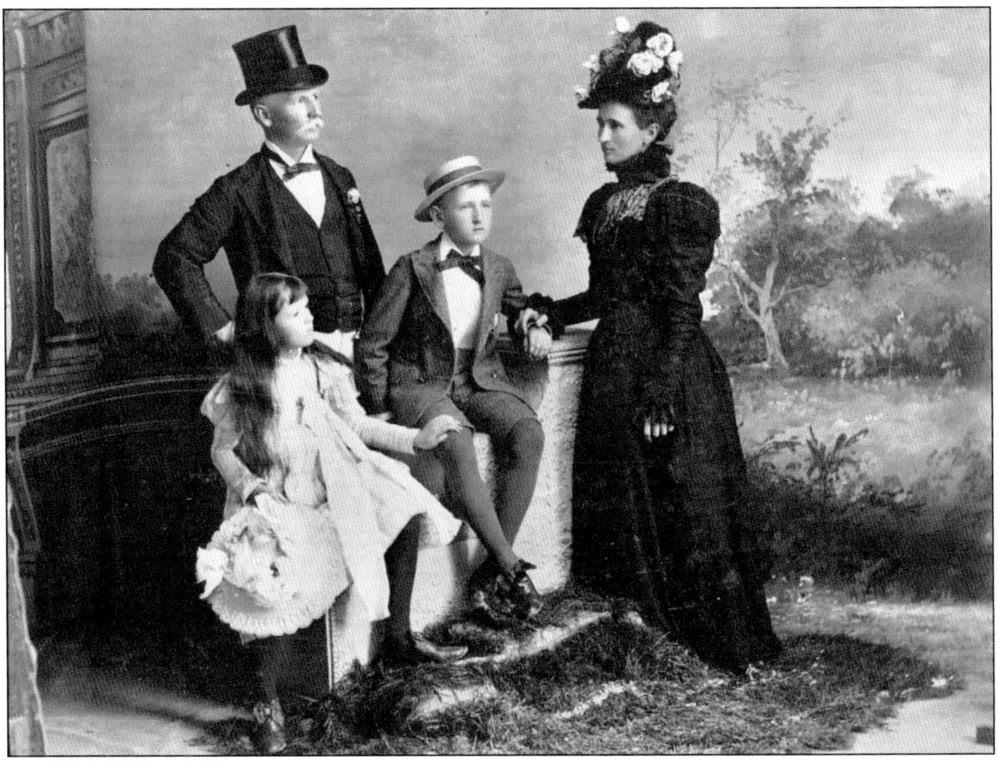

FAMILY PORTRAIT, C. 1895. Jule, Alice, Dore, and Gilmer pose for a family portrait around 1895. (JW.)

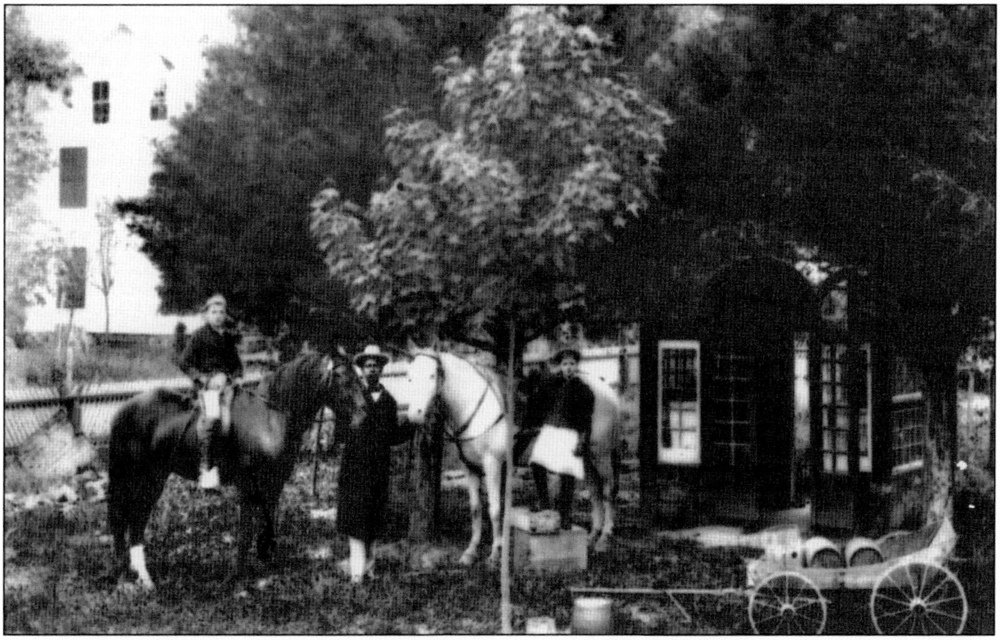

CHILDREN'S PLAYHOUSE. Gilmer and Dore enjoy their playhouse on the north lawn of the Folly with coachman John Carr and horses Boy and Daisy around 1897. (JW.)

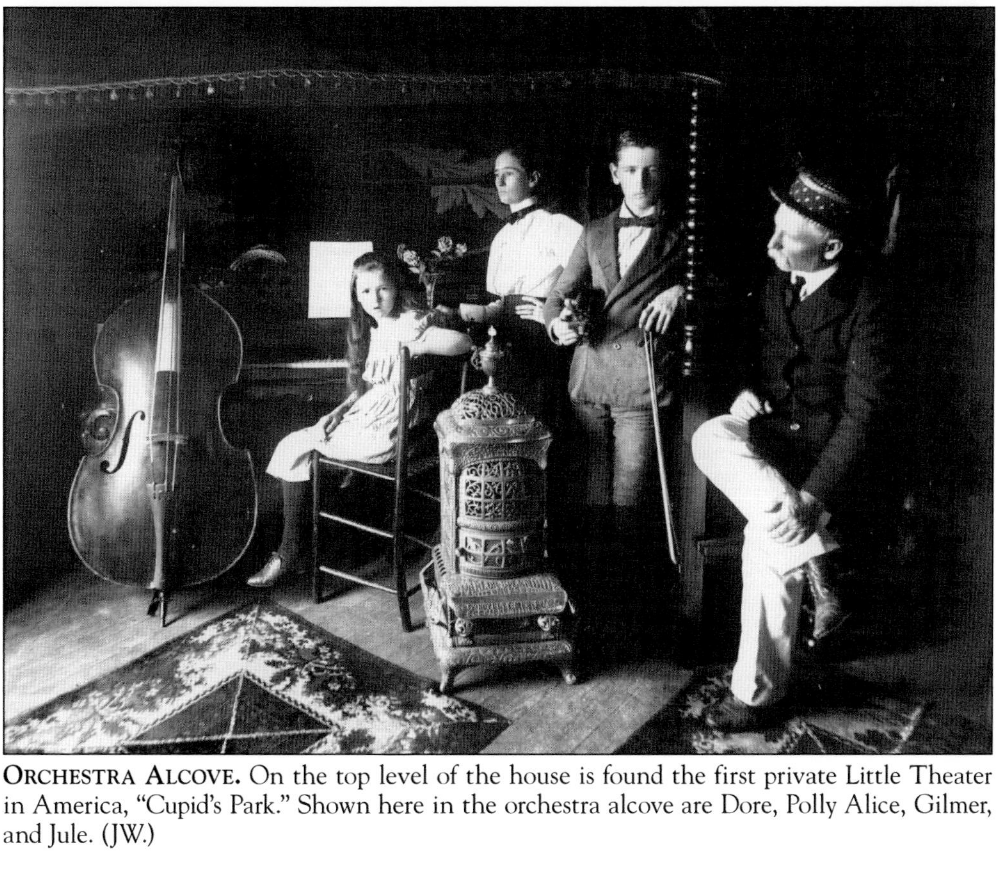

ORCHESTRA ALCOVE. On the top level of the house is found the first private Little Theater in America, "Cupid's Park." Shown here in the orchestra alcove are Dore, Polly Alice, Gilmer, and Jule. (JW.)

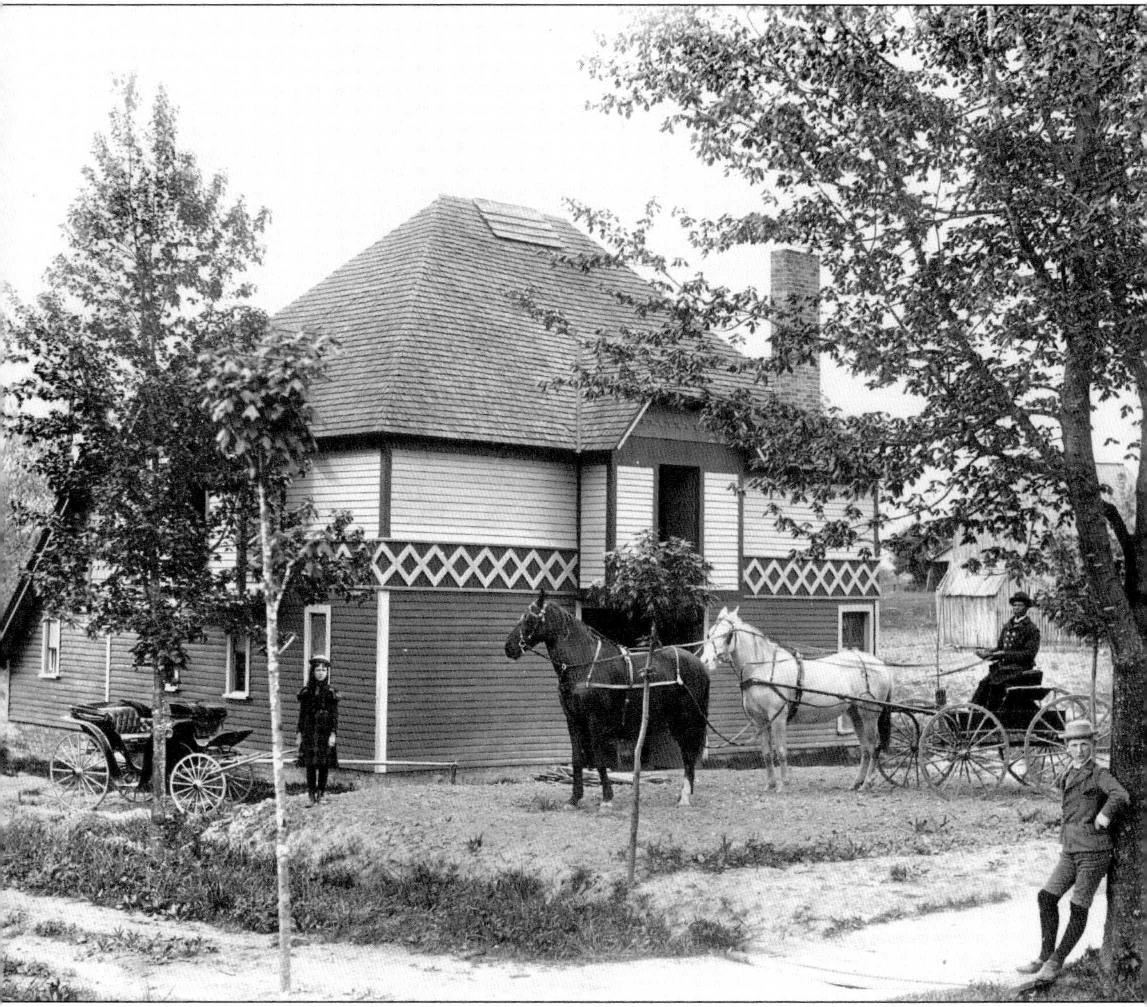

CHILDREN AT THE STABLES. This 1902 photograph shows Dore on the left and Gilmer on the right. Coachman John Carr drives tandem team Boy (black gelding) and Daisy (cream mare). (JW.)

JULE GILMER KÖRNER (1851–1924). Also known as "Reuben Rink," Jule was an artist, advertising genius, and interior decorator. This photograph was taken about 1908. (JW.)

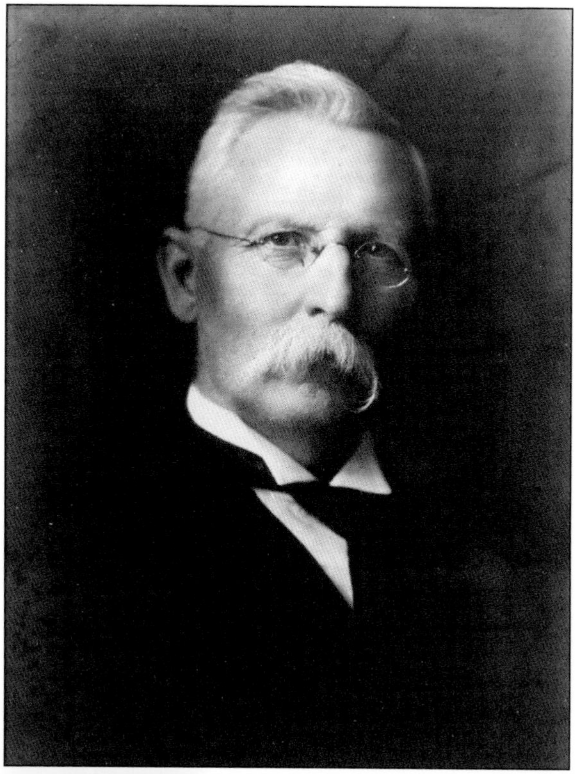

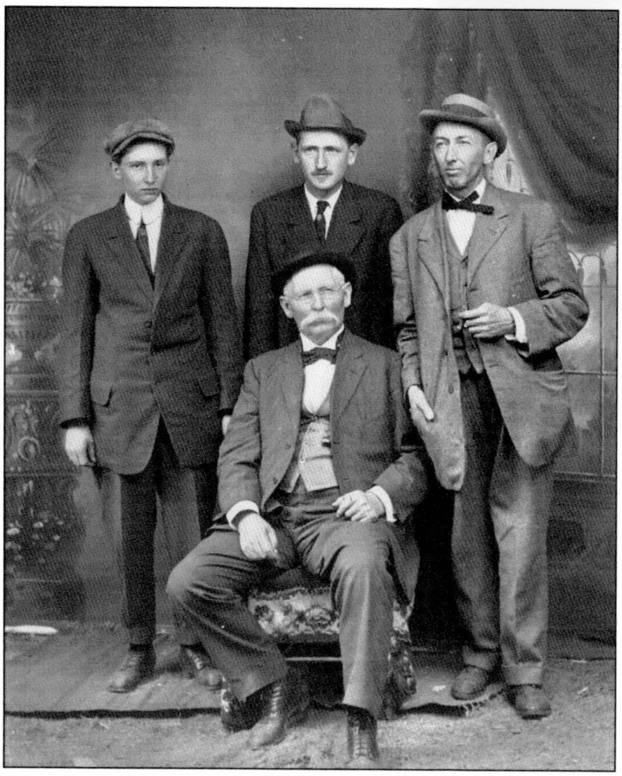

REUBEN RINK DECORATING COMPANY. The combined talents of the Reuben Rink Decorating Company can be seen in homes and churches in the Southeast. From left to right are Philip Körner (son of Henry), J. Gilmer Körner Jr. (son of Jule), and Henry C. Körner (brother of Jule, called "Little Reuben Rink"). Seated is Jule Gilmer Körner Sr. ("Reuben Rink" and builder of the Folly). The photograph was taken about 1911. (JW.)

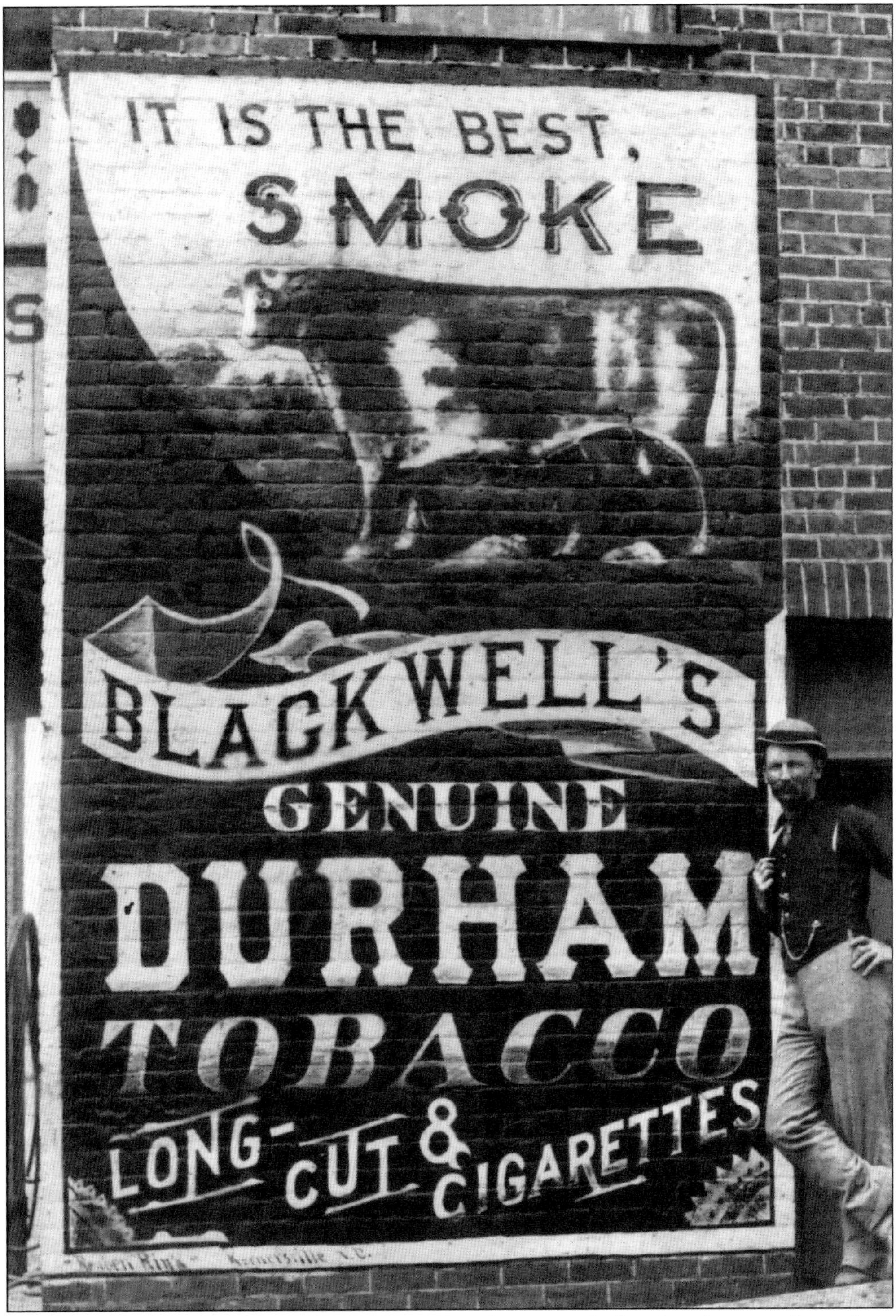

Jule and Bull Durham Advertising. As one of the developers of outdoor advertising, Jule made Dull Durham tobacco a household word with his unique design and advertising campaign. (JW.)

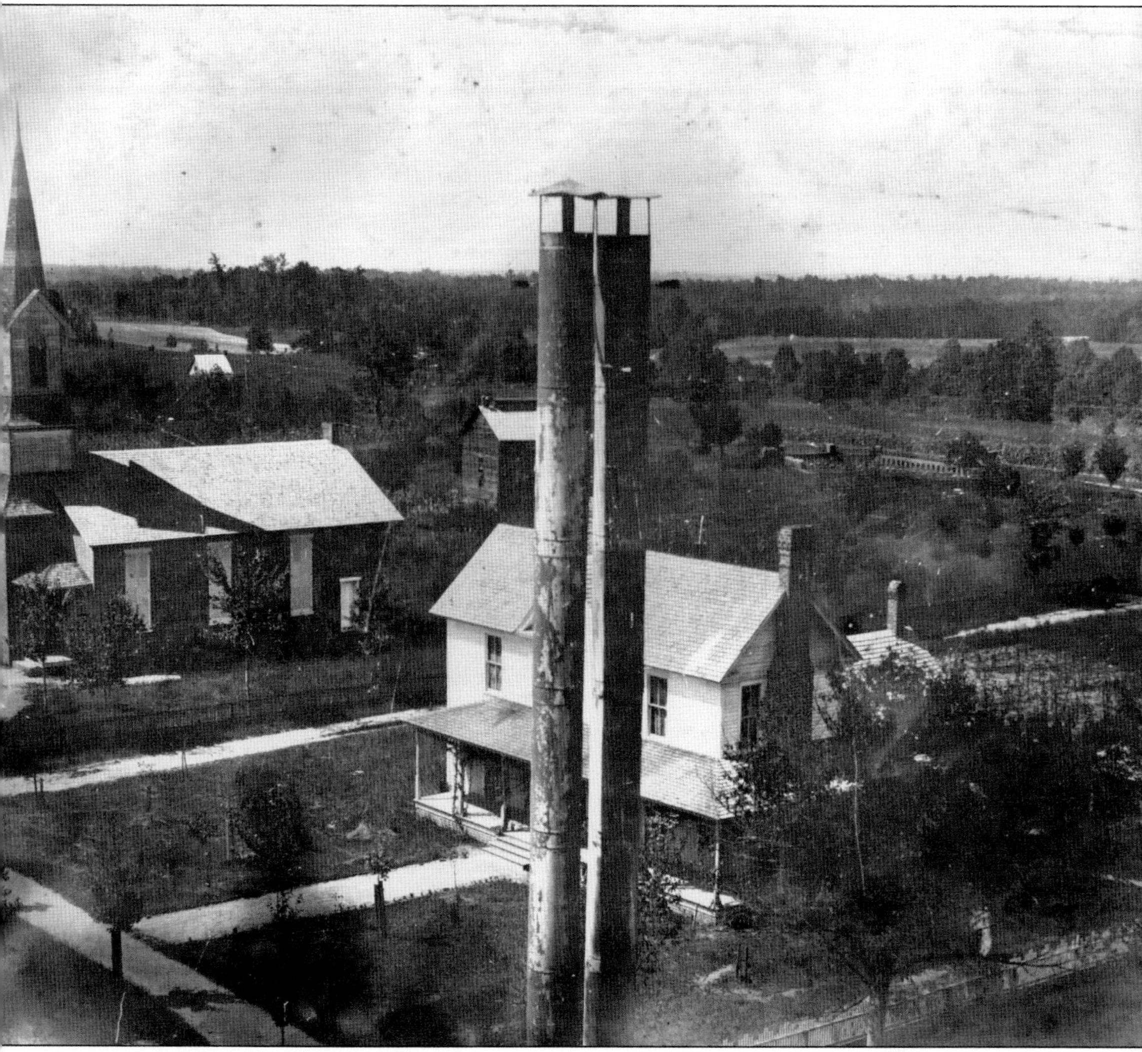

VIEW FROM KÖRNER'S FOLLY, 1899. This photograph was taken from the roof of Körner's Folly. The smokestacks were part of the Folly. The house belonged to James and Addie Kerner. The Kernersville Moravian Church steeple looms on the left. (JW.)

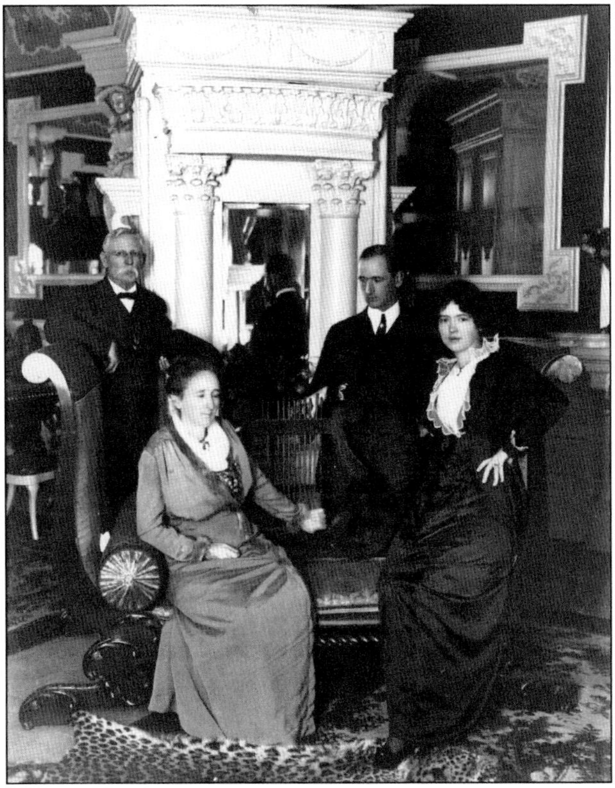

FAMILY, 1914. Jule, Alice, Dore, and Gilmer pose for a 1914 family portrait.

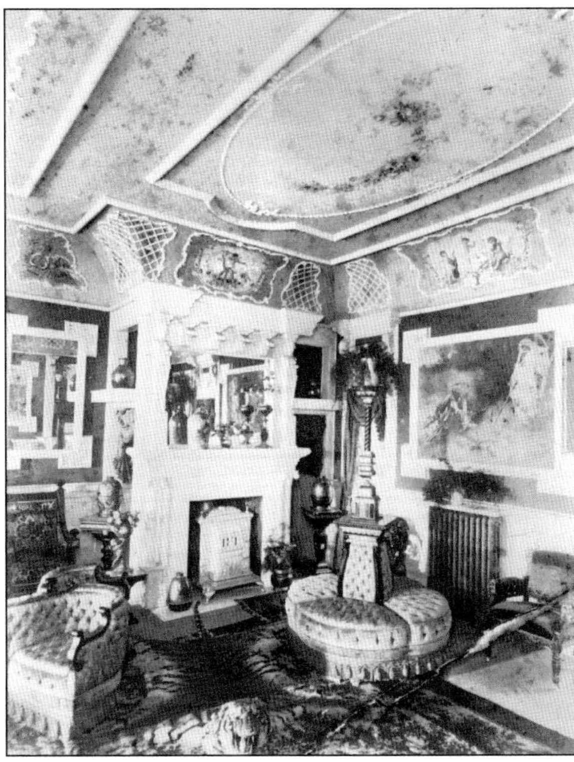

RECEPTION ROOM. The reception room at Körner's Folly is elegant with silk damask panels, hand-laid tile, and magnificent hand-painted murals and frescoes done by a German artist, Caesar Milch. (JW.)

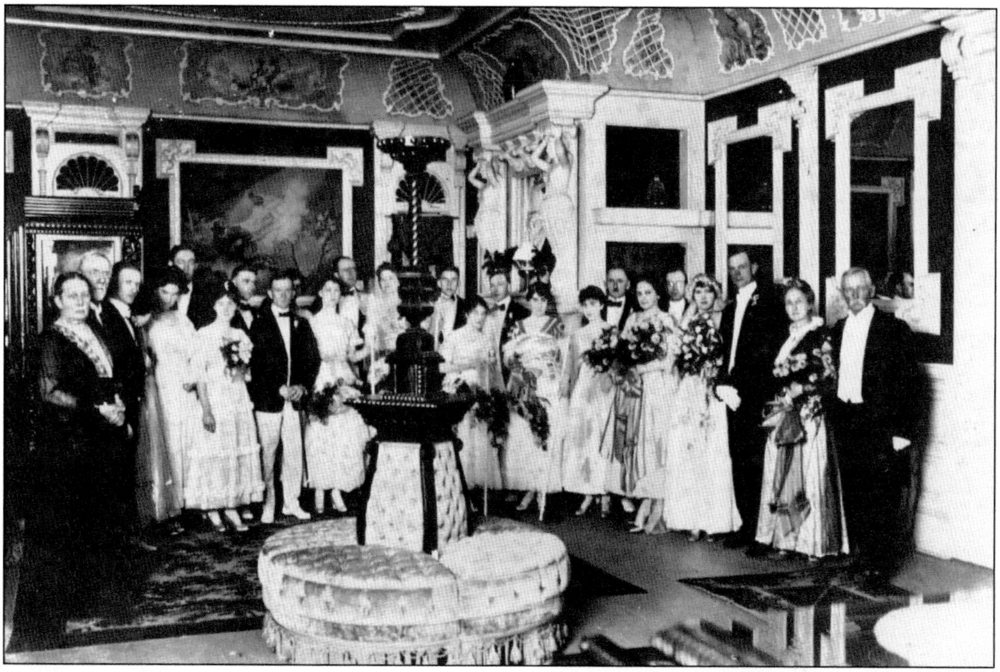

WEDDING, 1916. The wedding reception of Dore Körner and Lanier Donnell was held in the reception room after a wedding ceremony on the north lawn of the Folly. (JW.)

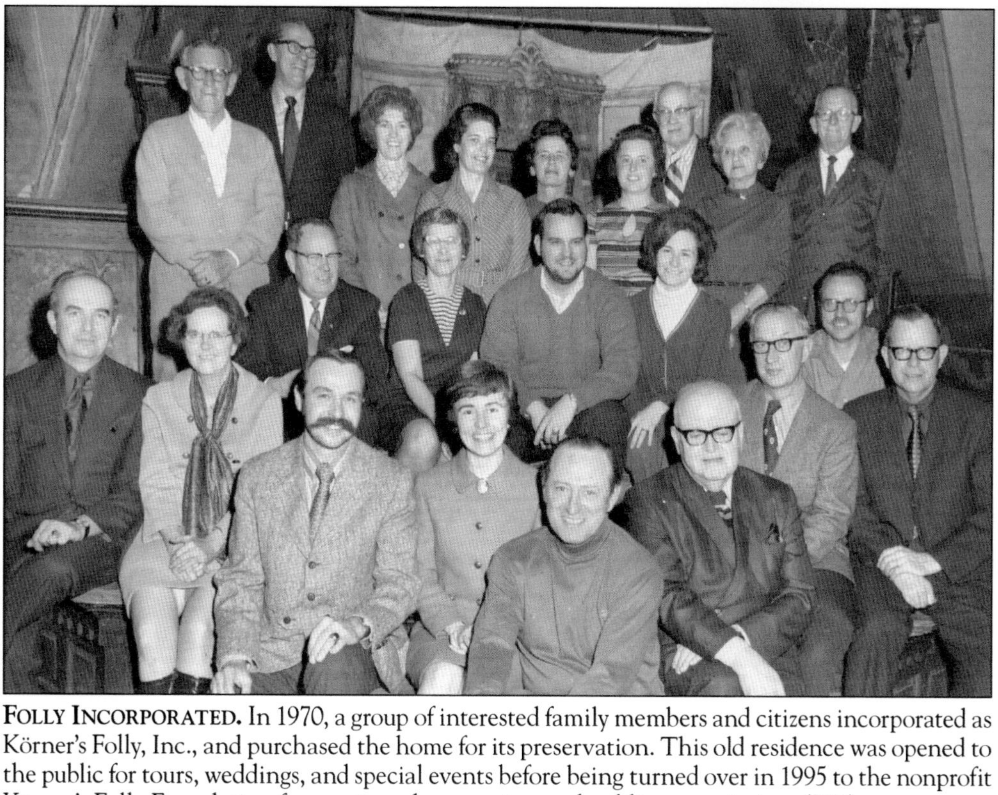

FOLLY INCORPORATED. In 1970, a group of interested family members and citizens incorporated as Körner's Folly, Inc., and purchased the home for its preservation. This old residence was opened to the public for tours, weddings, and special events before being turned over in 1995 to the nonprofit Körner's Folly Foundation for continued restoration and public appreciation. (JW.)

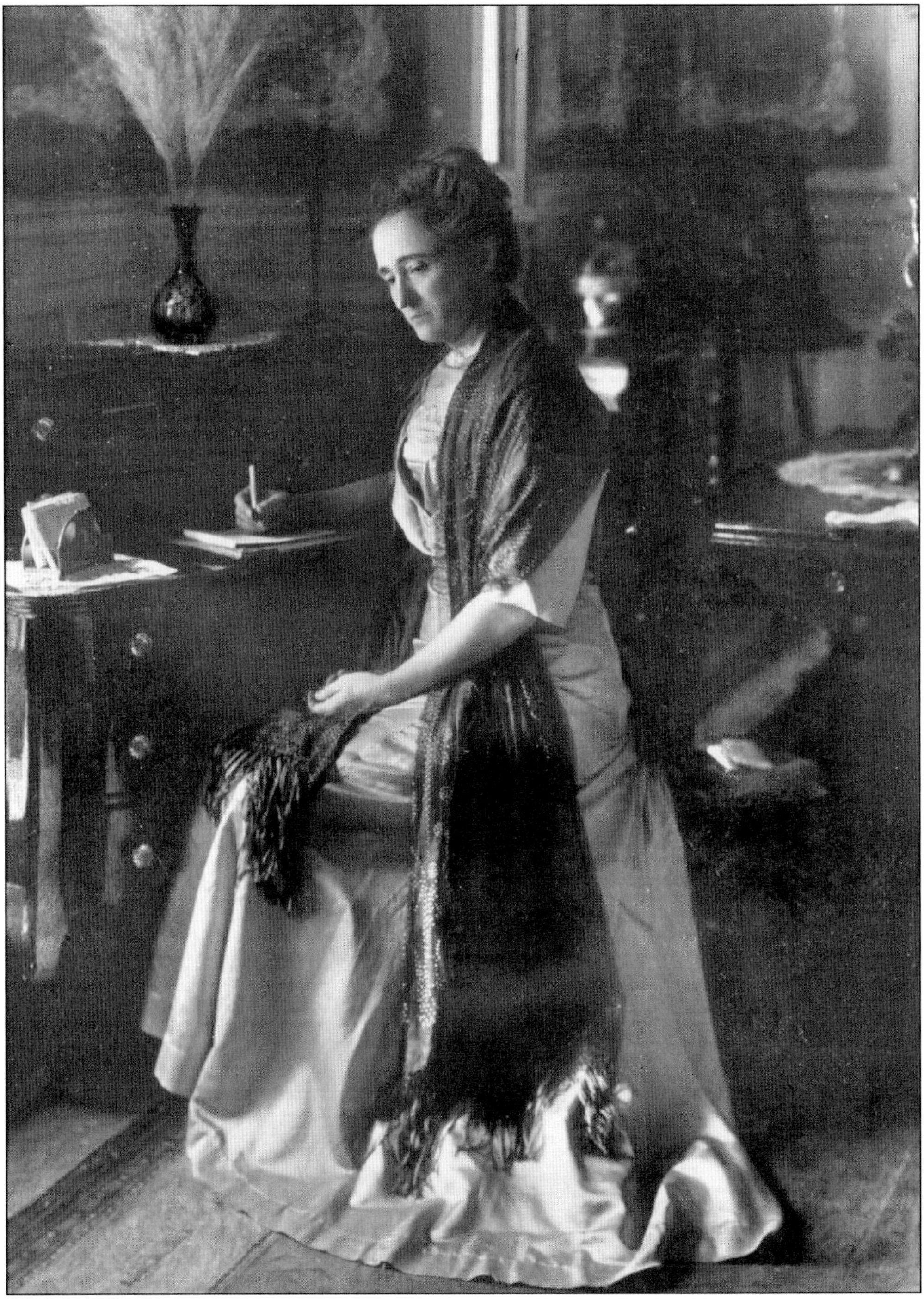

POLLY ALICE MASTEN KÖRNER AT HER DESK. A talented and energetic woman, Alice organized the first Little Theatre group in the United States. She named the upstairs rooms Cupid's Park and there produced original plays with local casts, dancing, orchestration, hand-painted scenery, and homemade costumes. (JW.)

Four

Community Interests and Involvements

As physical boundaries expanded and the railroad came to Kernersville, community interests and involvements escalated. Fires were fought with dependable and expensive equipment. Farmers produced wheat and tobacco. Their rural neighbors raised herds of dairy cows and delivered door-to-door milk orders. Other men and women took reliable jobs in mills, stores, lumber companies, tobacco warehouses, and schools. The canning factory, which processed tomatoes, paid a whopping 50¢ a day for 10 hours' work. A huge tower held the town's water supply. Banks opened for business. Mayors, clerks of court, and boards of aldermen attended to the daily business of the town.

Then there was time for extra service. Civic clubs sprang up and offered assistance to those needing help. Among those were the Lions Club, Extension Homemakers Club, International Order of the Rainbow for Girls, Civitan Club, Exchange Club, Veterans of Foreign Wars (with Ladies Auxiliary), Jaycees (with Jaycettes), and Local Order of Moose.

Parent-Teacher Associations organized as an outgrowth of the Women's Betterment Association, gasoline rationing became a sad reality, and students and teachers alike purchased savings stamps. The John T. Ring Post of the American Legion offered help to veterans and delegates to Boys' and Girls' State. Church activities for both adults and children increased.

The men, women, and children of Kernersville loved parades. They arrived early in droves to line the sidewalks and then watched in amazement as decorated floats, marching bands, old fire engines, and soldiers passed before their eyes.

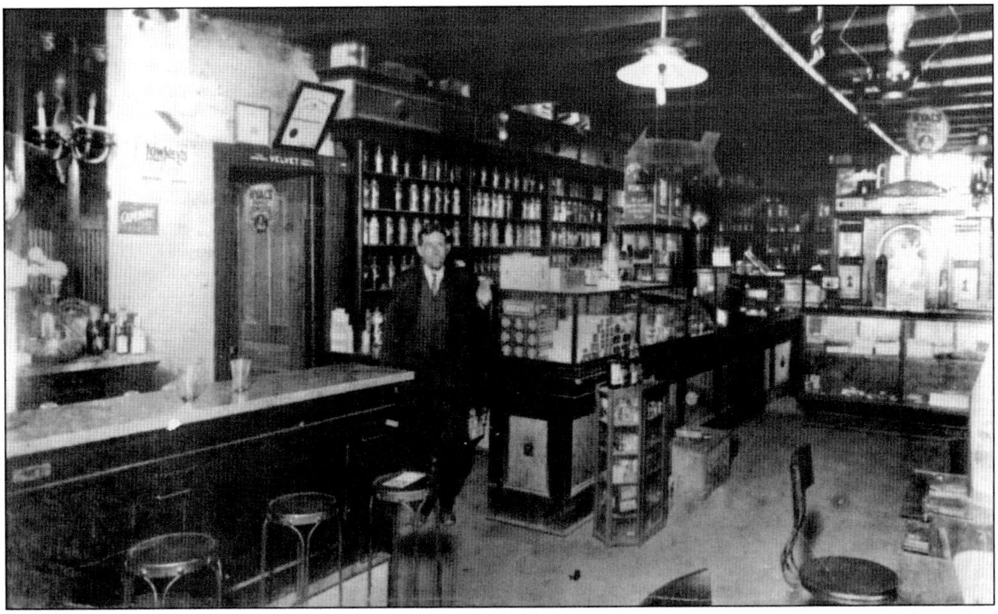

PINNIX DRUG STORE. Beginning in 1904, Pinnix Drug Store, owned and operated by John (Neighbor) Pinnix, was apparently the "place to be" in Kernersville. The back room soon became a favorite place for men to gather for a friendly game of checkers or a round of tall tales. A wood stove heated the entire building. Ice cream tables and booths were inviting to the ladies and children of the town. (JP.)

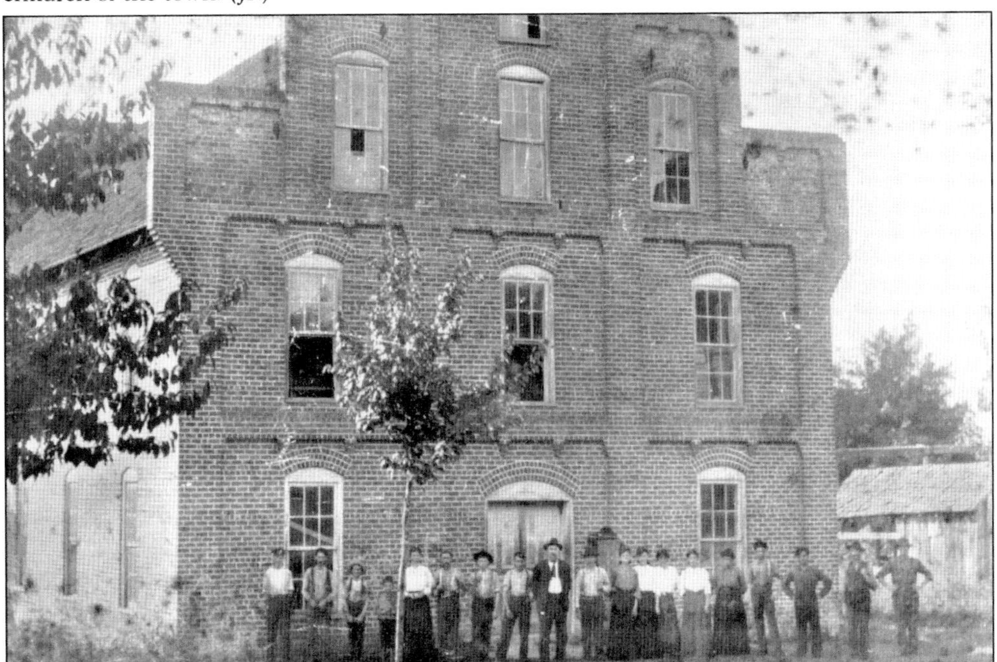

THE WOOLEN MILL. This early business on South Main Street produced blankets. The mill burned in 1909 while Crews Brothers of Walkertown occupied the premises. Originally this large brick building had housed Shore, Kerner & Adkins, Tobacco Manufacturers, run by James F. Kerner and his two sons-in-law, Henry Shore and James Adkins. (MRK.)

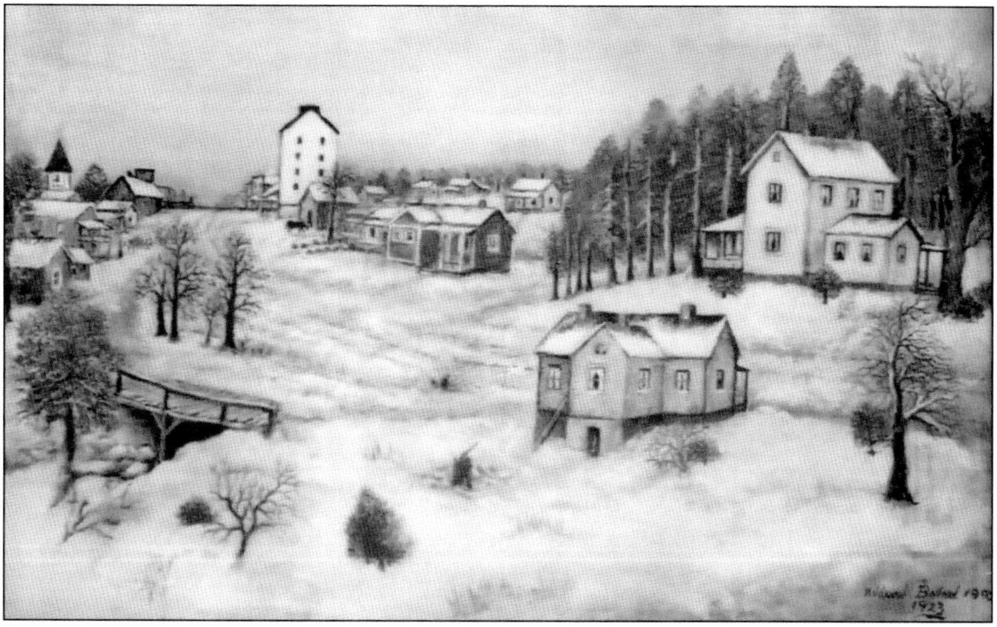

WINTER VILLAGE SCENE. This is Kernersville in winter 1923 as depicted by Kernersville's folk artist Mildred Ballard. (BB.)

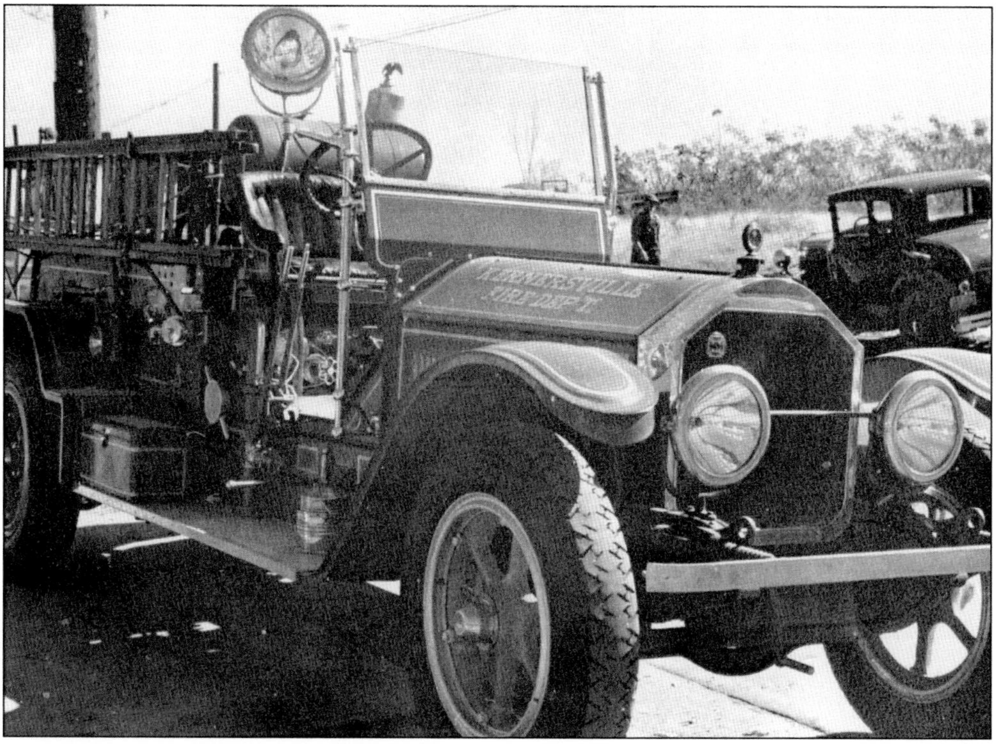

THE LAFRANCE. The town purchased its first fire truck, a 1923 LaFrance, for $6,500. In the early days, Ned Stuart, organizer of the Kernersville Volunteer Fire Department, kept the truck in his garage until a building was completed in 1928. The fire truck has been restored for special events such as antique shows and parades. (MVB.)

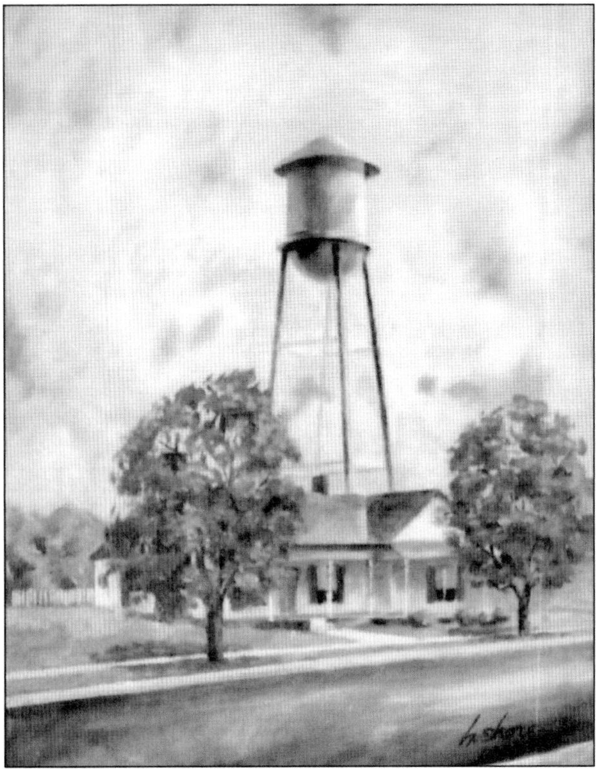

WATER TOWER. The fire alarm was situated on top of the town's water tower on West Mountain Street behind the Cooke House. (MRK.)

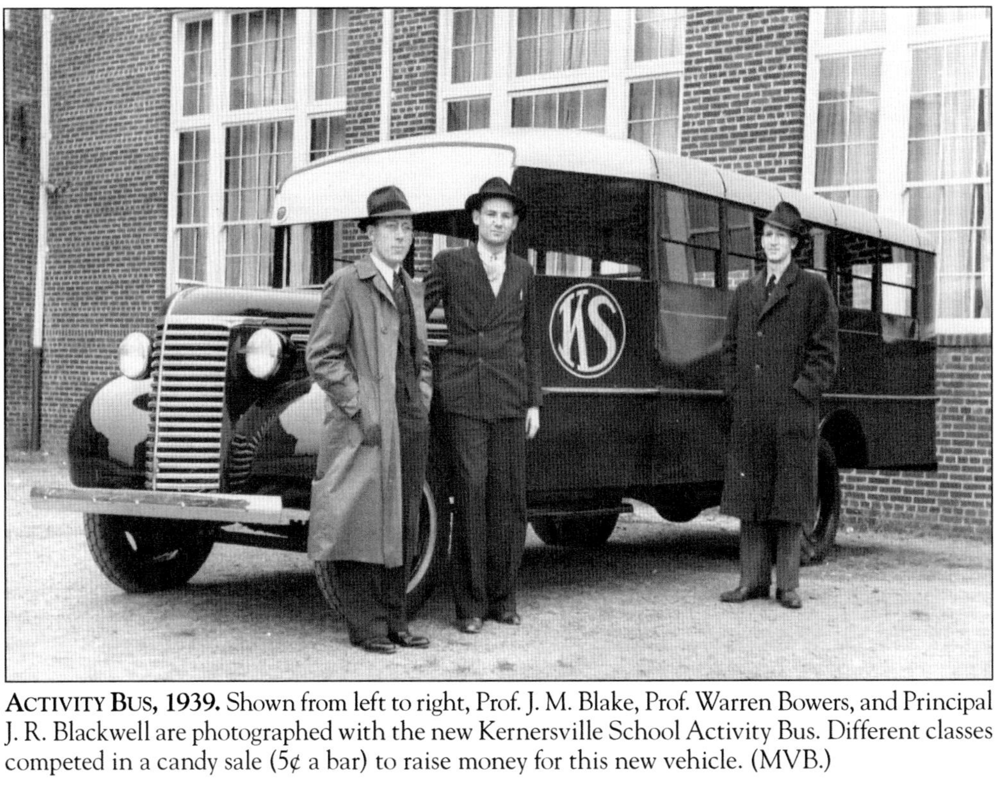

ACTIVITY BUS, 1939. Shown from left to right, Prof. J. M. Blake, Prof. Warren Bowers, and Principal J. R. Blackwell are photographed with the new Kernersville School Activity Bus. Different classes competed in a candy sale (5¢ a bar) to raise money for this new vehicle. (MVB.)

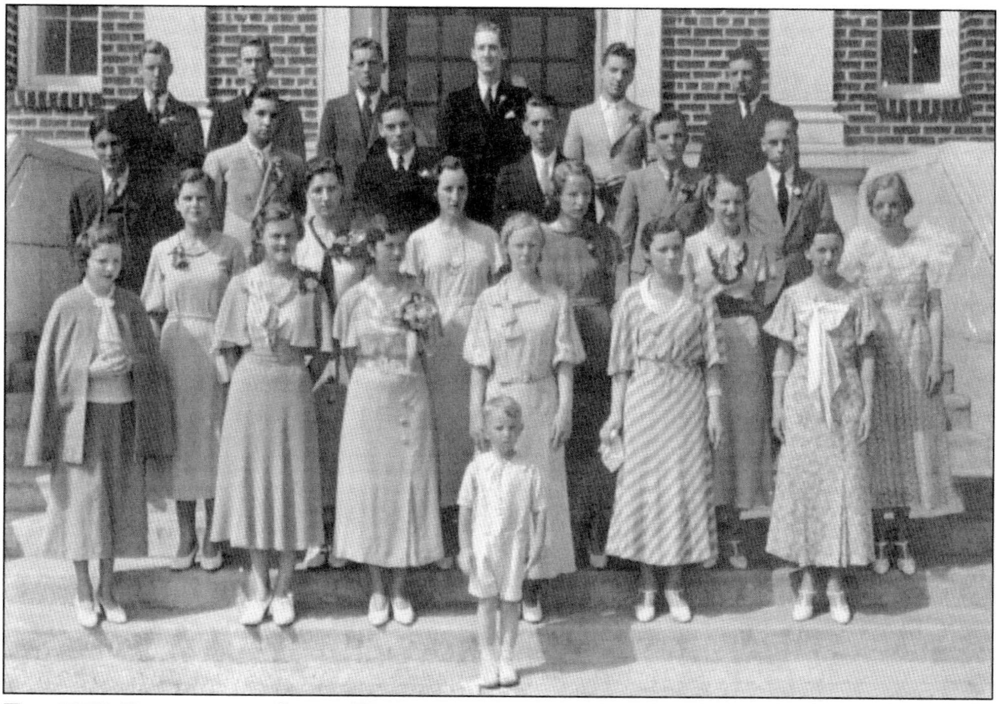

THE 1933 GRADUATING CLASS, KERNERSVILLE SCHOOL. Established by Rev. J. W. Pinnix on November 22, 1907, Kernersville's first high school burned in 1925. A new building was finished in time for the 1927 graduates to receive their diplomas. This photograph shows the 1933 graduates with Ed Shore as mascot. (ES.)

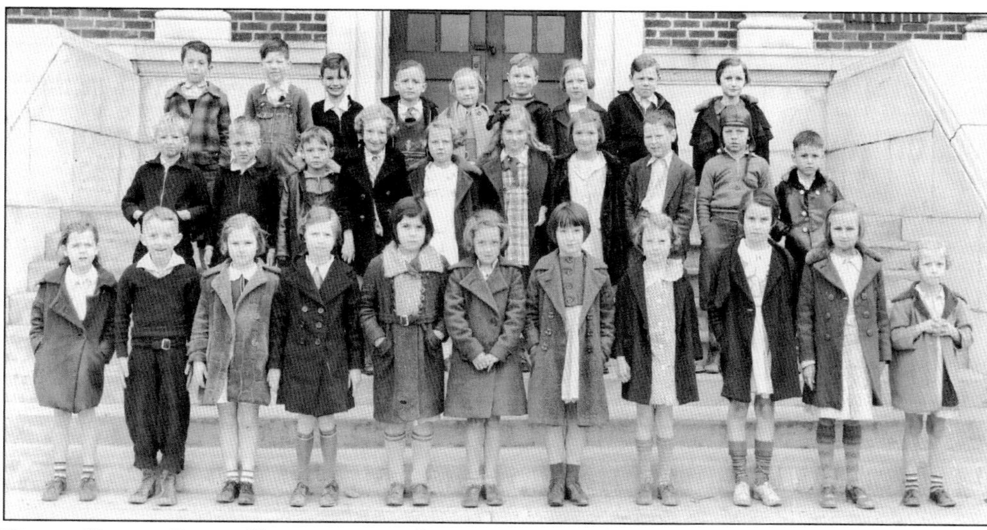

THIRD-GRADE CLASS, KERNERSVILLE SCHOOL, 1936. These third-grade children pose on the front steps of the school. Shown here from left to right are the following: (first row) Carolyn Cooke, Edgar Shore, Pauline Tilley, Maxine Idol, Mary Thomas, Sybil Thomas, Mary L. Mitchell, Joanne Pegg, Boyd Vass, Marie Crews, and Bernice Kirkman; (second row) Horace Nelson, Crawford Roddy, Charles Hubbard, Nancy L. Wicker, Laura M. Tuttle, Frances L. Meadows, Rachel Pardue, Conrad Barrow, Richard Stockton, and Robert Wells; (third row) Robert Joyce, Clay Blackburn, Ferney Baker, Leon ?, Alma Tatum, William Kerner, Bernice Idol, Zeb Vance, and Alice F. Wilson. (ES.)

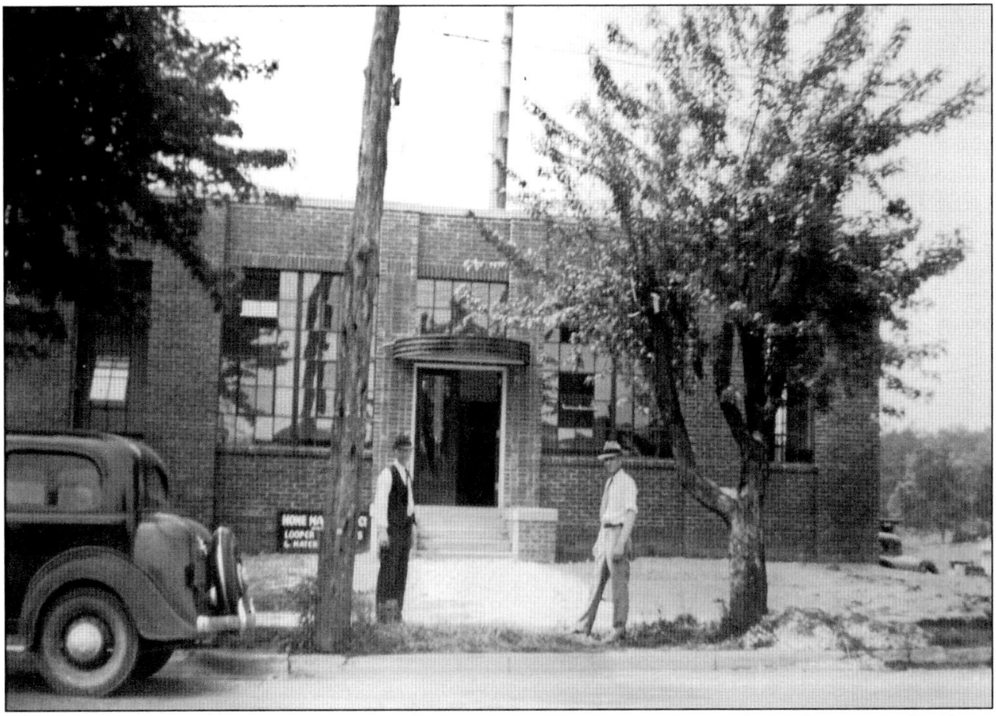

KERNERSVILLE LAUNDRY/SHORE BROTHERS HOMEMADE RUG COMPANY. Shown here are K. E. Shore (left) and E. E. Shore and their business. This photograph was taken about 1935. (ES.)

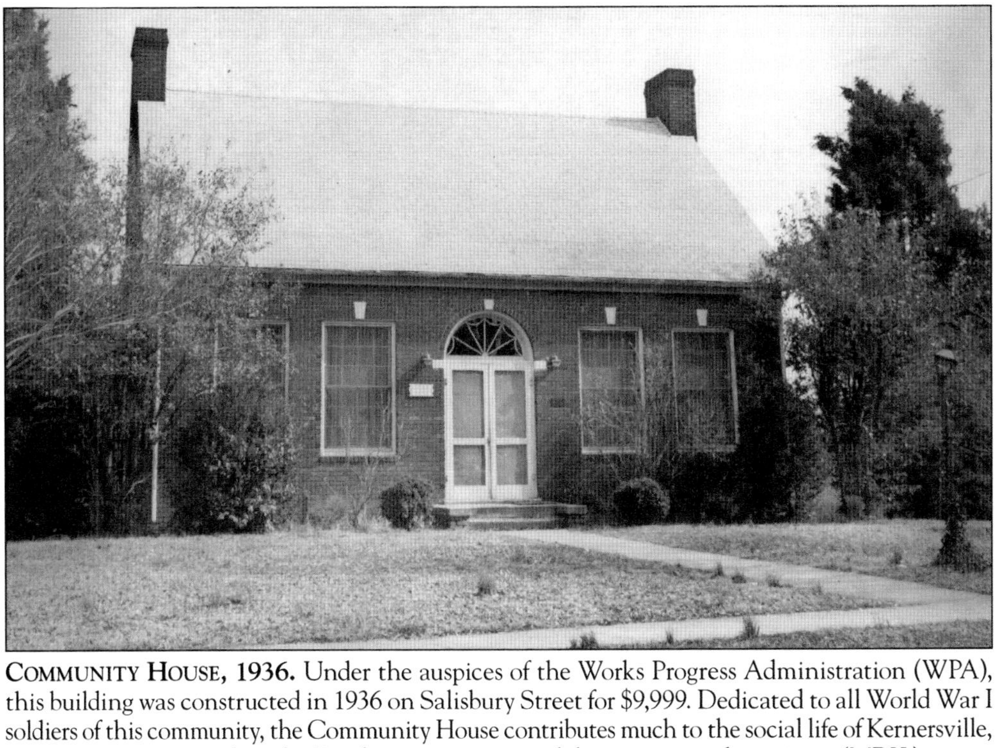

COMMUNITY HOUSE, 1936. Under the auspices of the Works Progress Administration (WPA), this building was constructed in 1936 on Salisbury Street for $9,999. Dedicated to all World War I soldiers of this community, the Community House contributes much to the social life of Kernersville, serving as a meeting place for Sunday services, civic clubs, parties, and reunions. (MRK.)

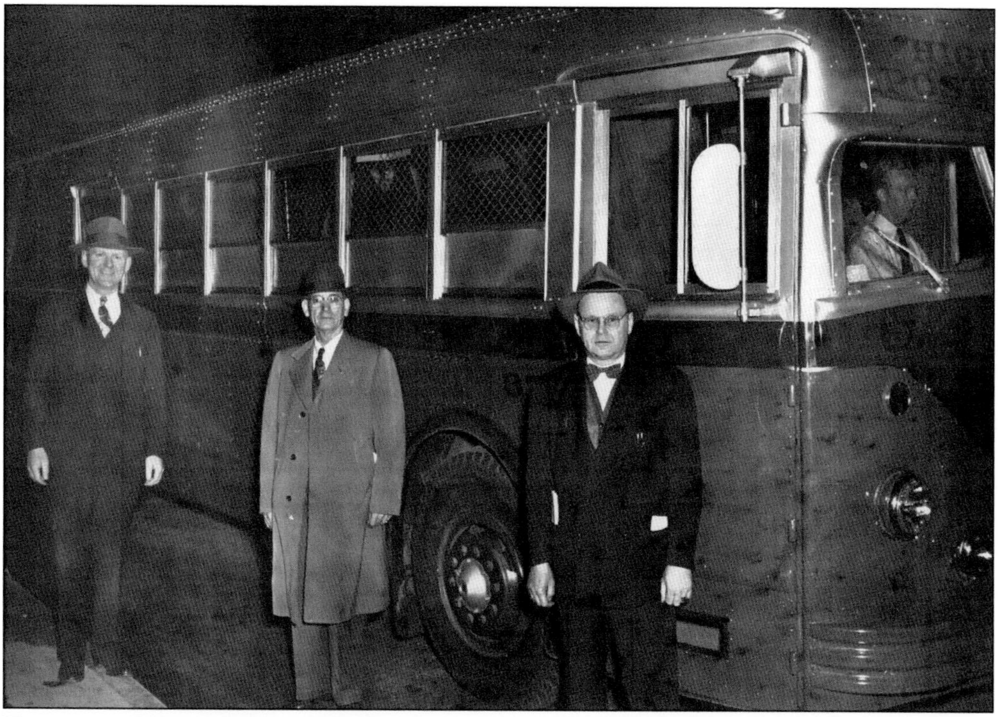

Traveling Post Office, c. 1940s. This mobile post office helped get mail to rural residents. Harmon Linville is pictured on the left. (MRK.)

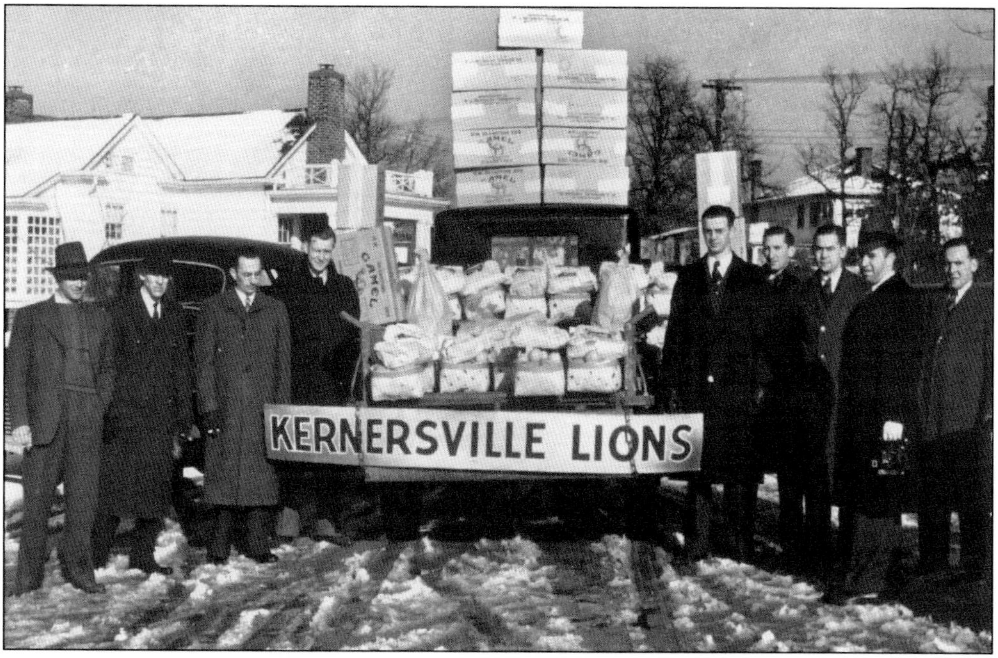

Kernersville Lions at Work. Chartered as the second club in Forsyth County and one of the first in the state, the Kernersville Lions Club's major goal has always been to offer assistance to the visually handicapped. Members are quick to volunteer their services in community and civic projects. (SC.)

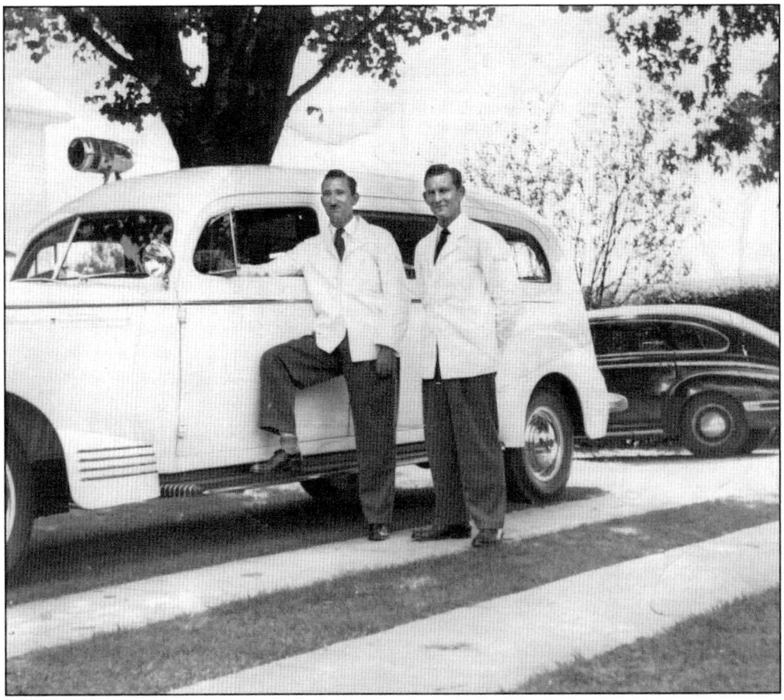

Ambulance Crew, c. 1940s. Charlie James Ragland (left) and Philip Körner (right) take their ambulance duty seriously. These two men were associated with Linville Funeral Home. (MKH.)

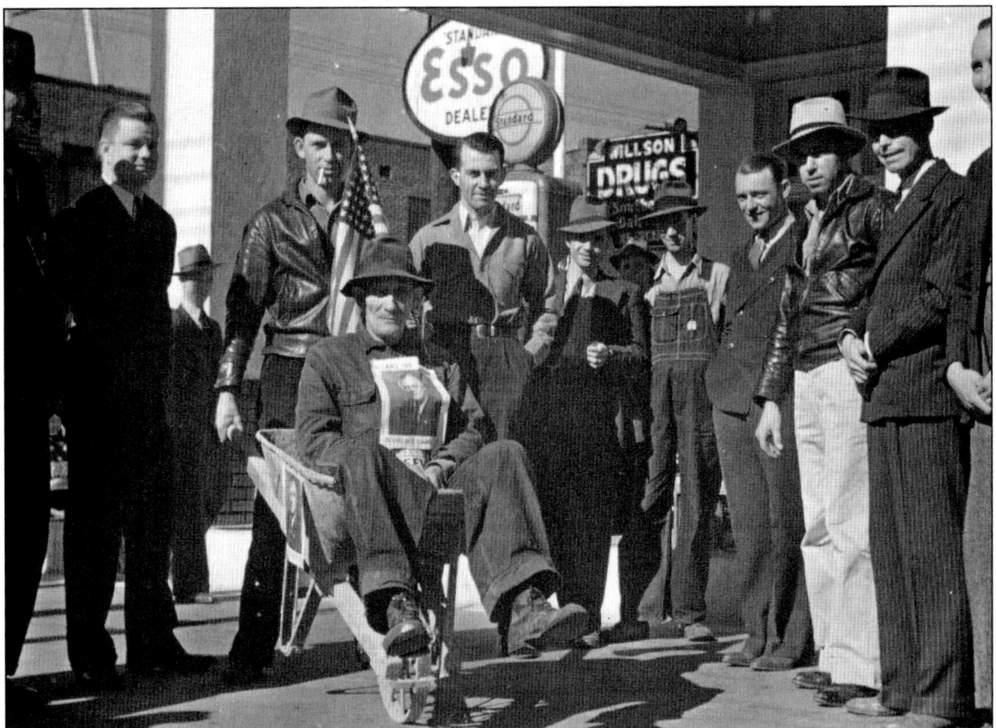

Political Rally. With enthusiasm and fervent political concern, these citizens held a political rally at Main and Mountain Streets. Note the poster of F. D. Roosevelt, who advocated the New Deal. (MVB.)

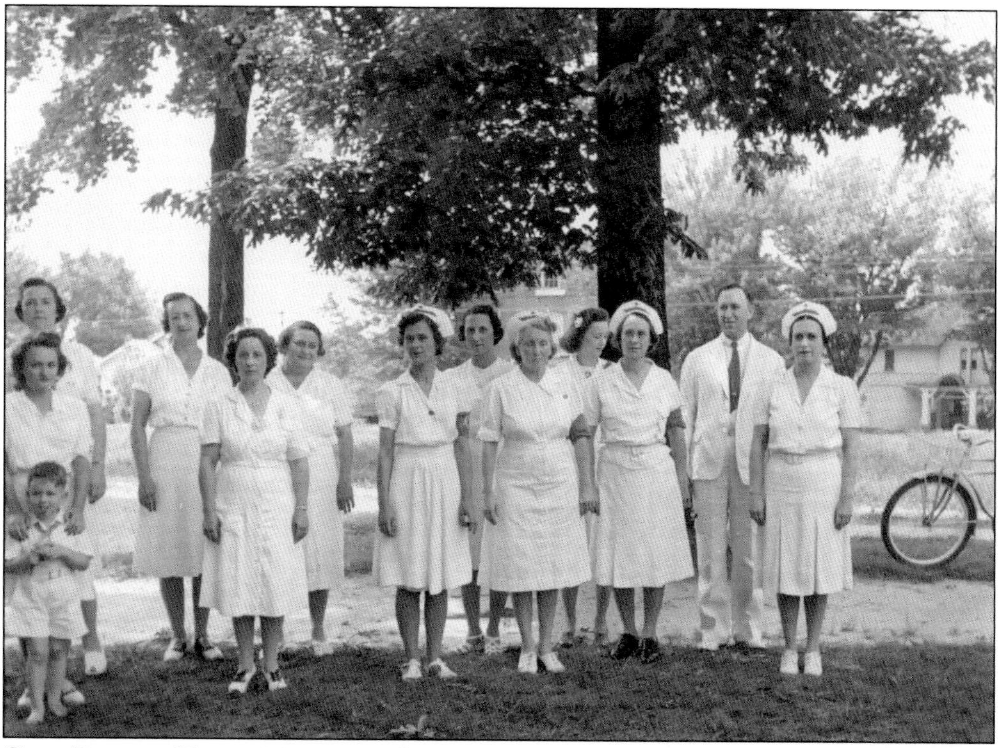

CIVIL DEFENSE UNIT, 1940–1941. These patriotic citizens comprised the Civil Defense Unit. They are from left to right as follows: Virginia Linville, Frances Parrish Wrenn, unidentified boy, Glancey Parrish, unidentified, Otavia Körner, Mary Porter, Ida Roberts, Collie Pegg, Josephine Sims Barbour, Nancy Allen, Dr. Richard Whitaker, and Annabelle Stuart. (MRK.)

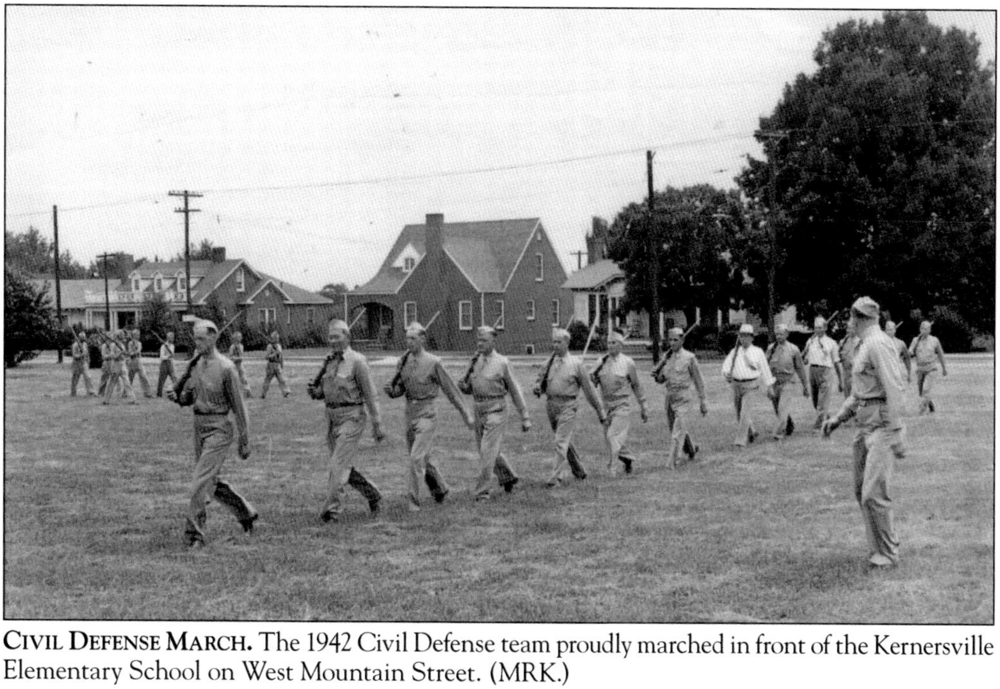

CIVIL DEFENSE MARCH. The 1942 Civil Defense team proudly marched in front of the Kernersville Elementary School on West Mountain Street. (MRK.)

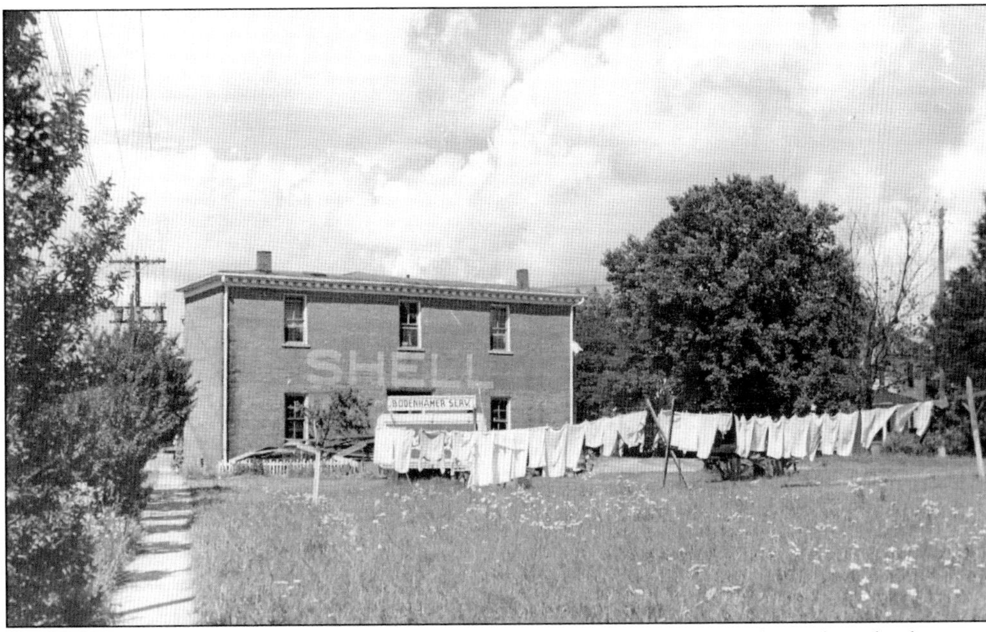

BACK OF BODENHAMER STORE. This rear view of Bodenhamer Store shows laundry hanging on a nearby resident's clothesline. Originally, E. Y. (Yancy) Marshall and his wife, Iocelia, operated a general store and lived upstairs. Then the business became a Shell service station. In the early 1930s, Harvey Bodenhamer restored it to a general store. Today the building contains various offices. (MVB.)

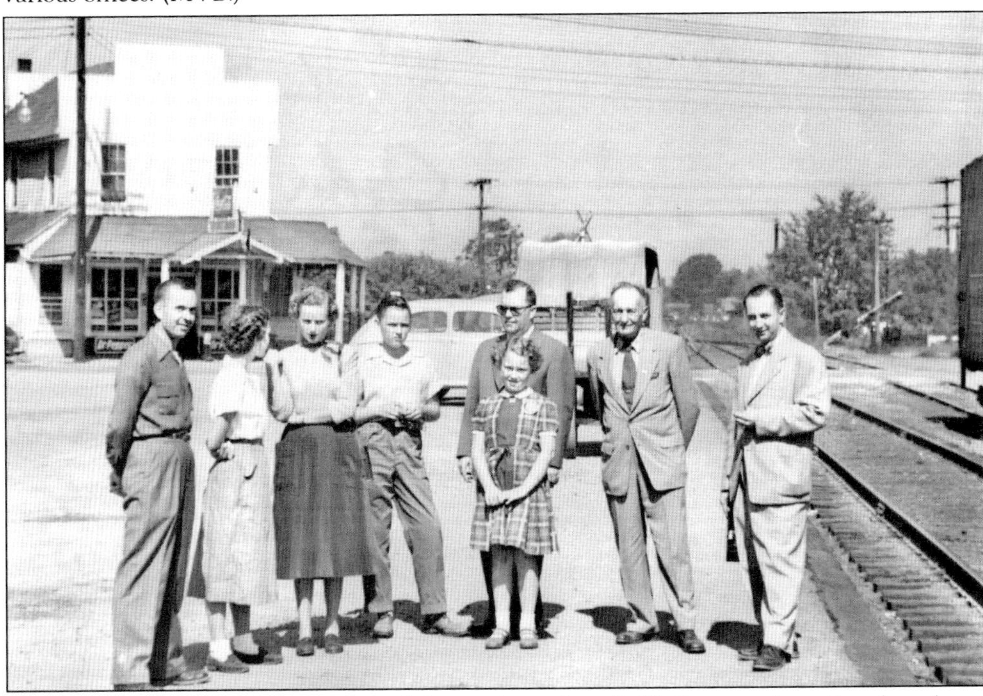

JINX BULL'S STORE. Posed here, from left to right, at Jinx Bull's Store at the railroad tracks are John Vance, Sarah Vance, Virginia Snow, Sam Vance III, Sam Vance, Beatrice Vance, Philip Körner, and Charlie Snow. (MVB.)

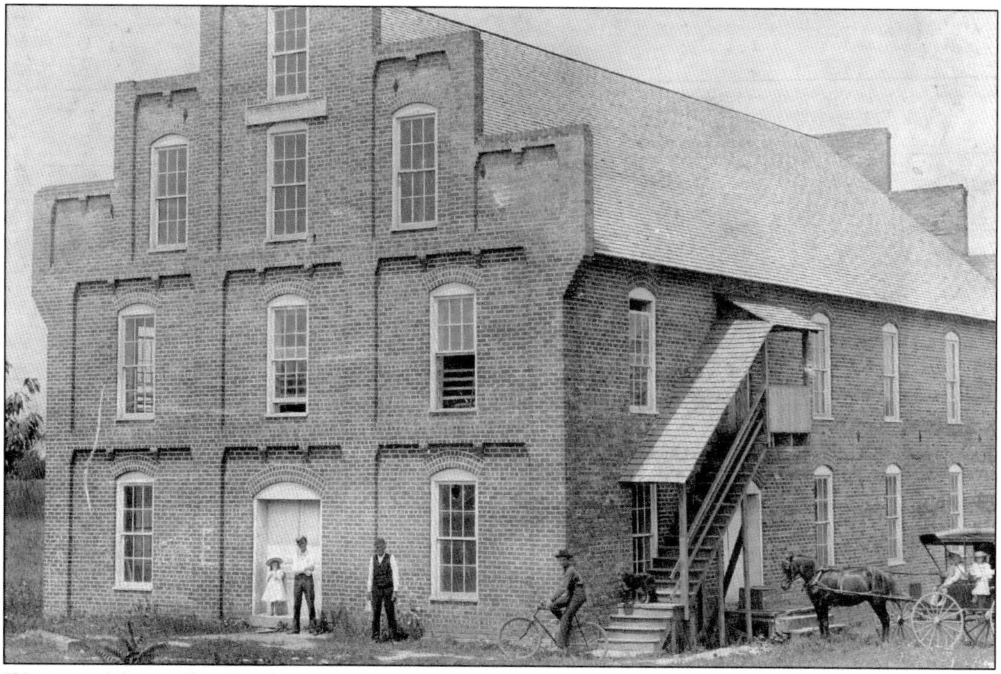

WOOLEN MILL. The Woolen Mill on South Main Street made blankets. Shown here from left to right are Maude Kerner Ring, James F. Kerner, Dr. Elias Kerner, George G. Kerner, Robert Shore, and Ed Shore. The mill burned in 1909. (MVB.)

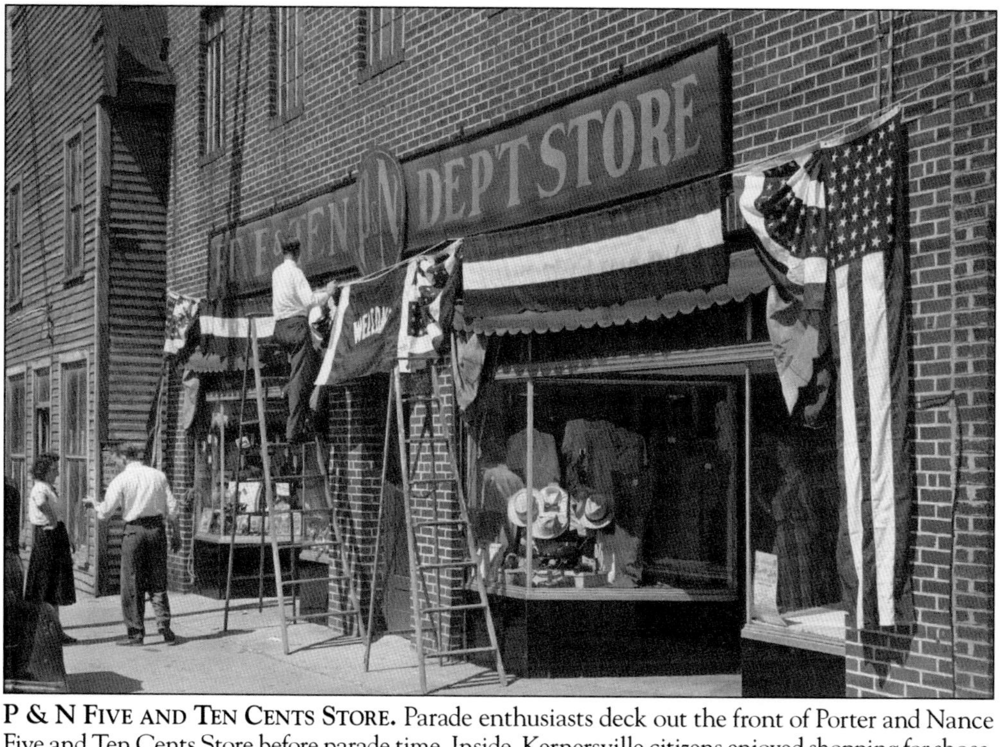

P & N FIVE AND TEN CENTS STORE. Parade enthusiasts deck out the front of Porter and Nance Five and Ten Cents Store before parade time. Inside, Kernersville citizens enjoyed shopping for shoes, clothing, toys, and household items. The candy counter lured both children and adults. (MRK.)

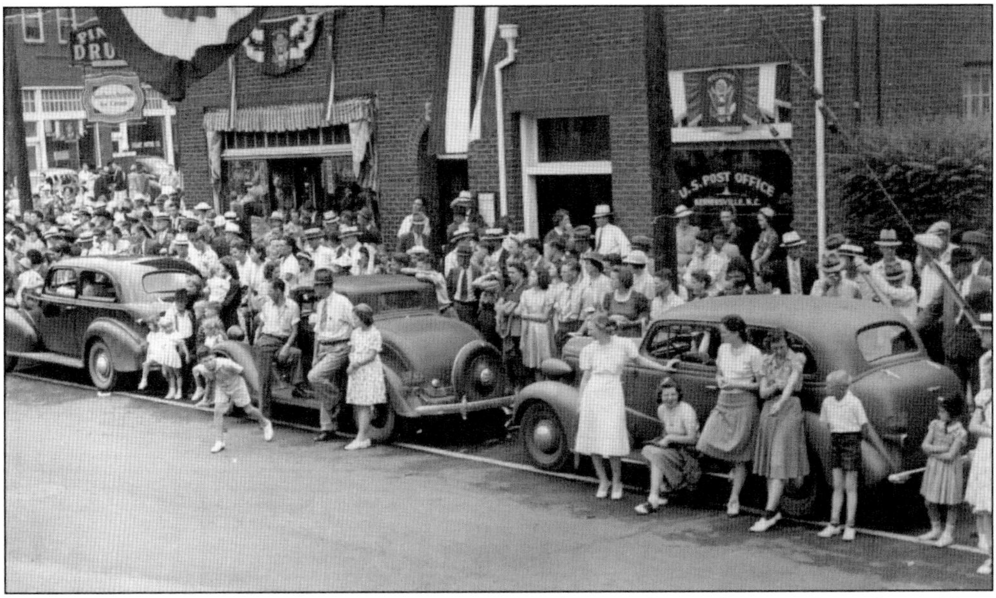

PARADE WAITING. An excited pre-parade crowd gathers in front of Pinnix Drug Store. Note the Southern Dairies Ice Cream and old Coca-Cola signs. The boy in the street peers eagerly for the first float. (MRK.)

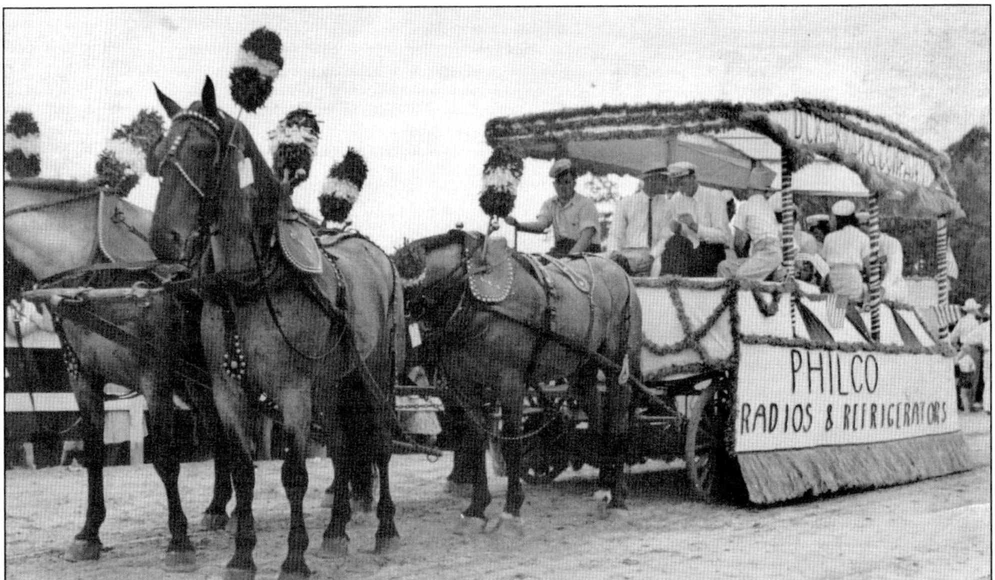

D. C. KIRKMAN AND COMPANY. Pulled by horses with gala plumes, the D. C. Kirkman and Company float advertises Philco radios and refrigerators. (MRK.)

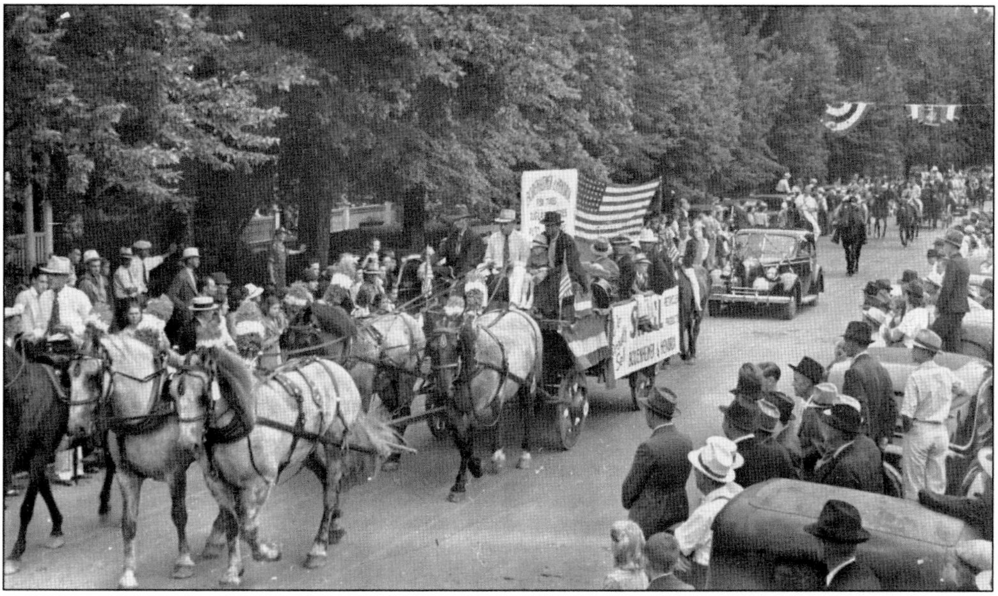

BODENHEIMER AND HENDRIX. This Bodenheimer and Hendrix parade wagon, proudly advertising Shell petroleum products, carries a group of folks. The American flag flies proudly. The team of horses sports fancy plumes. (MRK.)

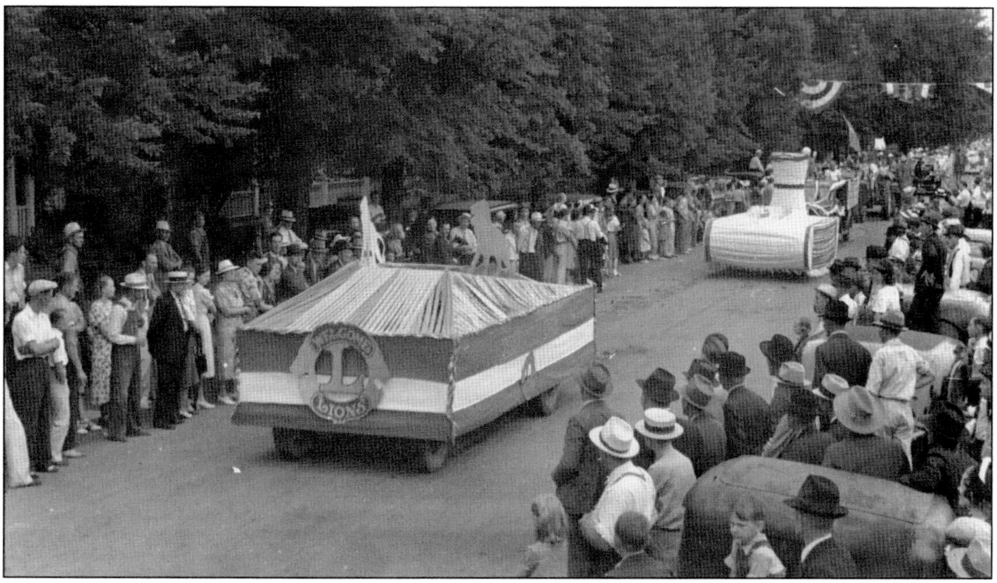

THE LIONS CLUB. The Kernersville Lions Club float, decorated with large stand-up lions, gets the attention of the parade watchers. (MRK.)

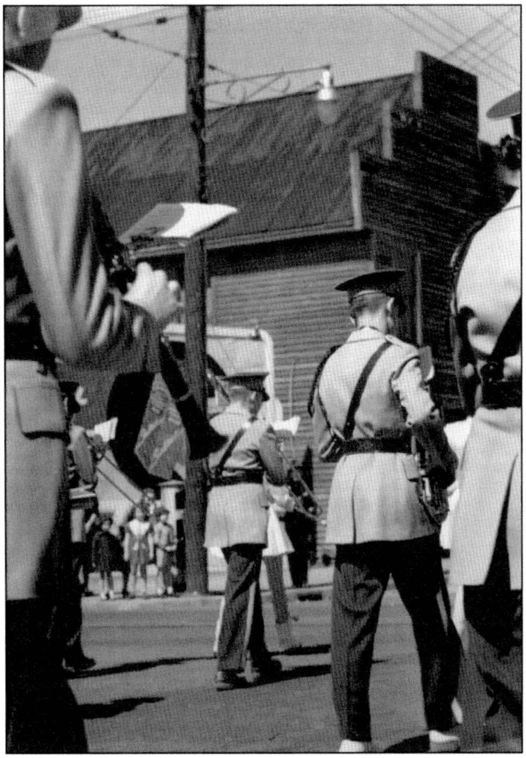

Oak Ridge Military Academy. Children in the background gaze in rapture as the Oak Ridge Military Academy marching band goes by. (MRK.)

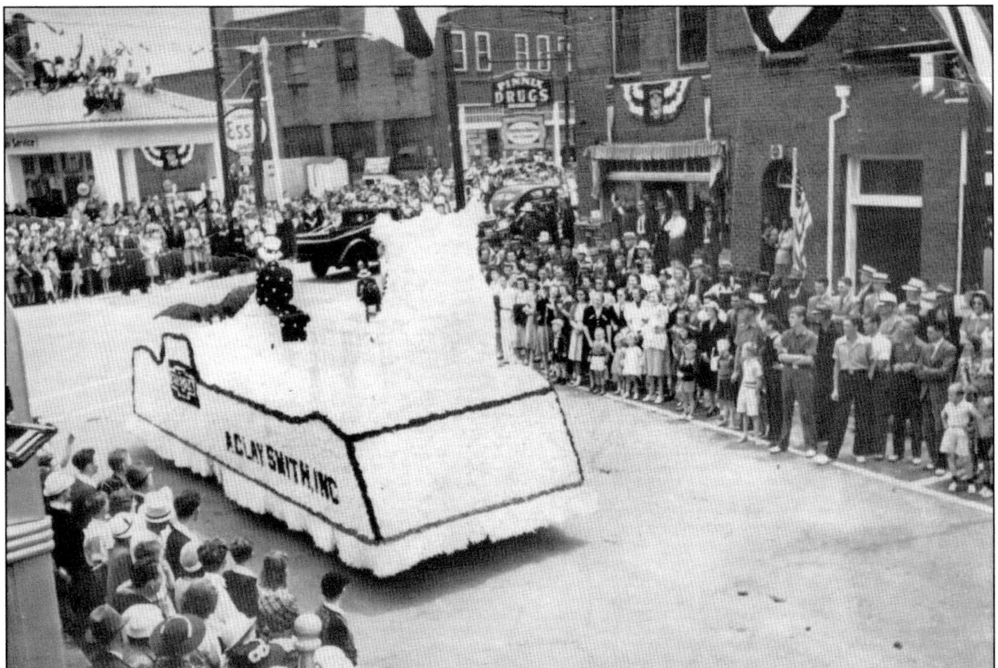

Clay Smith Float. The elegance and beauty of the Clay Smith float thrills the crowd. Note the crowd perched atop the Esso station; both male and female spectators sport their best clothes and hats. (MRK.)

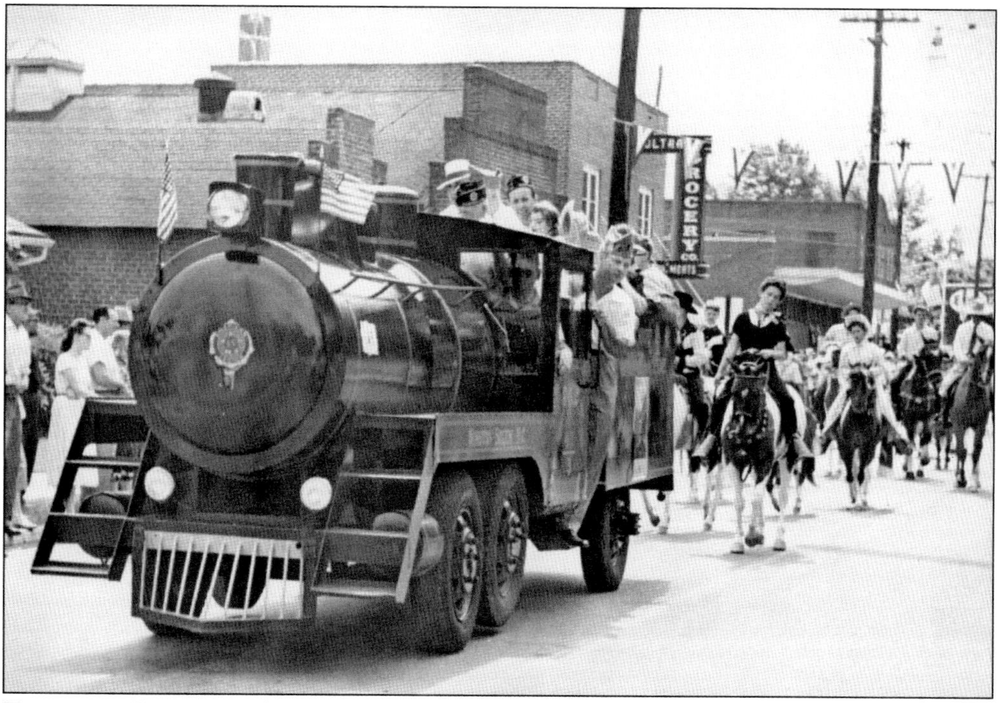

TRAIN ON PARADE. The Winston-Salem train engine is popular in this July 4, 1940, Kernersville parade. (MVB.)

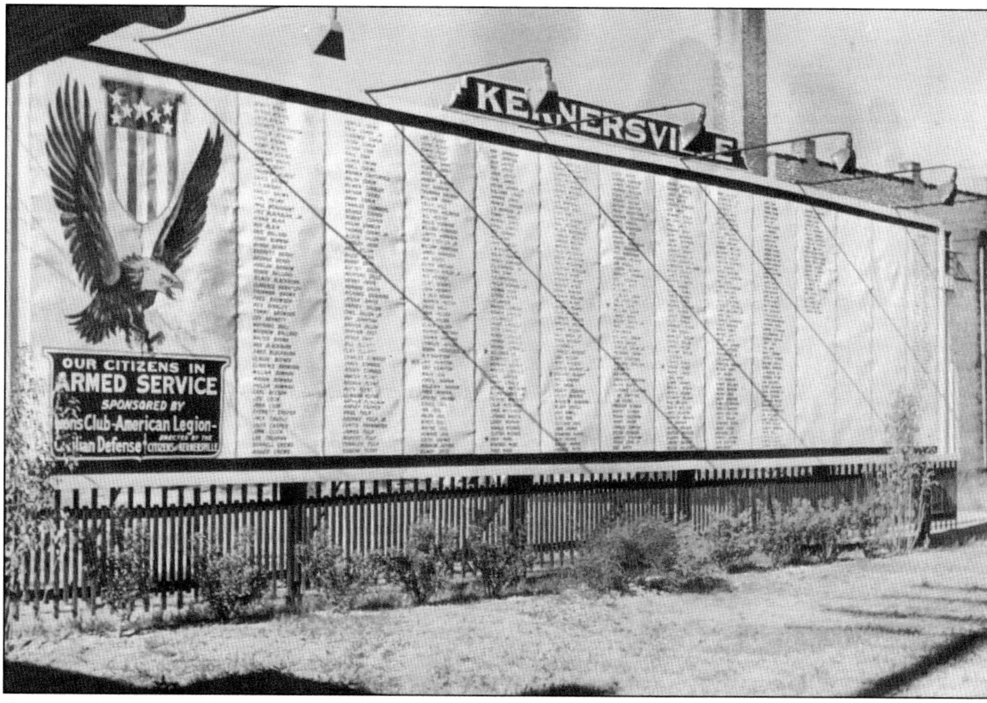

BILLBOARD. Erected by citizens of Kernersville and sponsored by the Lions Club, American Legion, and Civilian Defense, this billboard showed the names of Kernersville boys serving in the Armed Service. It was located on West Mountain Street in front of the old water tower. (MRK.)

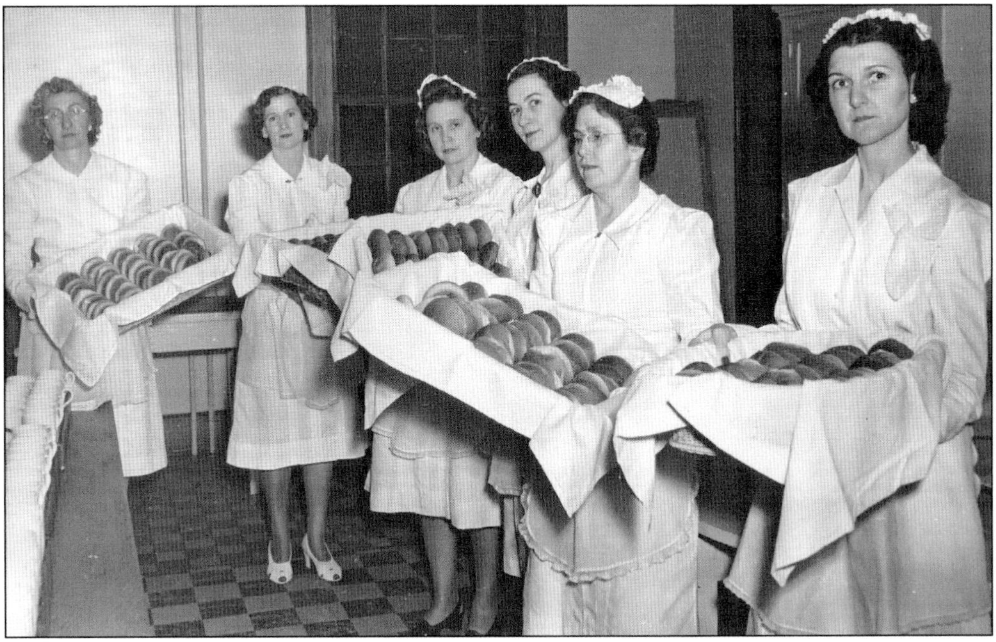

MORAVIAN DIENERS, C. 1948–1949. The Moravian Love Feast originated in Old Salem by the Moravian Germans who settled there. This feast is held at various times during the church year and consists of a traditional Moravian spiced bun and coffee or hot spiced cider as a beverage. The server is called a diener. Pictured from left to right are Neva Linville, Grace Holder, Lula Shore, Mary Stanley Flynn, Eileen Smith, and Mary Phillips. (MRK.)

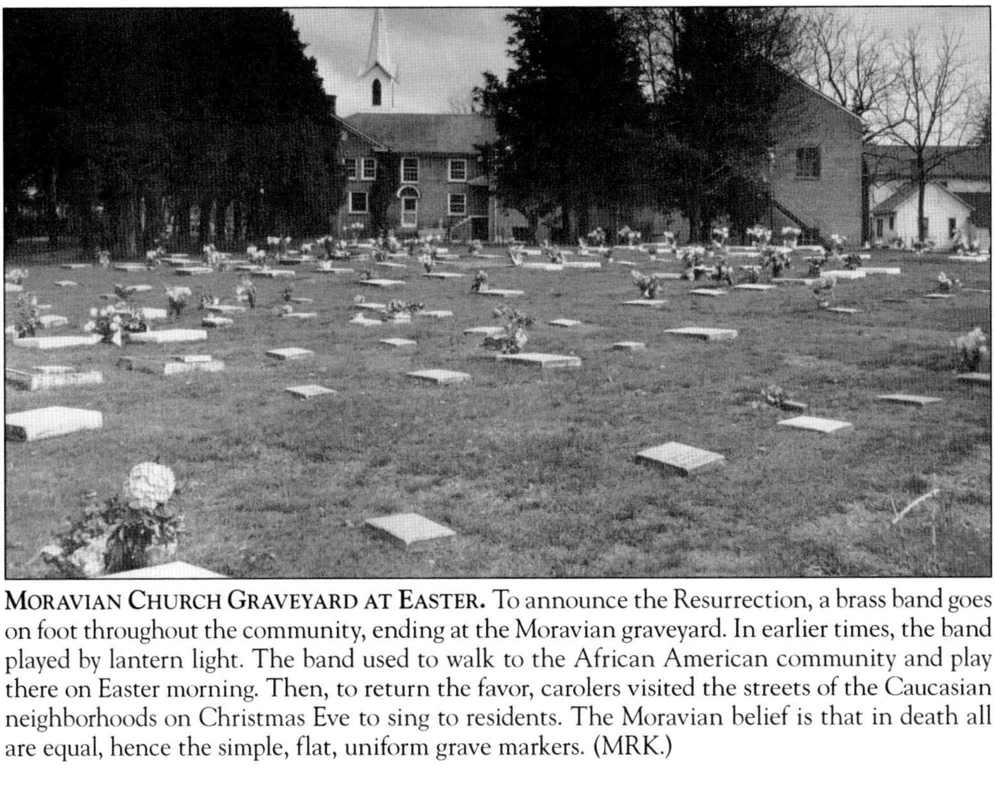

MORAVIAN CHURCH GRAVEYARD AT EASTER. To announce the Resurrection, a brass band goes on foot throughout the community, ending at the Moravian graveyard. In earlier times, the band played by lantern light. The band used to walk to the African American community and play there on Easter morning. Then, to return the favor, carolers visited the streets of the Caucasian neighborhoods on Christmas Eve to sing to residents. The Moravian belief is that in death all are equal, hence the simple, flat, uniform grave markers. (MRK.)

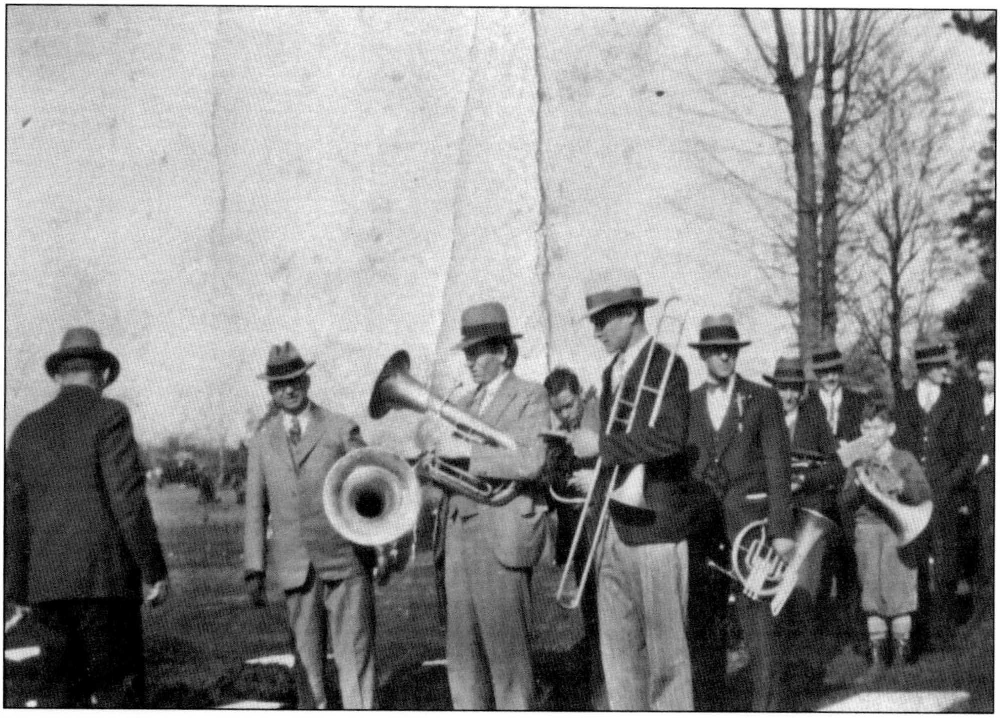

MORAVIAN BAND, 1930S. The first Moravian Band was organized in 1891. Members in the 1930s are shown here and include Carl Kerner, John Vance, Philip Körner Sr., Philip Körner Jr., W. O. Doggett, and Ted Kerner. (MRK.)

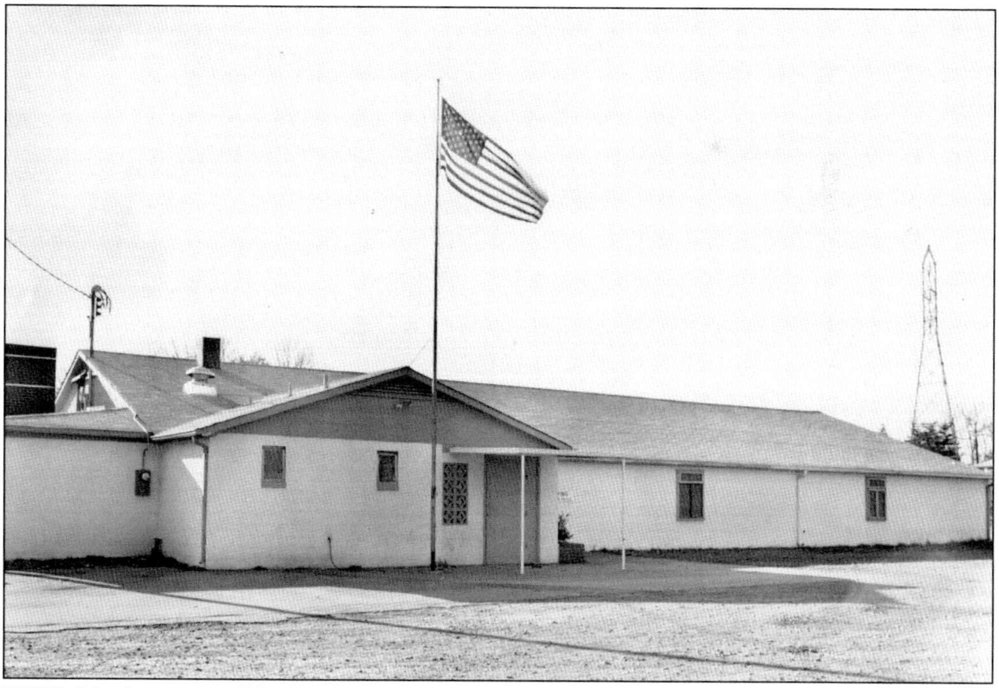

VFW. The Veterans of Foreign War Post 5352 was organized in 1946 with 28 members. (MRK.)

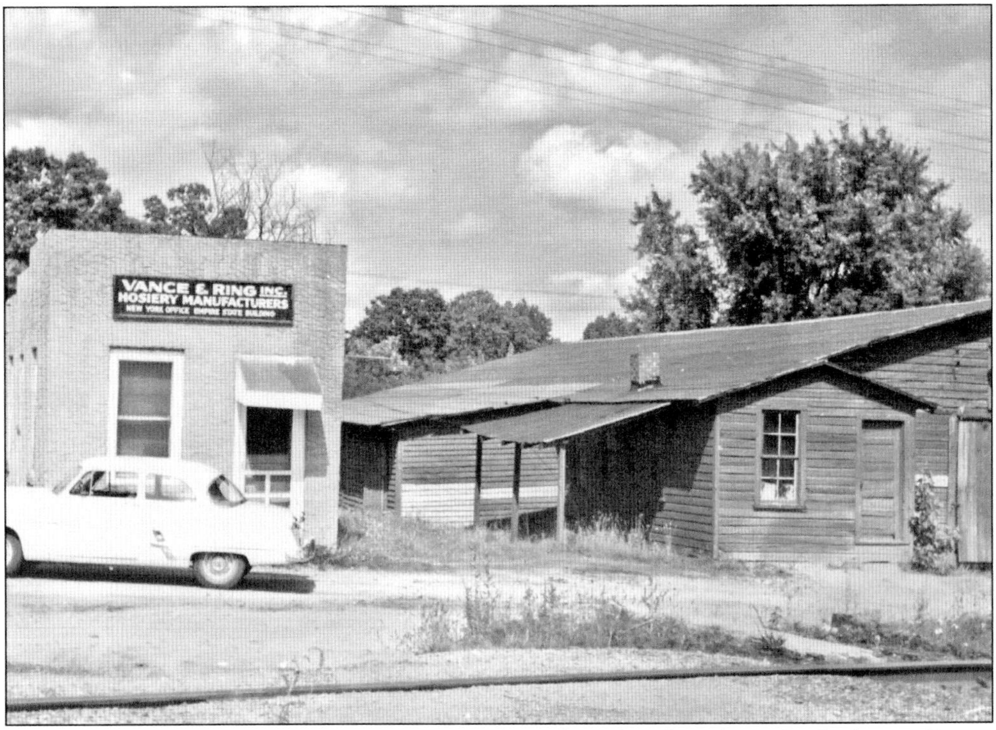

VANCE AND RING. This hosiery mill, located along the railroad tracks on Bodenhamer Street, employed many local citizens. (MVB.)

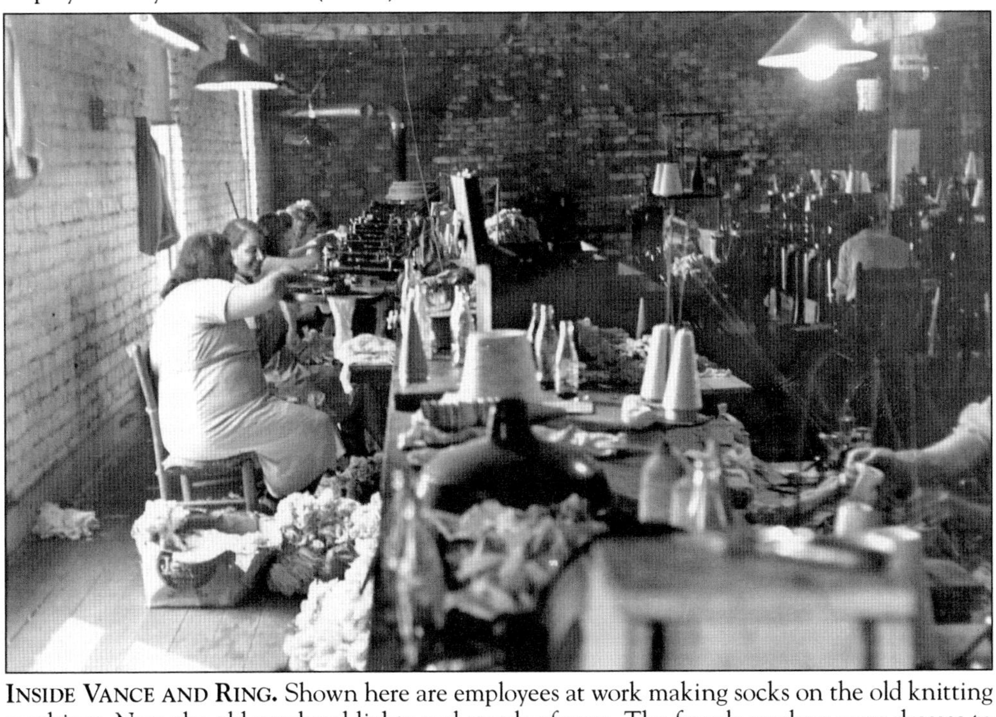

INSIDE VANCE AND RING. Shown here are employees at work making socks on the old knitting machines. Note the old overhead lights and spools of yarn. The female workers wore dresses to work in the mill. (MVB.)

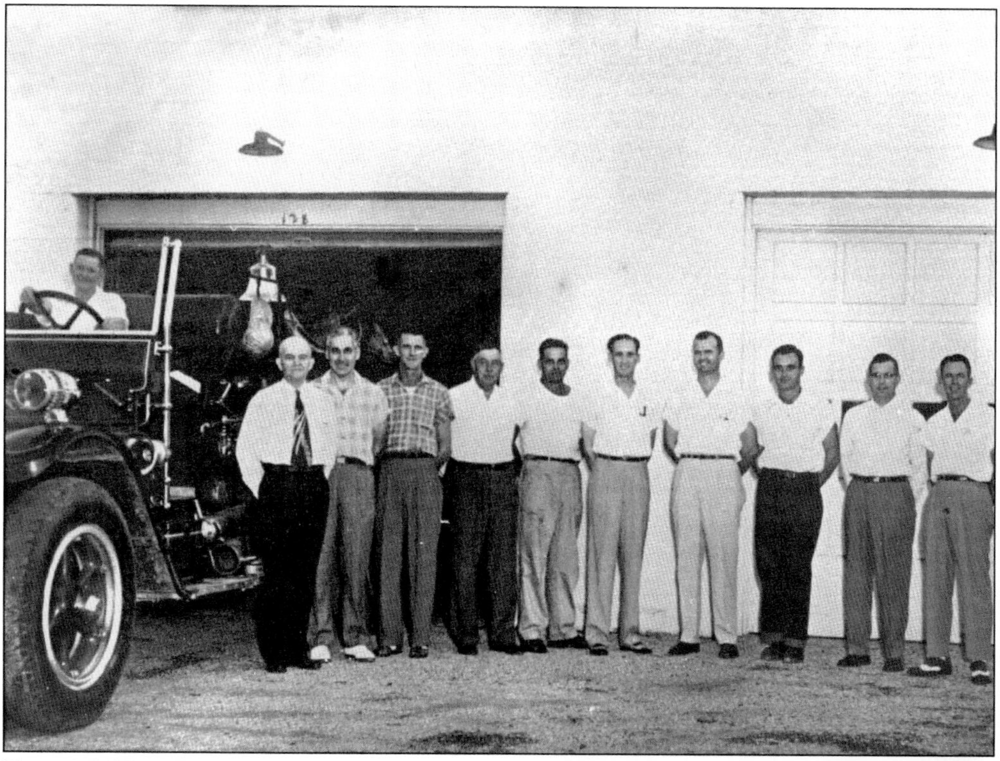

THE 1956 FIRE DEPARTMENT. By this time, the town's second fire truck needed to be replaced, so planning began to requisition a new vehicle with up-to-date communications equipment. In 1957, the town authorized the purchase of this truck and also incorporated a policy that paid firemen to be on duty at all time.

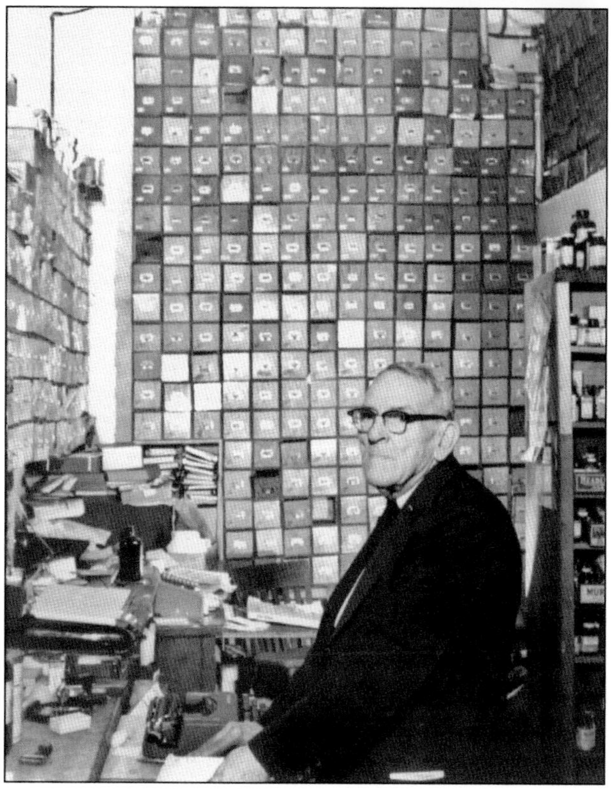

JOHN PINNIX, 1957. By this time, John "Neighbor" Pinnix has been "on the job" for a total of 43 years. (JP.)

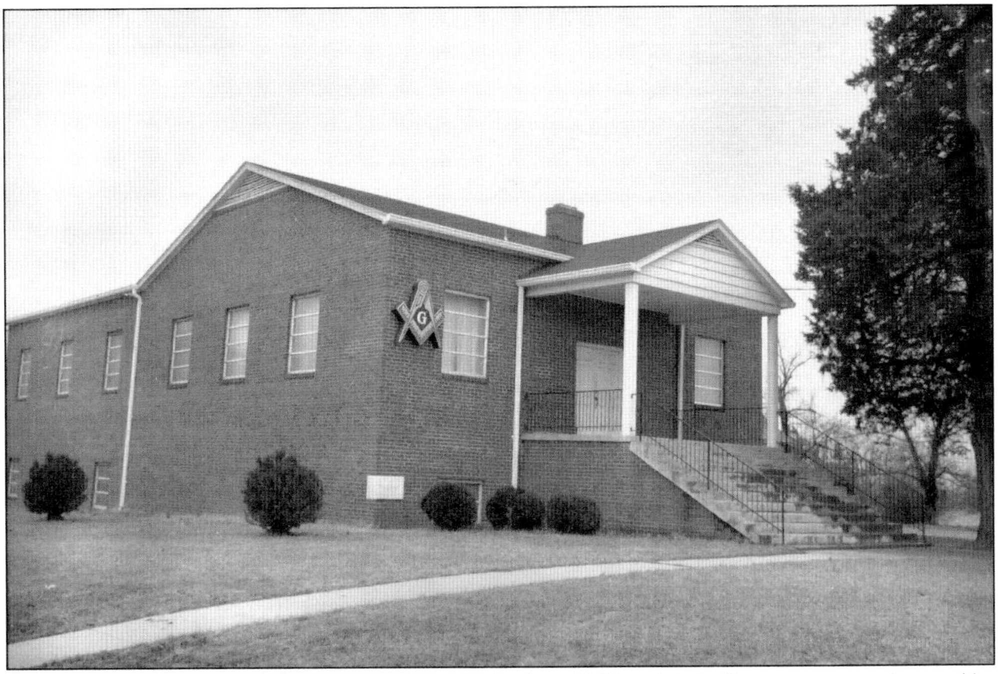

MASONIC LODGE, 1957. The Masonic Temple, built in 1957 on Main Street property donated by Bern C. Stafford, became the new meeting place for the Ancient Free and Accepted Masons in Kernersville. Since its 1931 organizational meeting, members had gathered on the second floor of Snow Brothers Mercantile. (MRK.)

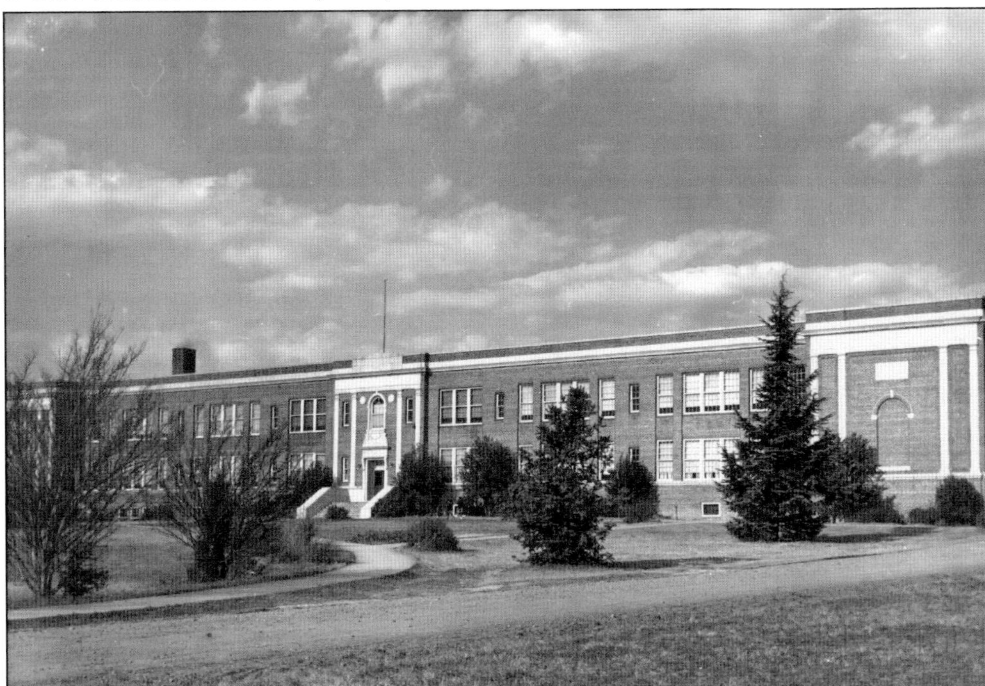

KERNERSVILLE SCHOOL. Located on West Mountain Street, this building housed grades 1 through 12 from 1927 to 1962. Today it is Kernersville Elementary School. (MRK.)

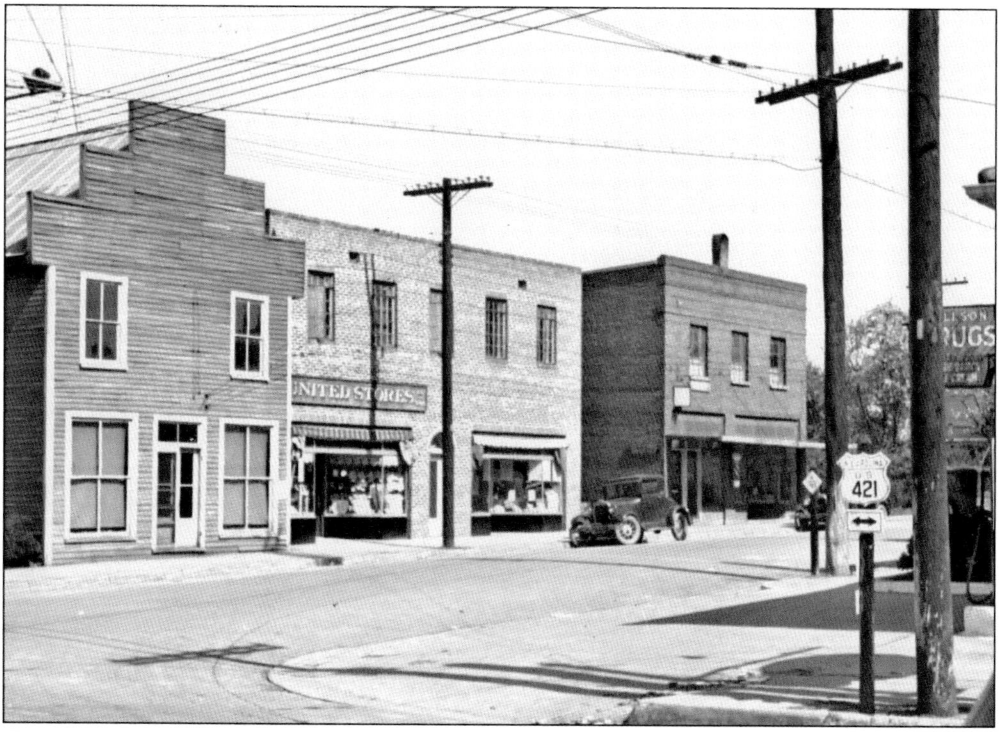

TOWN BUSINESSES. Shown here are Mrs. Lizzie Lowry's Store, Porter's P & N (before Charlie Snow's), Joe Smith's Barber Shop, and the Masonic Lodge over the barber shop. (MVB.)

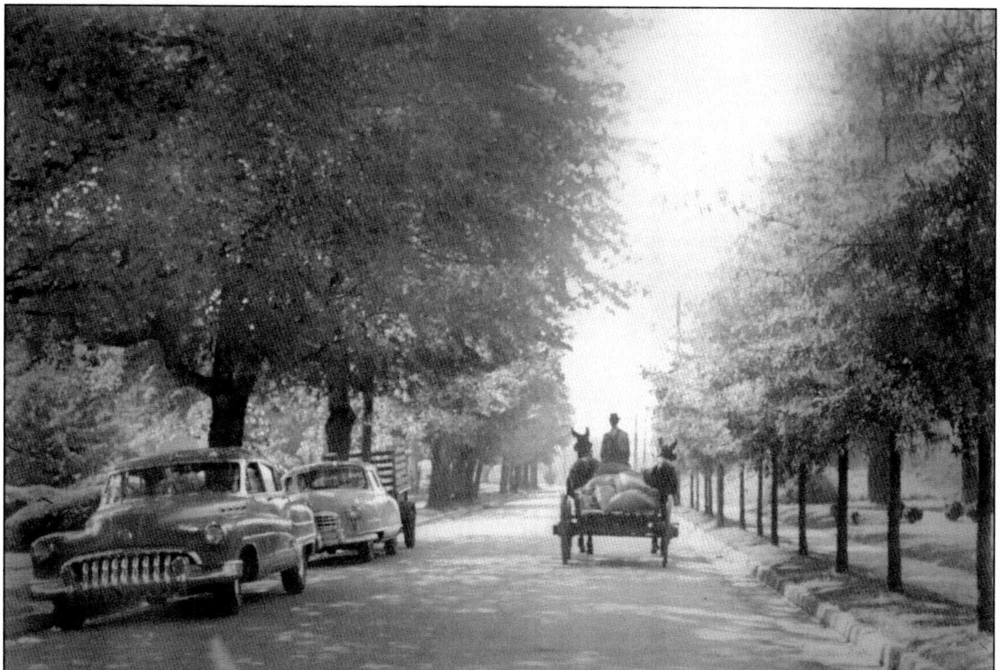

FARMER. In the mid- to late 1940s, this farmer drives his donkey cart to town to pick up supplies. He travels along the tree-lined street beside shiny new automobiles. (MRK.)

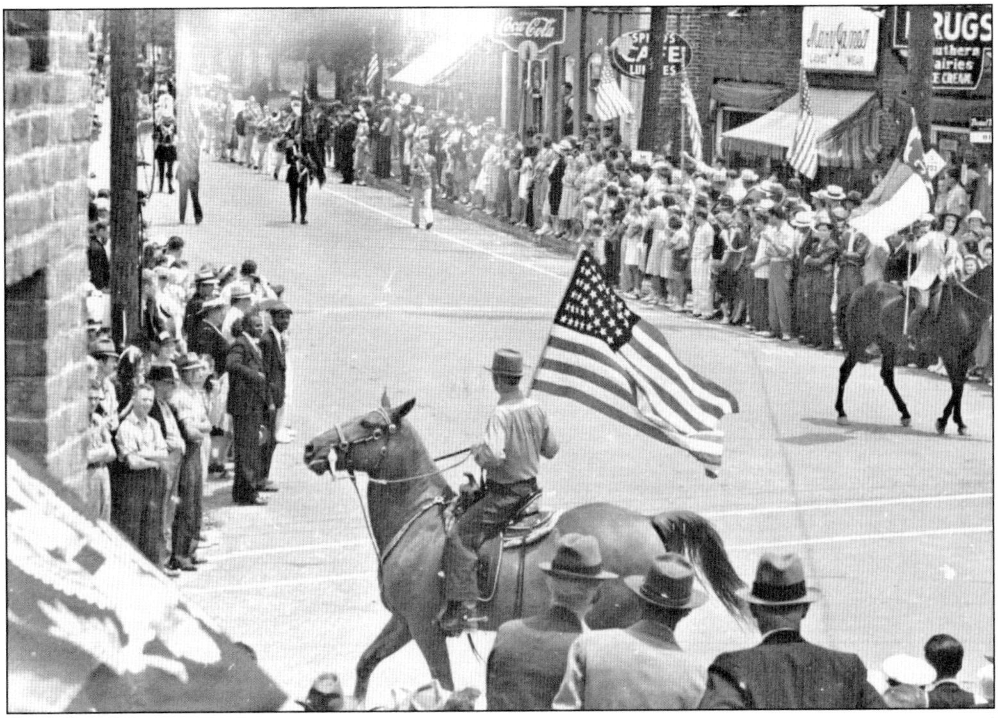

FOURTH OF JULY PARADE, 1940. This parade photograph was taken at the corner of Main and Mountain Streets. (MVB.)

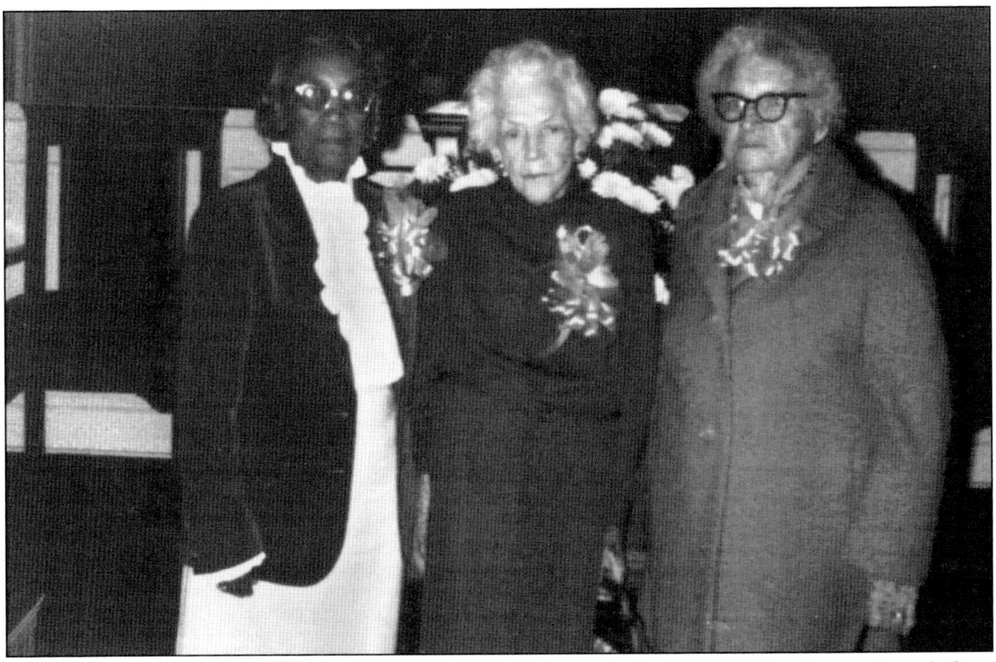

WORLD DAY OF PRAYER. The World Day of Prayer was begun in 1952 by these three ladies, Mrs. Leone Friende of St. Paul's United Methodist Church; Miss Eugenia Stafford of Kernersville Moravian Church; and Mrs. Doskie Nelson of the Friends (Quaker) Church of Kernersville. This picture was taken on the World Day of Prayer 30th anniversary in 1982. (SH.)

Five

Friends, Neighbors, and Extracurricular Activities

Friends and neighbors liked to gather at the Esso Station, Pinnix Drug Store, Pickfair Theatre, and Depot. On their Main Street strolls, couples paused to speak to neighbors or enjoy the budding trees. Children enjoyed having their photographs taken with siblings and pals. Sam Vance could usually be seen with his trusty camera.

Folks took time to enjoy buggy rides, picnics, lawn parties, hayrides, ice cream socials, and field trips to nearby Winston-Salem for entertaining streetcar rides. Church revival meetings, baptisms, funerals, and Sunday morning and evening services doubled as religious and social activities. Political rallies intrigued many citizens. In 1906, William Jennings Bryan made a whistle-stop in Kernersville.

Tennis matches, Model T Ford rides, and bicycle trips provided wholesome entertainment. Various talented individuals and groups presented musicals. Spirited soccer teams, championship basketball and baseball teams, and accomplished glee clubs became the news of the day.

Parades continued to draw crowds as decorated floats, cars, horses, flag bearers, and string bands made their way down the middle of Main Street. For a few harsh years during the early 1930s, these beloved parades ceased. Then, in 1938, when the celebration resumed, 25,000 lined the streets once more to enjoy their favorite pastime. Again, from 1941 to 1947, the parade route was stilled as war loomed in the somber hearts of Kernersville citizens. However, on July 4, 1948, the traditional Independence Day gala resumed with all its glory.

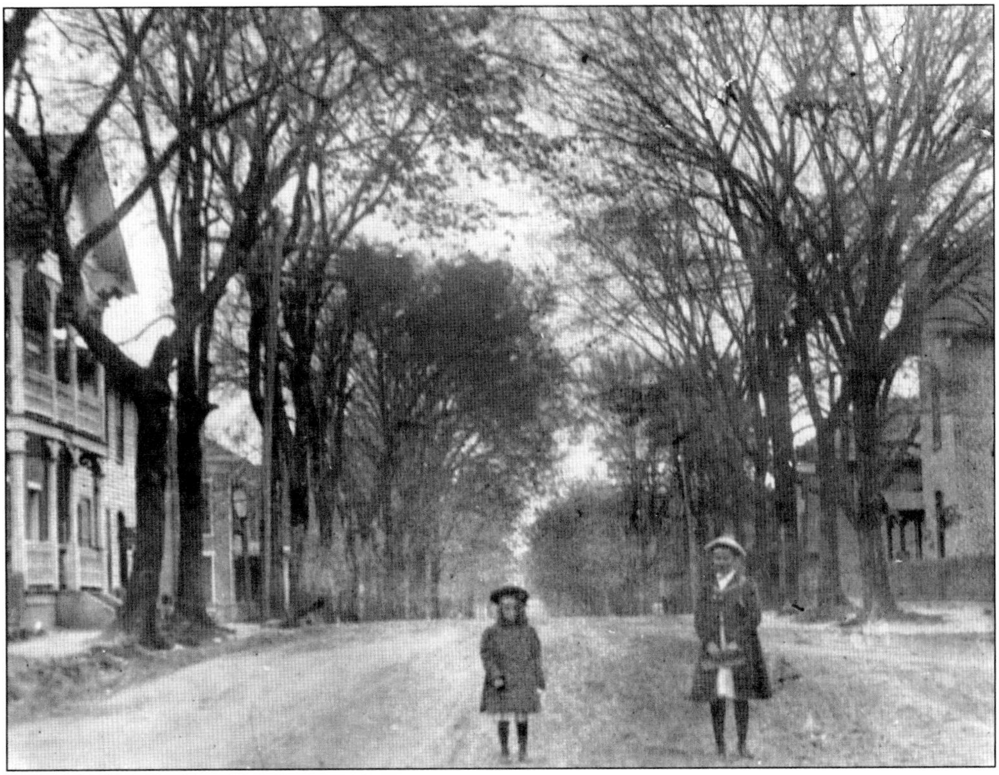

SISTERS. Helen and Ruth Humphrey pose at the corner of Main and Salisbury Streets. This photograph was taken about 1900. The Israel Kerner house is on the left. (BW.)

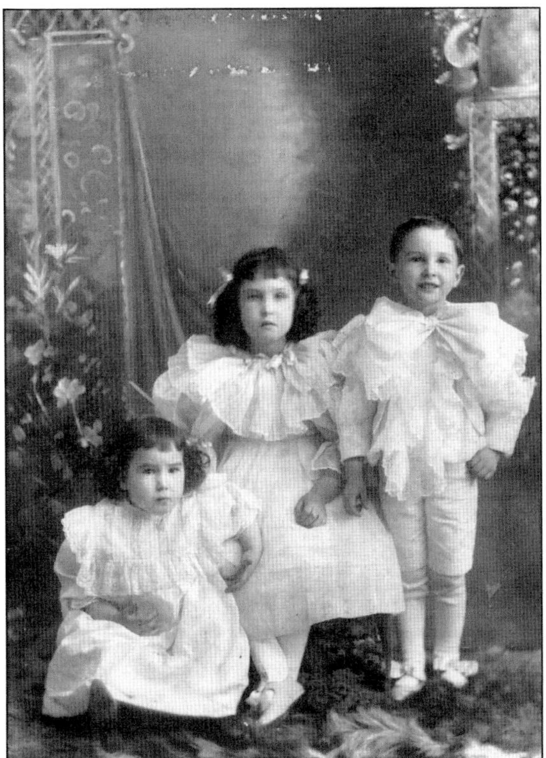

PHILIP KÖRNER CHILDREN. Mattie Lee (left), Philip (right), and Kathleen Körner (center) pose for the camera. (BW.)

STILL AT WORK. J. M. Pinnix is still at work in Pinnix Drug Store in the 1950s. (JP.)

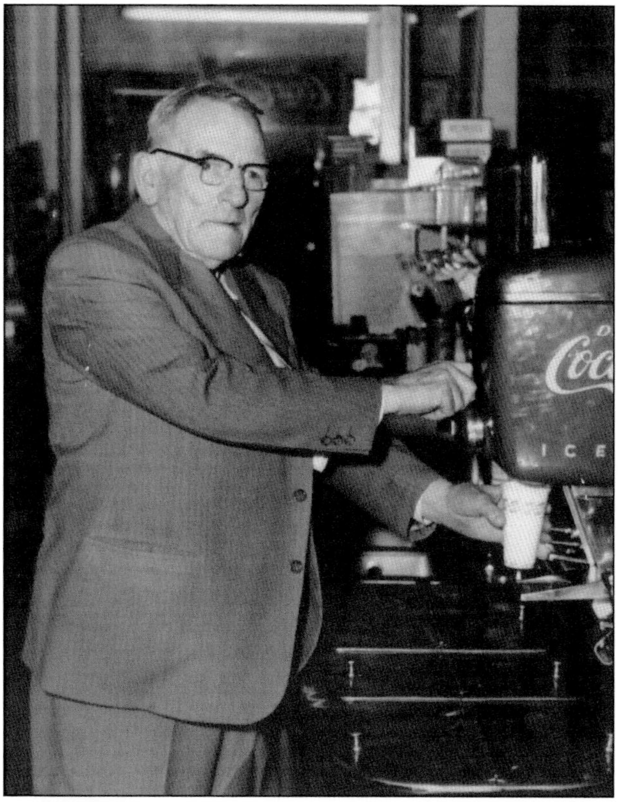

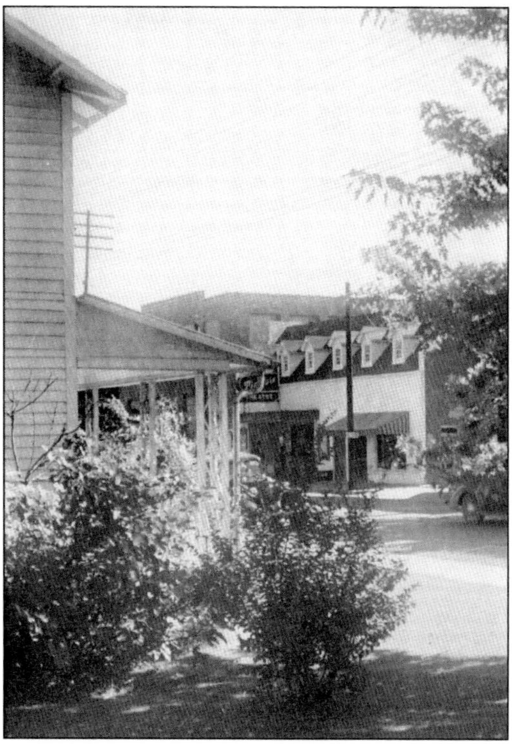

JUSTICE THEATRE. A bird's-eye view of the Justice Theatre can be seen to the right of Mamie Guire's Main Street boarding house. Even today, men and women have fond memories of Saturday cowboy movies, the giant popcorn popper, the projection booth in the balcony, and their first viewing of *Gone With the Wind.* (MVB.)

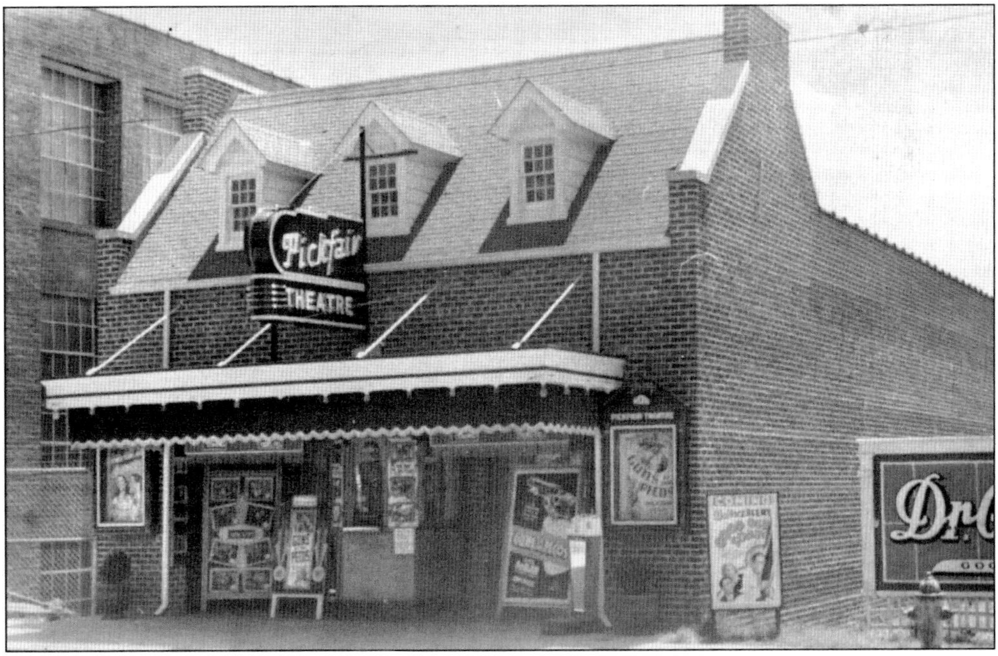

PICKFAIR THEATRE. One of the most popular spots in town is the movie theatre on North Main Street. Named after Douglas Fairbanks and Mary Pickford, the Pickfair opened in 1934. It later became the Justice Theatre. (MRK.)

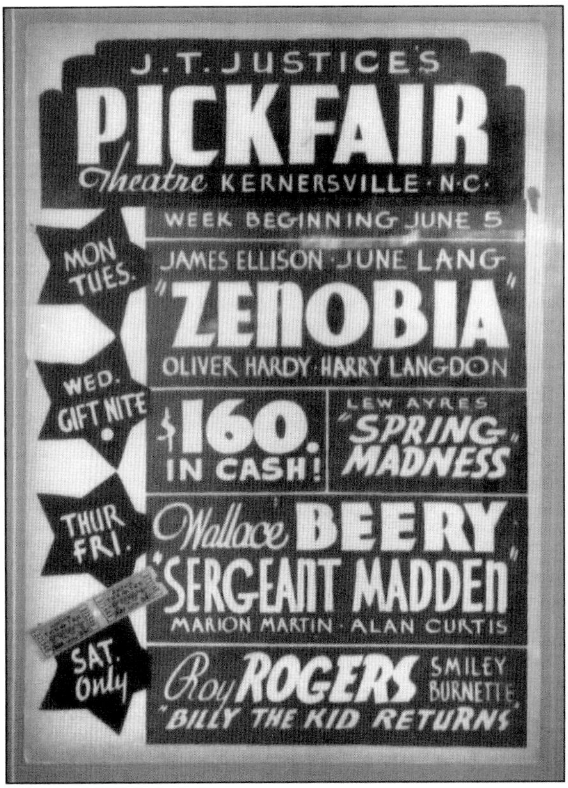

PICKFAIR THEATRE POSTER. J. T. Justice's Pickfair Theatre advertises movie titles such as *Zenobia*, *Sergeant Madden*, *Spring Madness*, and *Billy the Kid Returns*. To add to the fun, the cash giveaway pot is $160. (BB.)

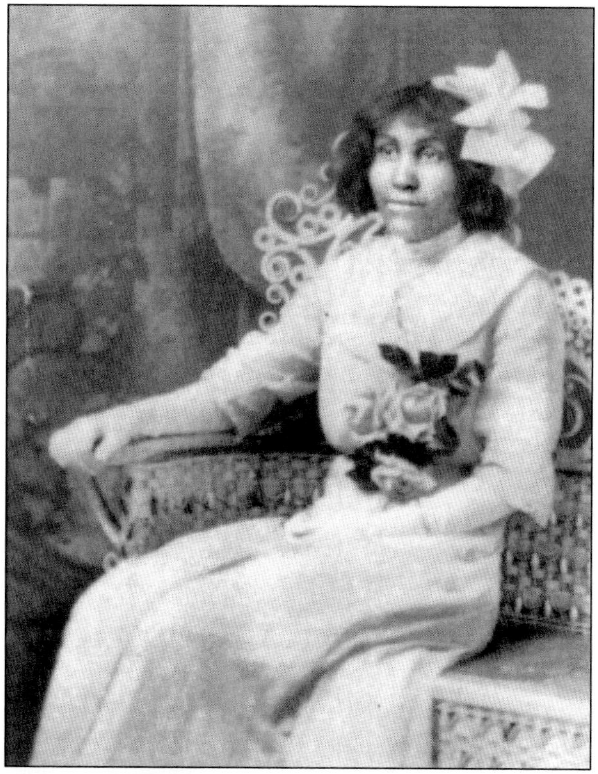

LEONE MATTHEWS FRIENDE. Leone Matthews Friende, age 16, was the daughter of Rhoda and Thomas Matthews and was an influential part of this community. She made the outfit she is wearing. (SH.)

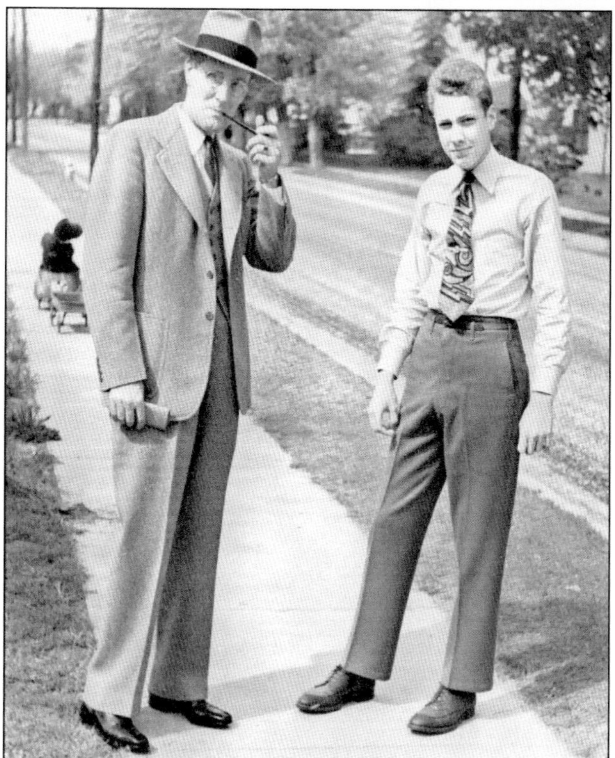

FATHER-SON OUTING. Clay Ring Sr. and Clay Ring Jr. enjoy their walk about town. Clay Sr. married Maude Kerner. Clay Jr. married Ann Crews. The Rings ran a housing mill and also sold coffins and veneer lumber. (MVB.)

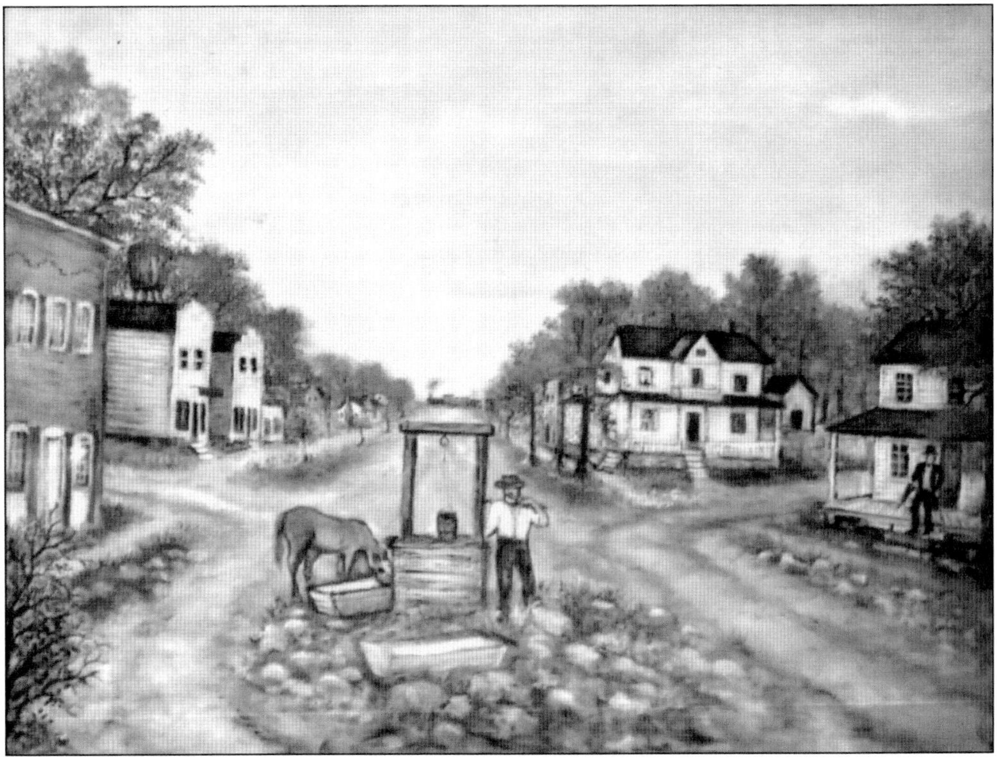

VILLAGE SCENE. Local folk artist Mildred Ballard painted this scene of early Kernersville. (BB.)

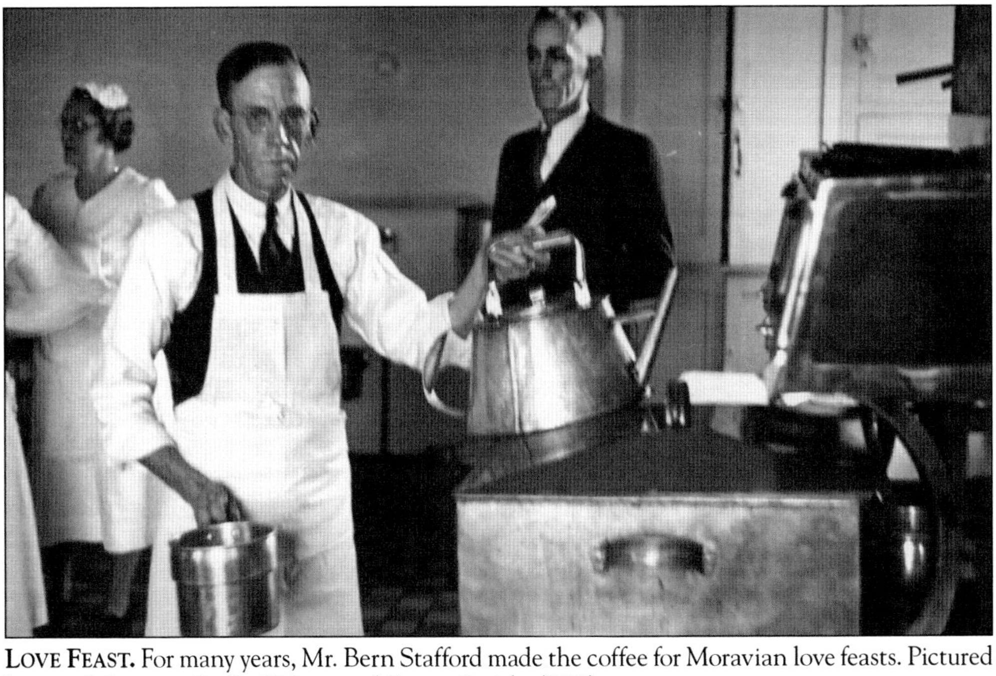

LOVE FEAST. For many years, Mr. Bern Stafford made the coffee for Moravian love feasts. Pictured here with him are Stella Wilson and Ernest Smith. (BW.)

TOM THUMB WEDDING. These young girls and boys participate in a Tom Thumb wedding, a pretend ceremony involving children who portray adults involved in a wedding party. This form of entertainment was popular in the South in the 1940s. (MVB.)

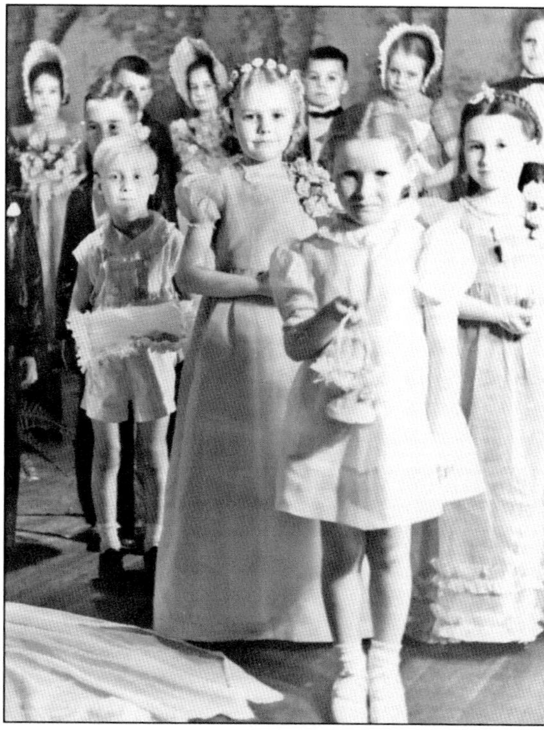

MOTORCYCLE MAN. A young man shows off his new Harley Davidson in front of the local Esso station. (MVB.)

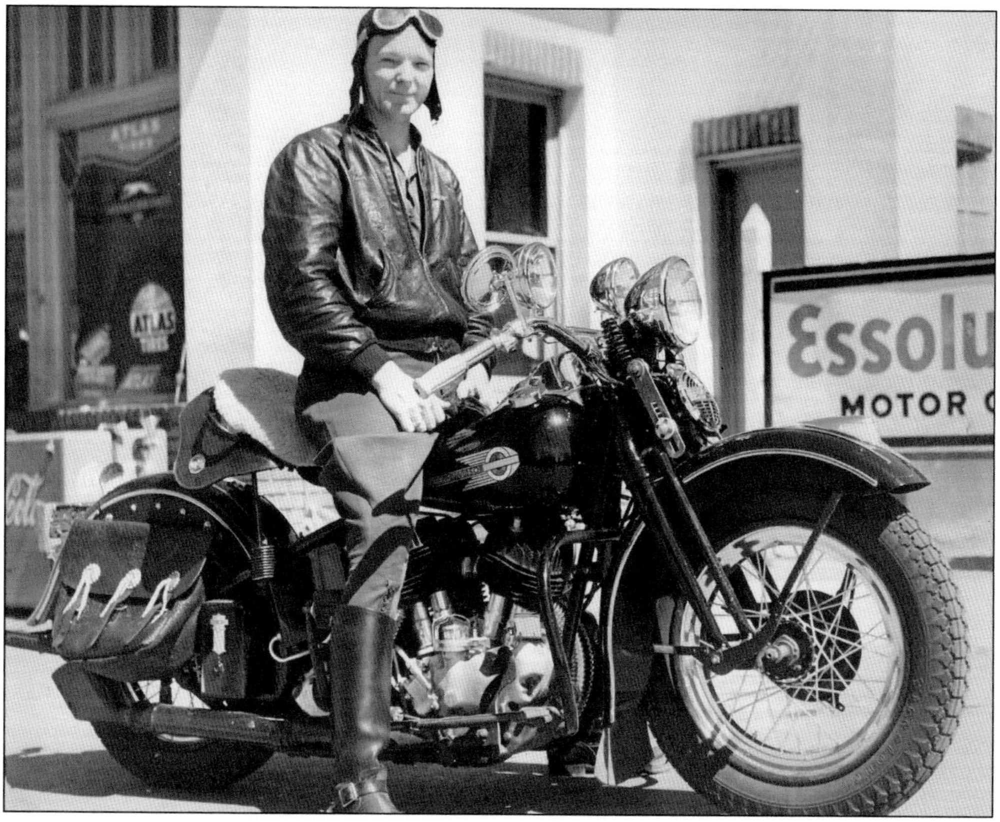

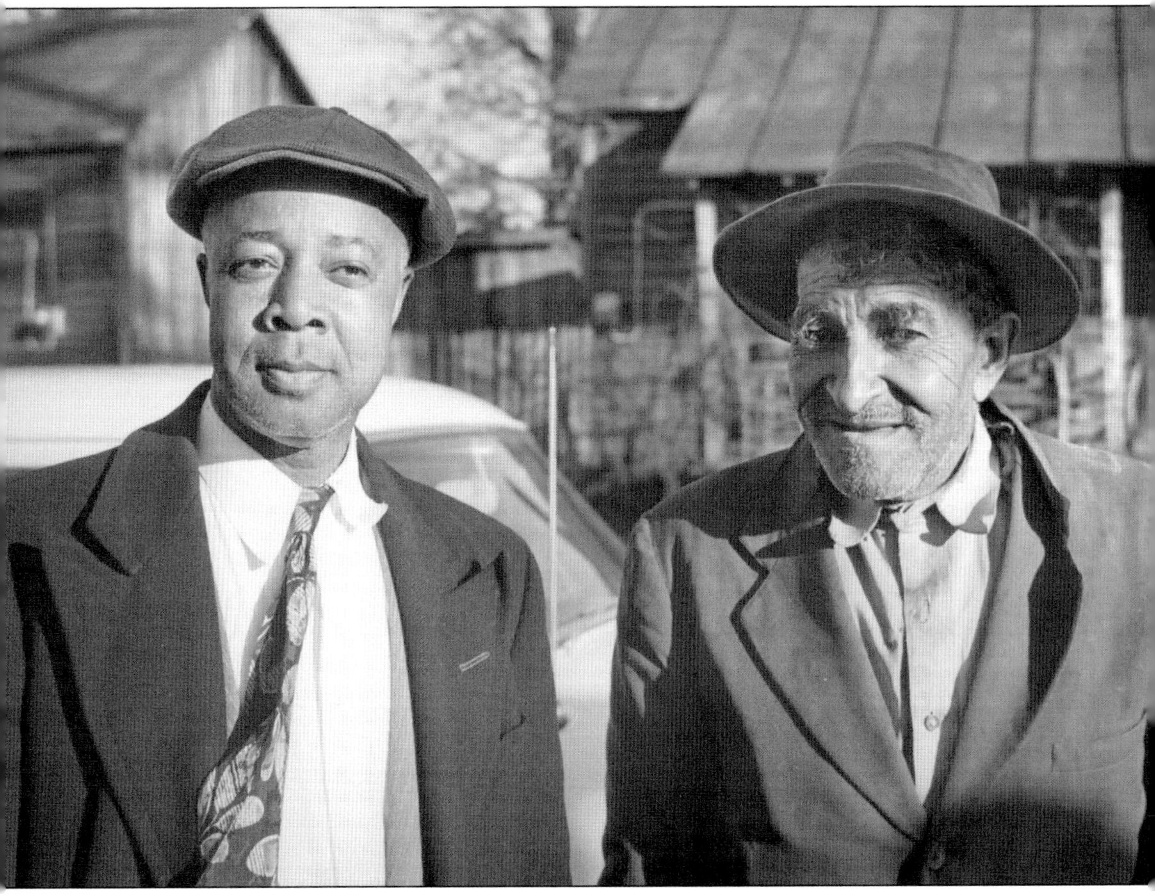

BUDDIES. Millard Stafford (left) and Sam Brooks enjoy their daily walk. During segregation, Stafford operated the ticket booth from which African Americans bought their tickets at the Justice Theatre, and he managed the balcony where they sat. Stafford lived in a little yellow house on Piney Grove Road, and he could be seen daily walking through town in a suit and tie. He always carried his cane. Artist Richard Hedgecock painted a picture of him with the Justice Theatre in the background. Brooks, a businessman in the African American community, owned an "ice house" on the corner of Nelson and New Streets. In addition to selling ice, he stocked candies and snacks. Kernersville residents remember buying these sweets when they were children. (MVB.)

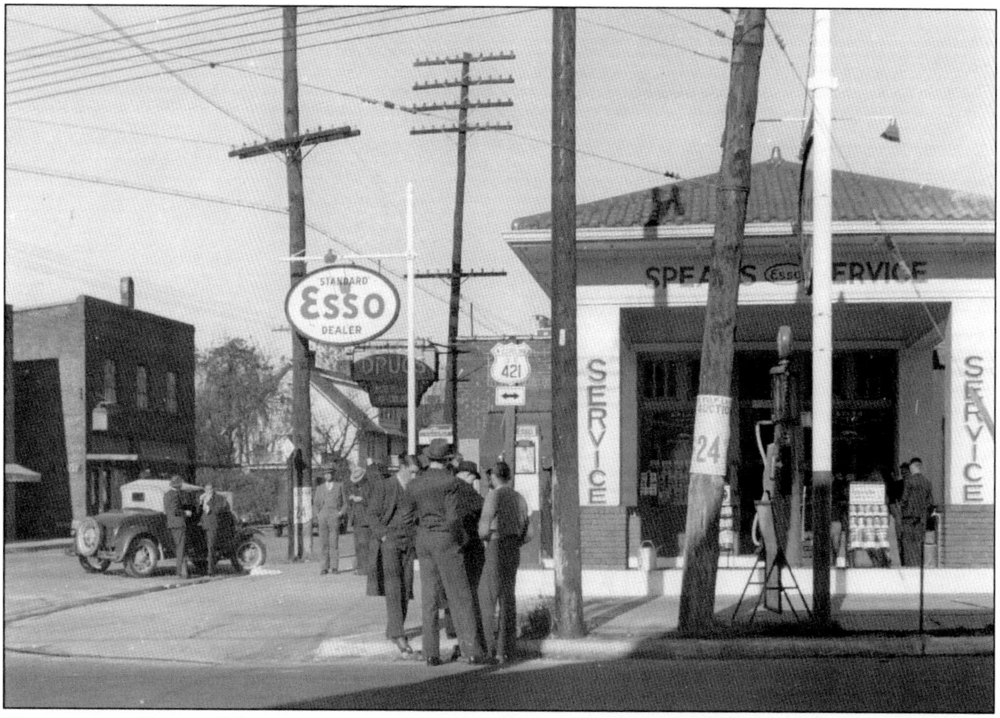

GATHERING PLACE. These men congregate at the Esso station to share town news. (MVB.)

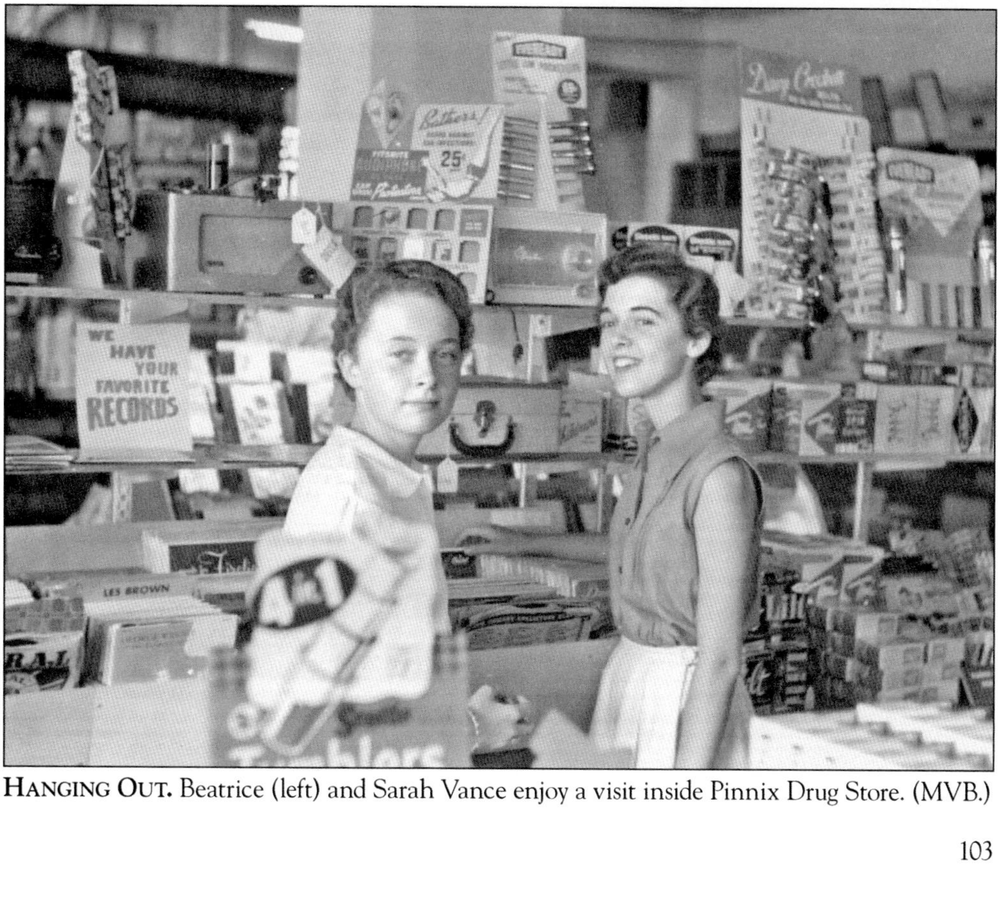

HANGING OUT. Beatrice (left) and Sarah Vance enjoy a visit inside Pinnix Drug Store. (MVB.)

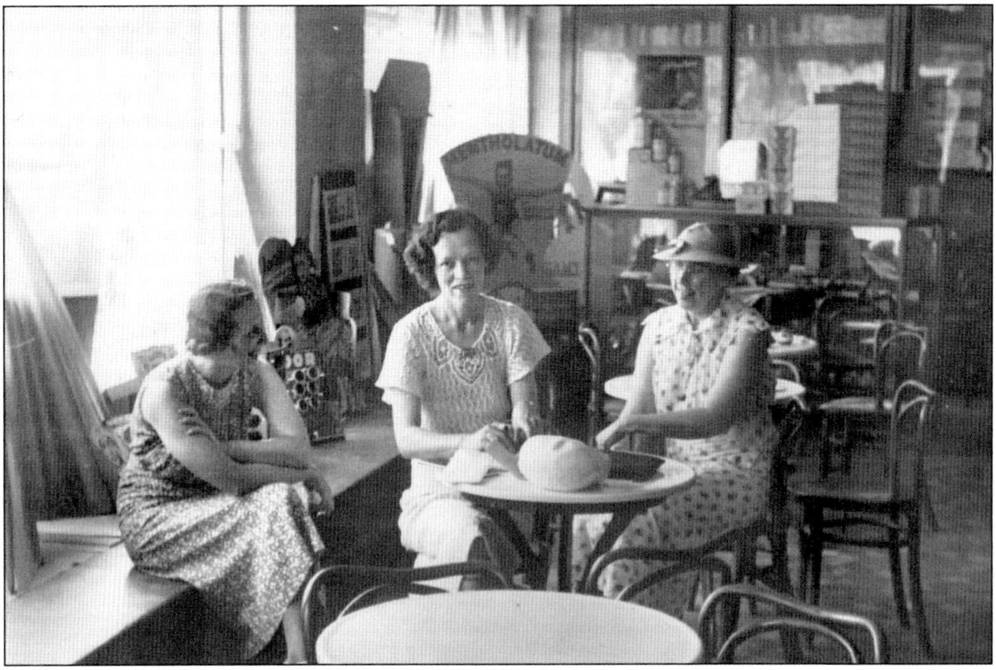

VISITING LADIES. A group gathers inside Pinnix Drug Store for refreshments and conversation. While the ladies of the town used to call upon each other at their homes, Pinnix Drug later became the idea spot to relax around one of the ornate ice cream tables, enjoy a fountain Cherry Coke, and catch up on current events. Note the antique glass showcases. (MVB.)

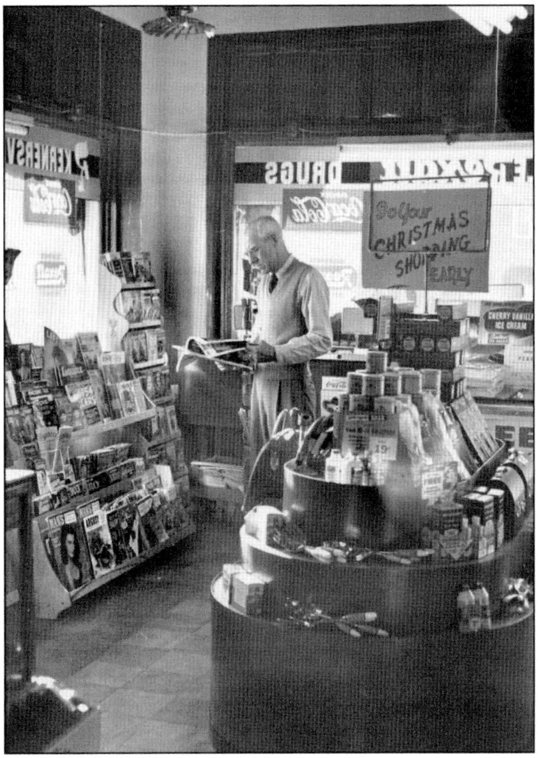

FREQUENT CUSTOMER. Mr. Ed Shore Sr., inside Pinnix Drug Store in 1954, selects his favorite reading material from the wooden magazine rack. (MVB.)

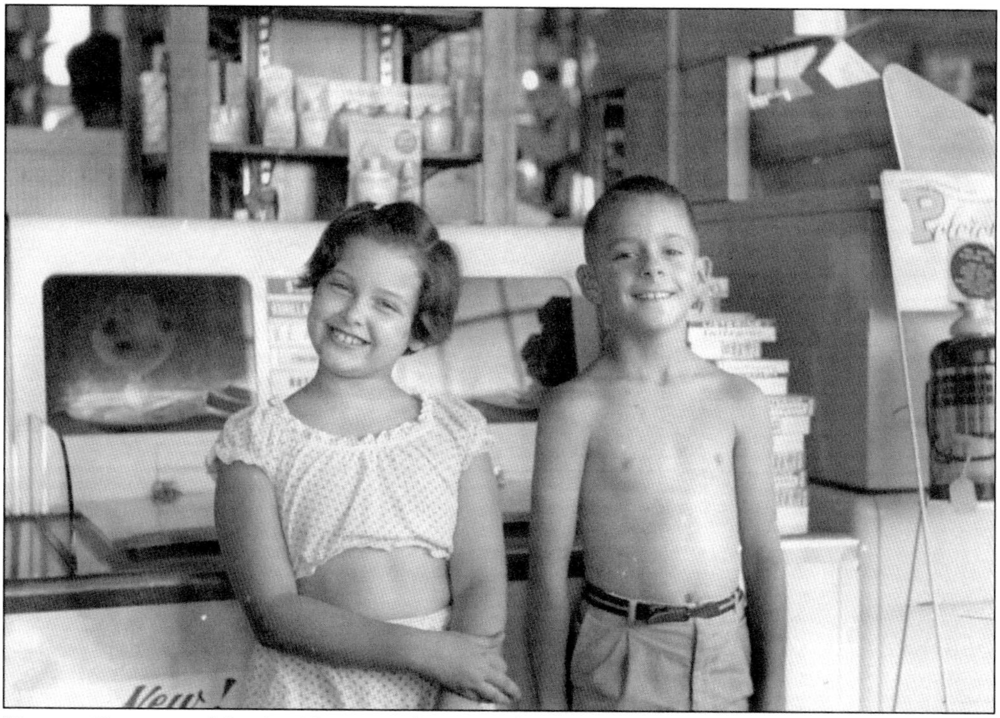

YOUNG FRIENDS. Martha Vance and Joe Leak Pinnix grin for the camera inside Pinnix Drug Store. (MVB.)

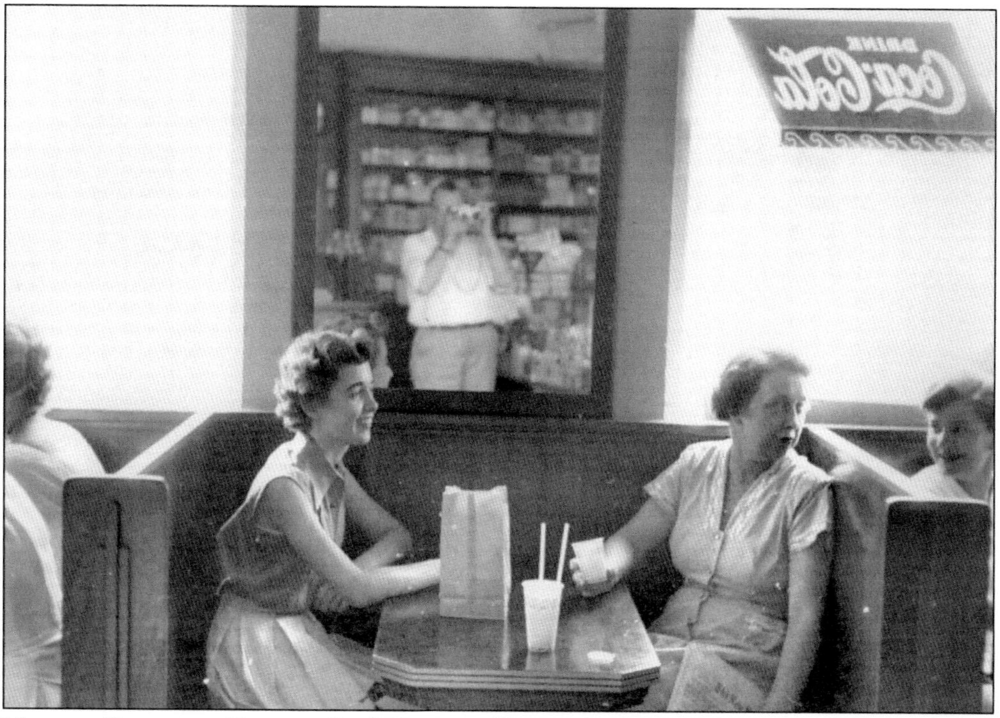

MOTHER-DAUGHTER OUTING. Sarah Vance and her mother Bea stop for a cold drink in one of the booths at Pinnix Drug. Sam Vance took this picture. Note his reflection in the mirror. (MVB.)

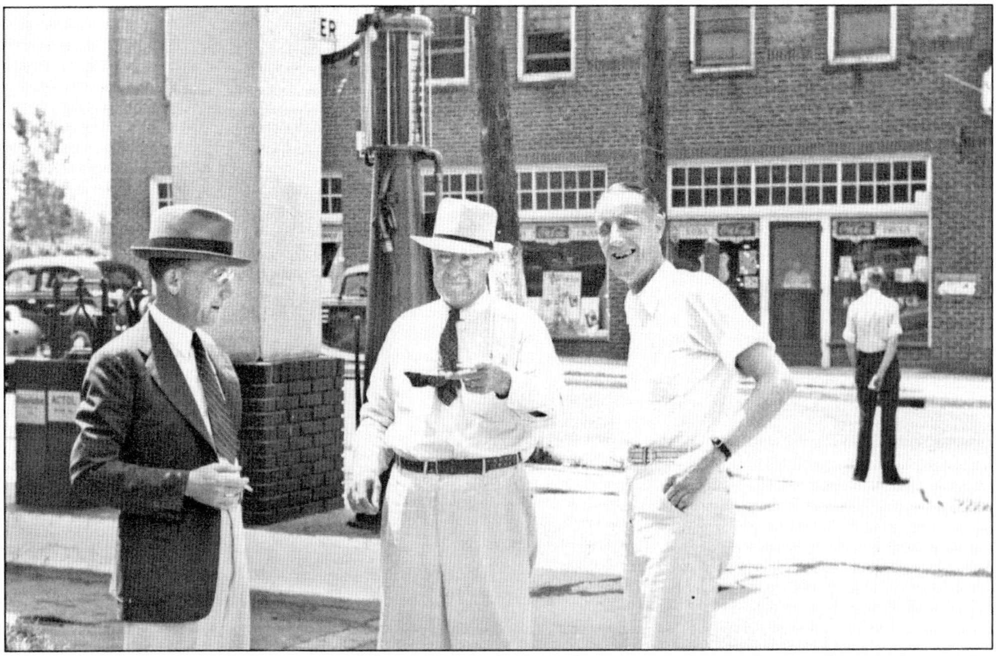

MAN TALK. A group of outgoing folks stop to chat at the Esso station. Shown from left to right are Ralph Fagg, Chester Morris, and Clay Ring Sr. (MVB.)

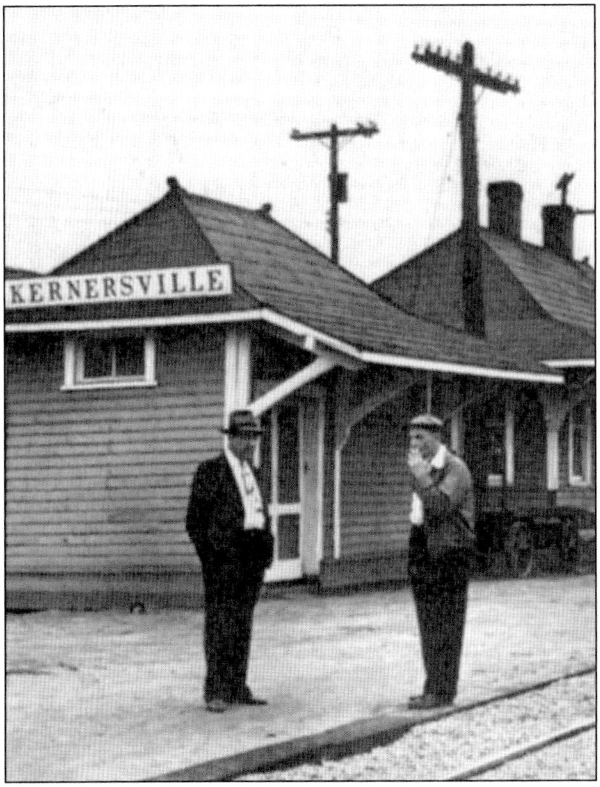

NEW DEPOT. George Marine (left) and Arch Perdue visit at the new depot. The railroad was a significant part of Kernersville's growth through the years. Passenger trains made daily runs through town, but this service was later discontinued. The Norfolk-Southern Railroad demolished this 1910 depot. (KBB.)

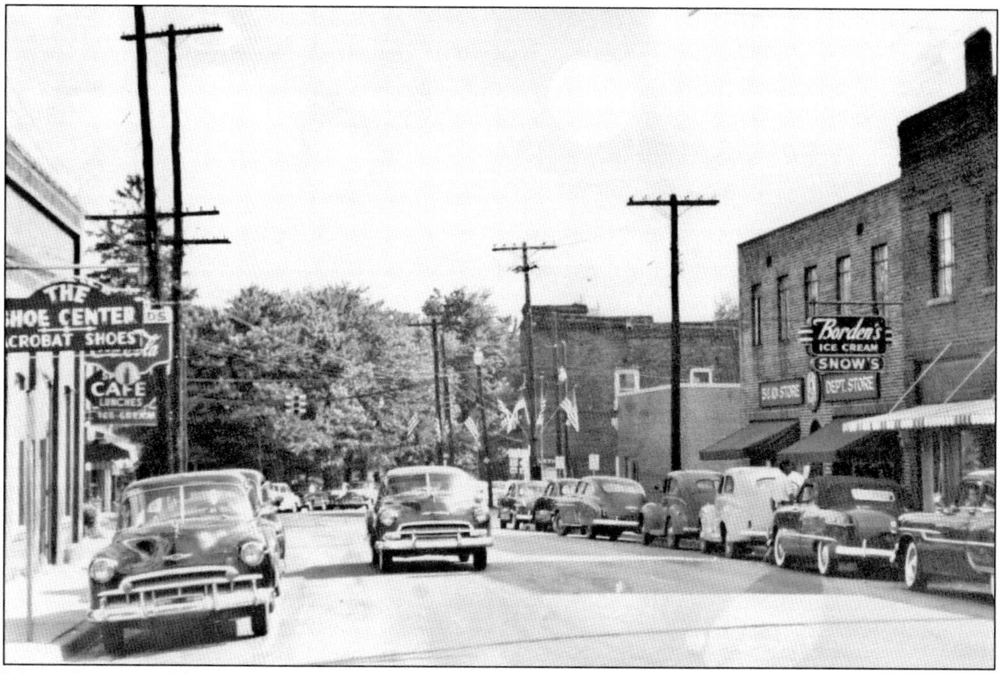

MAIN STREET. This view of Main Street looks south past Snow's ice cream shop, P & N Five and Ten Cents Store, Spiro's Cafe, and the Shoe Center. (MVB.)

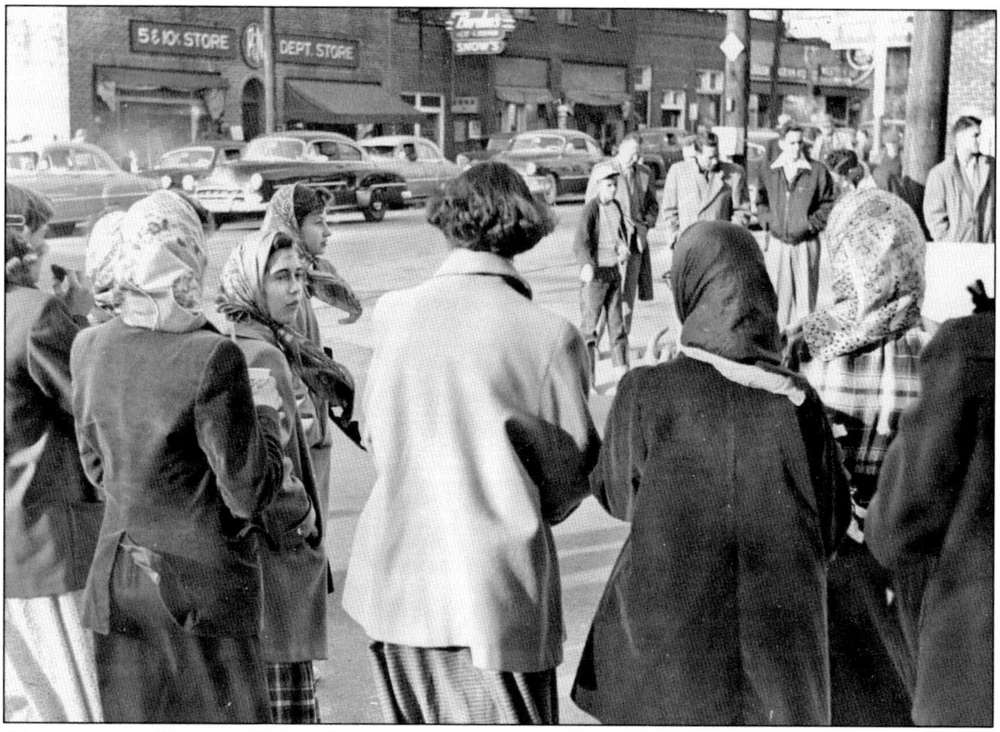

HOMECOMING PARADE. Sylvia Smith, Sarah Porter, and Joyce Porter are among the young women bundled up and waiting for the Homecoming Parade of 1952. (MVB.)

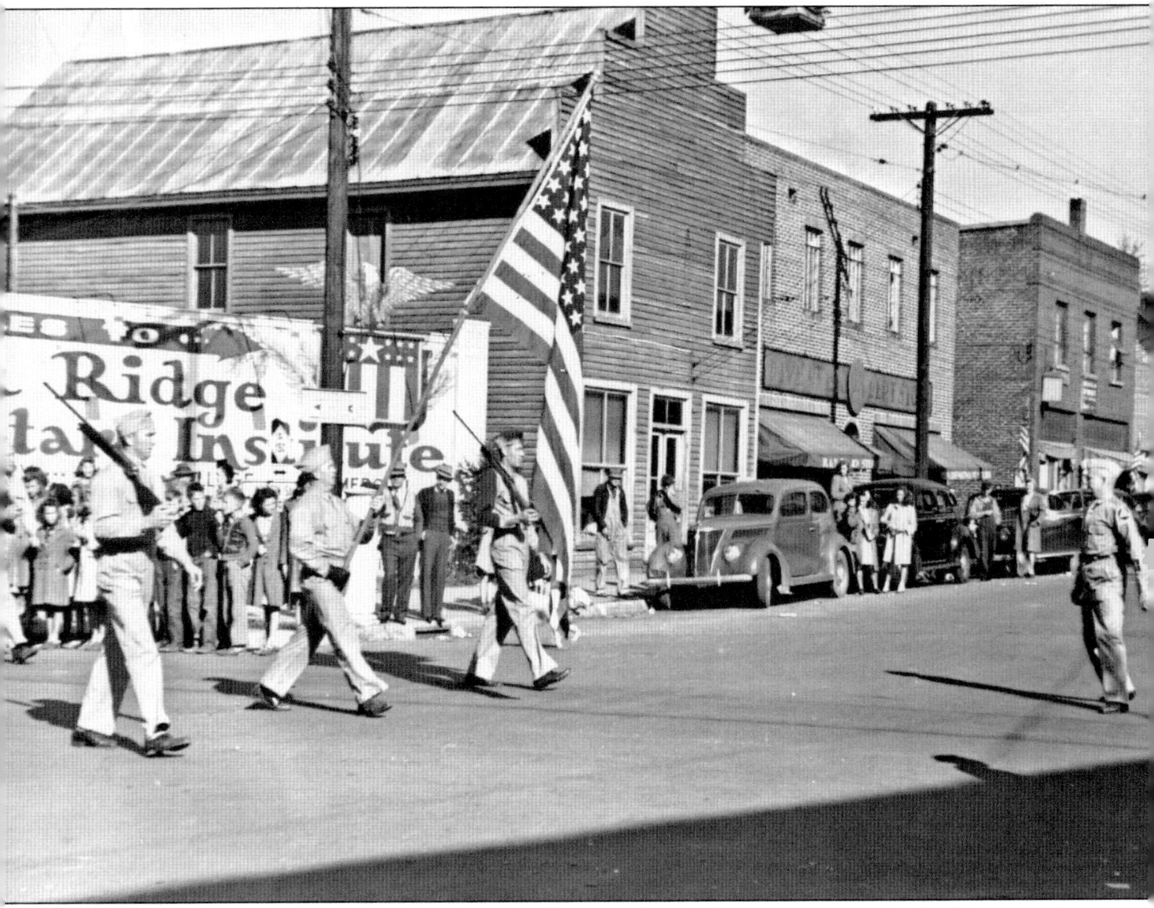

SOLDIERS MARCH BEFORE SIGN. An Oak Ridge Military Institute sign is the backdrop as this brigade gears up for a parade during World War II. These patriotic marchers will soon pass Rainy Beeson Dry Goods Store and the P & N in the background. The famous sign stated, "Six miles to Oak Ridge Military Institute." (MVB.)

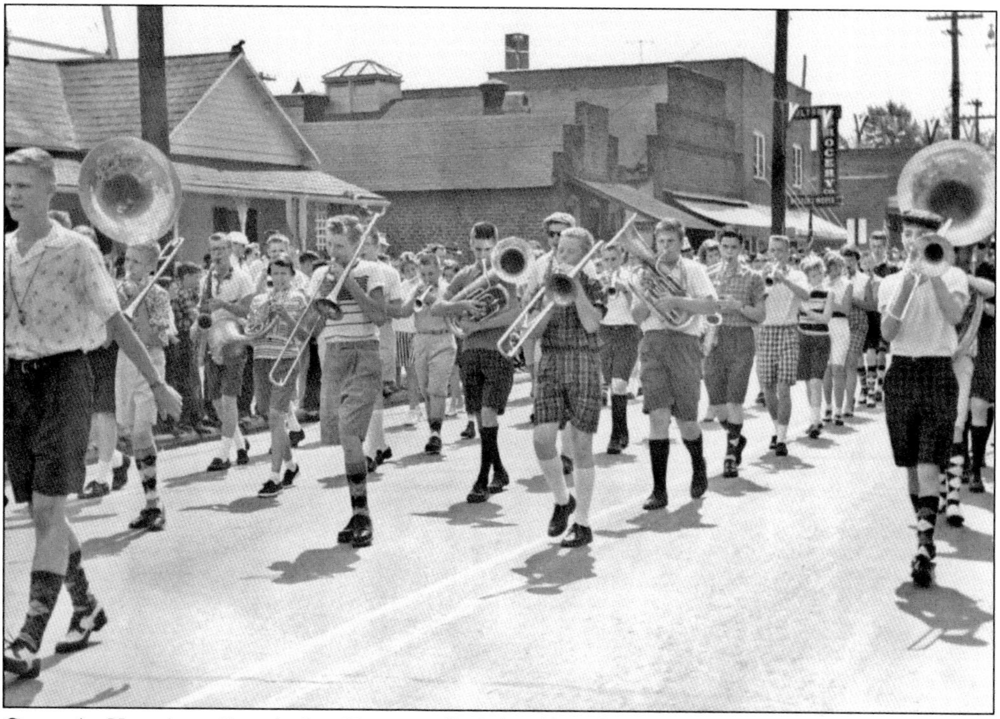

COME AS YOU ARE. Even before Kernersville School band members had uniforms, they marched proudly and played joyously. (MVB.)

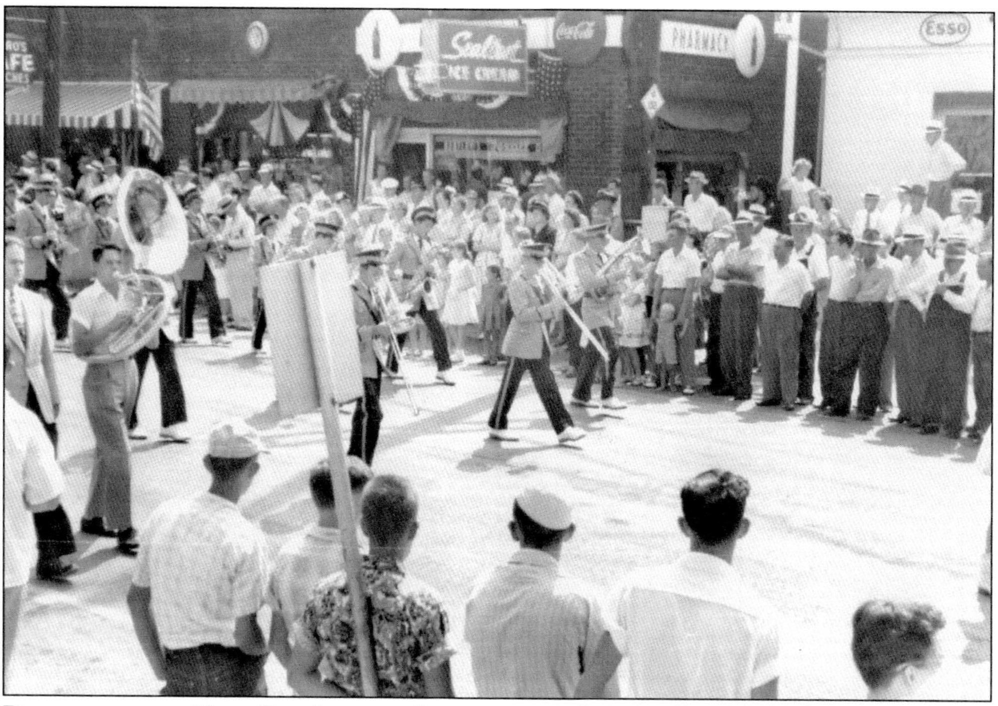

DRESSED TO THE HILT. Brand new uniforms give a sophisticated sense of refinery, dignity, and professionalism to the Kernersville School marching band. (MVB.)

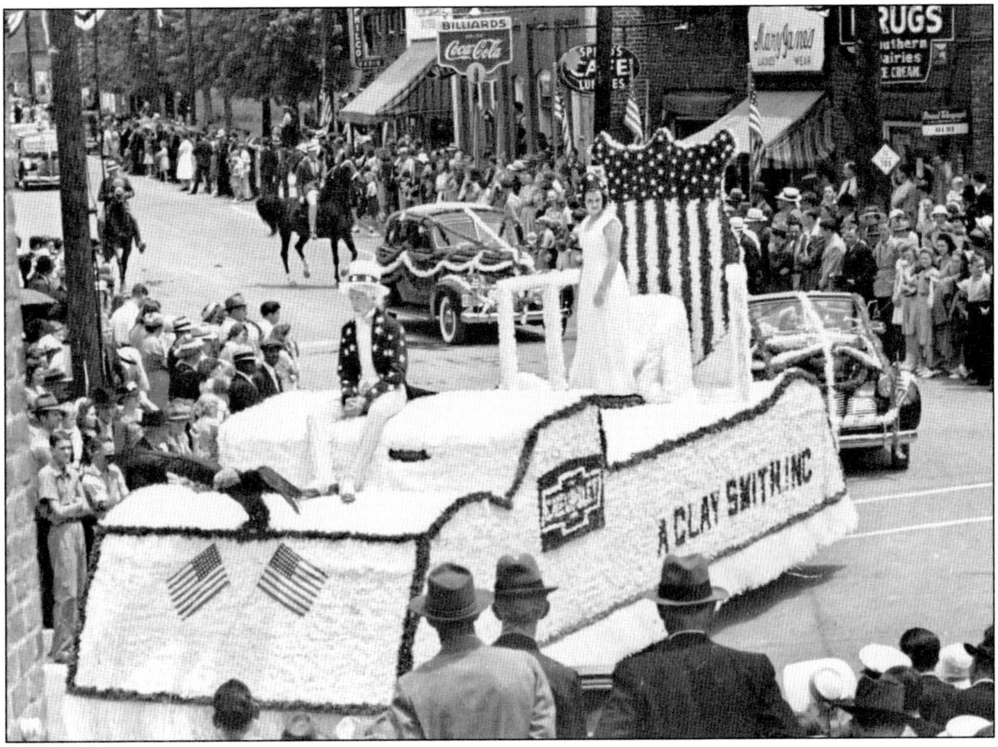

FLOAT. Sponsored by Clay Smith, Inc., an elaborately decorated float with a patriotic motif features Betsey Ann Ring as "Miss America" and Berkely Taylor as "Uncle Sam" in this 1940 parade. (MVB.)

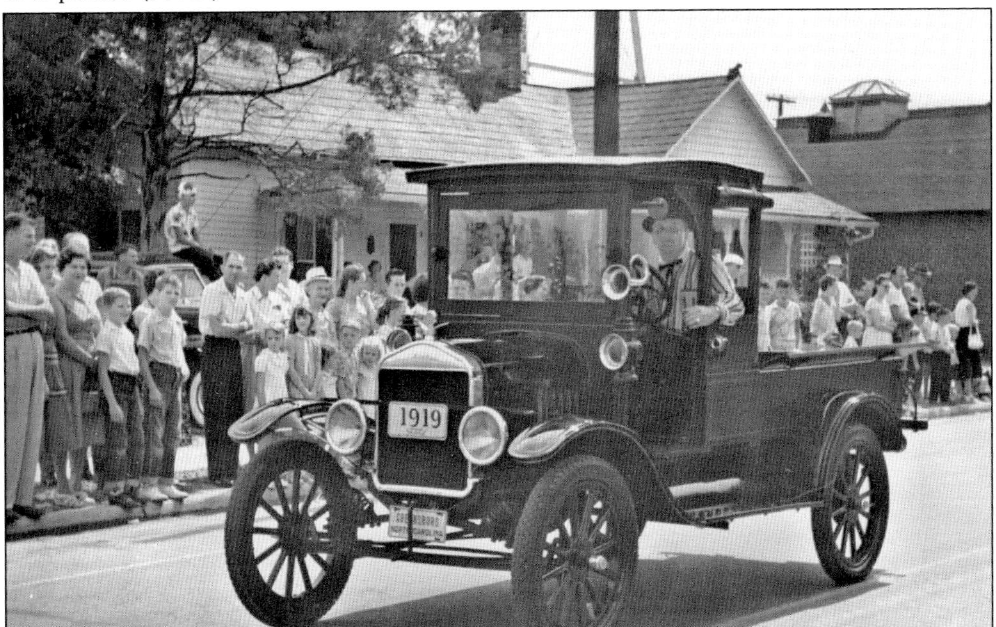

PARADE IN FRONT OF COOKE HOME. Interested viewers line the sidewalks and watch this restored car pass by in front of the Cooke house. (MVB.)

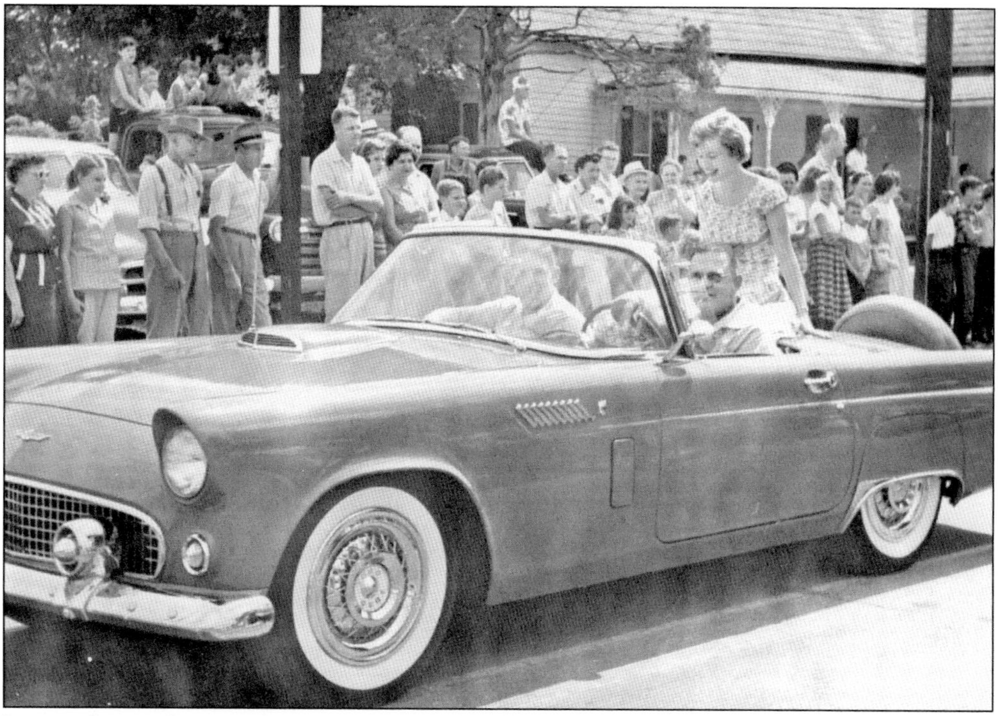

Lovely Lady. A gowned young woman is chauffeured on the back of this convertible as parade watchers stand on the sidewalks and behold her beauty. (MVB.)

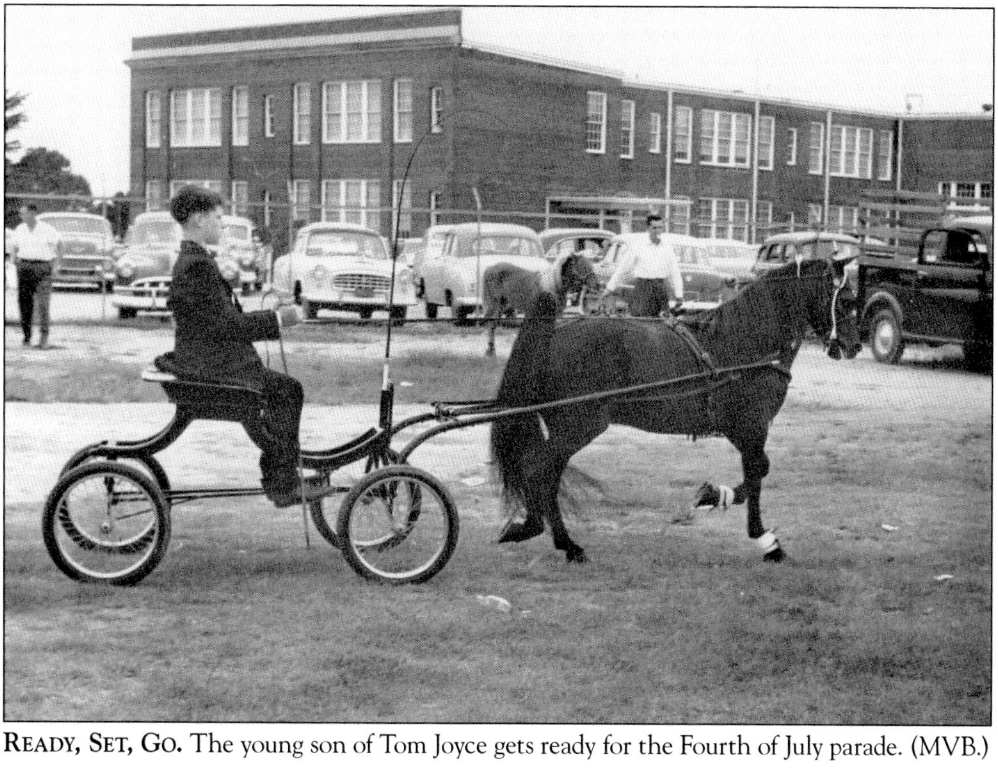

Ready, Set, Go. The young son of Tom Joyce gets ready for the Fourth of July parade. (MVB.)

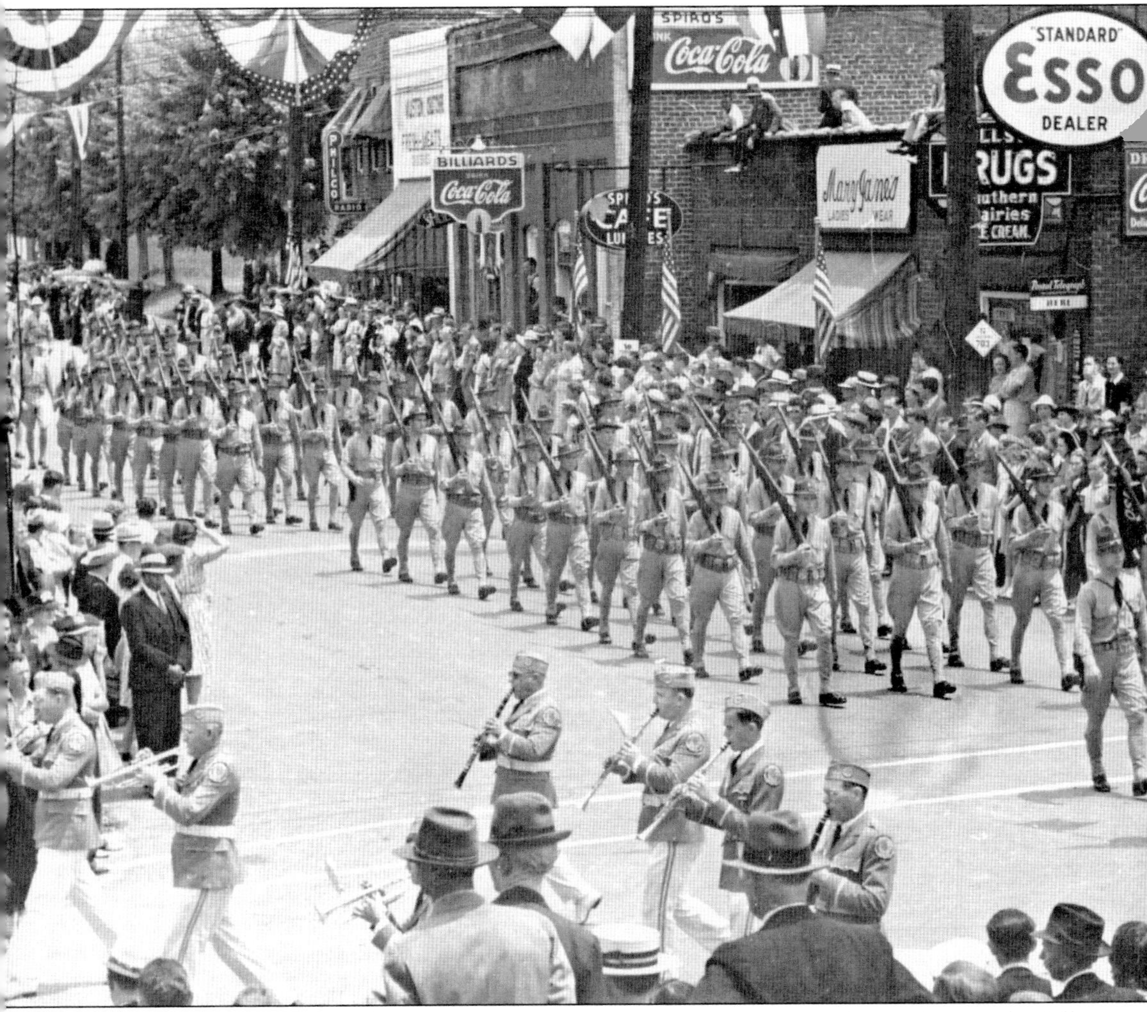

SOLDIERS. Troops march through the town's business district during a July 4, 1940, parade. Folks gather on both sides of Main and Mountain Streets to view the 1940 Fourth of July parade. Even in the heat of summer, men wear suits and dress hats. (MVB.)

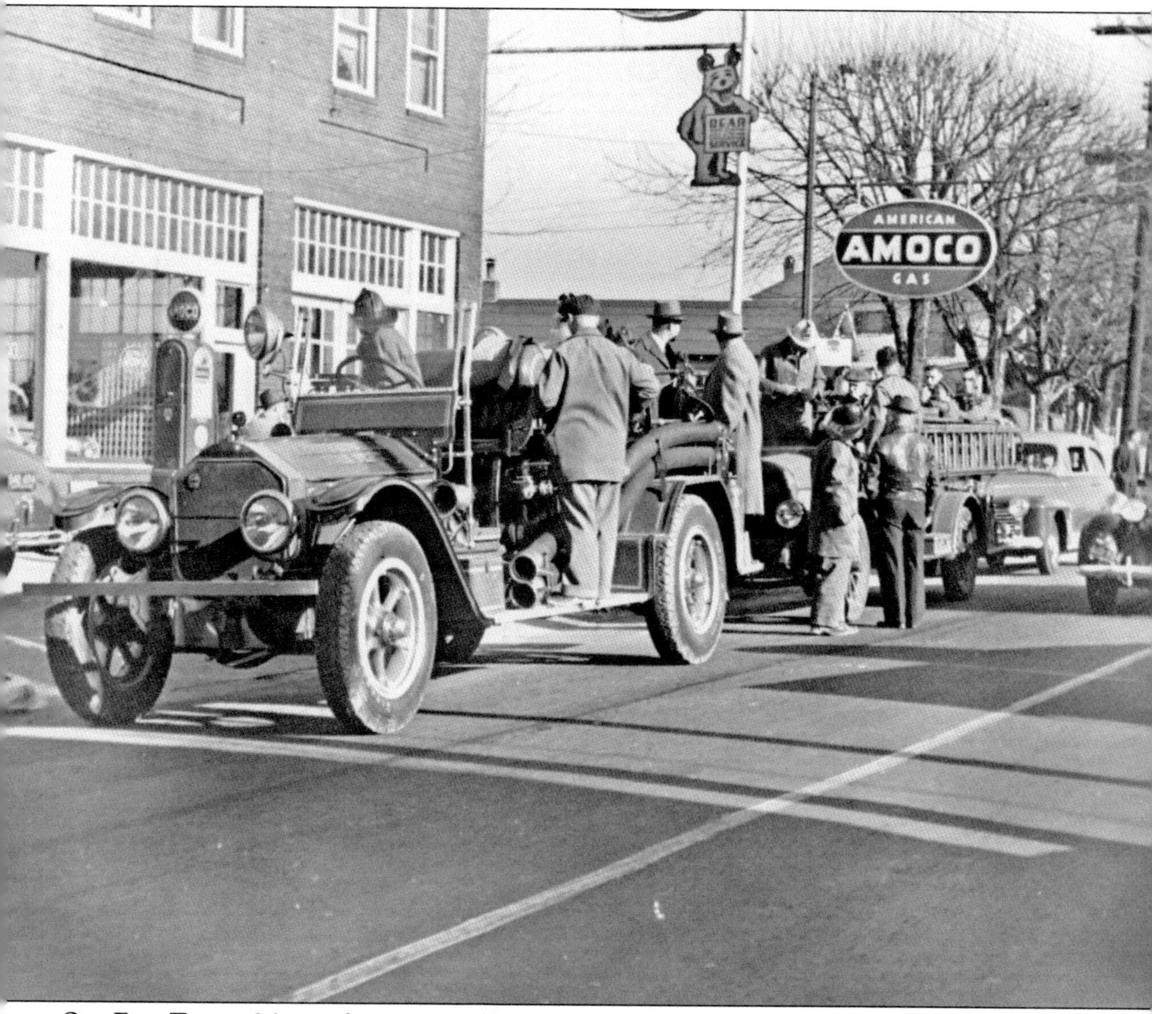

OLD FIRE TRUCK. Men in dress suits and hats cling to the sides and back of this old fire truck as it chugs past the Amoco station and the Stuart Building. (MVB.)

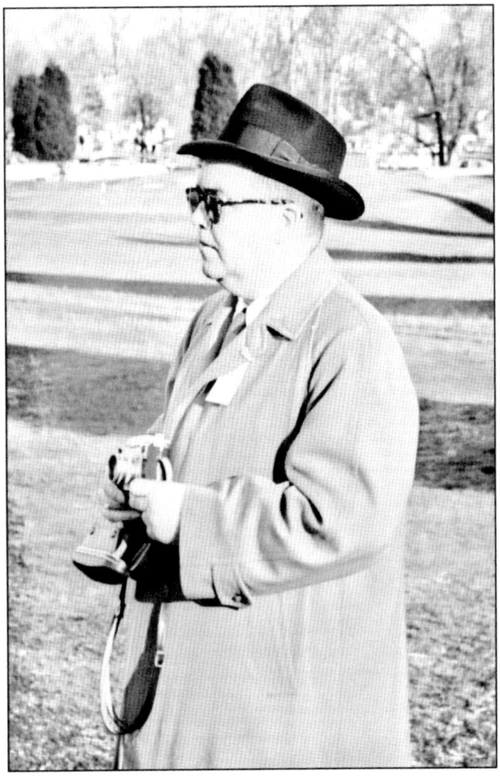

CANDID CAMERA. Shown here is Sam Vance with his trusty camera. Sam is responsible for taking many of the photographs that appear in this book. (MVB.)

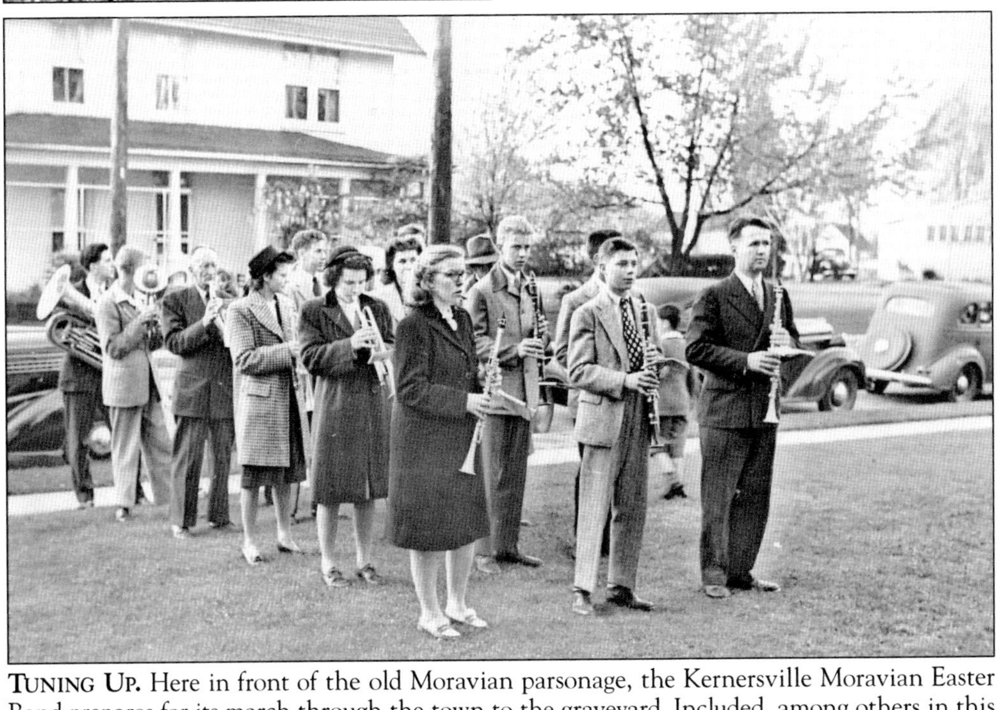

TUNING UP. Here in front of the old Moravian parsonage, the Kernersville Moravian Easter Band prepares for its march through the town to the graveyard. Included, among others in this group, are Philip Körner, Pat Cummings West, Ernestine Smith, Elsie Burke Menzel, and a Graves boy. (MVB.)

CHURCHGOERS. From left to right, Bea Vance, Marian Joyner Myers, Slaydon Myers, and Edgar Shore stop for a minute to greet each other after a Moravian church service. (MVB.)

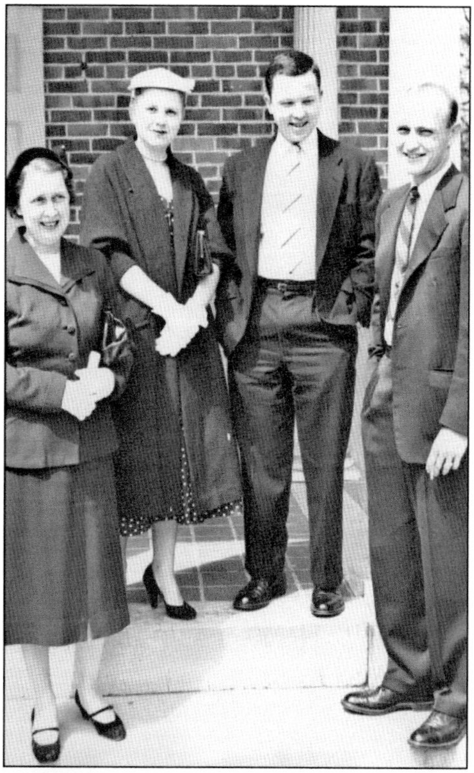

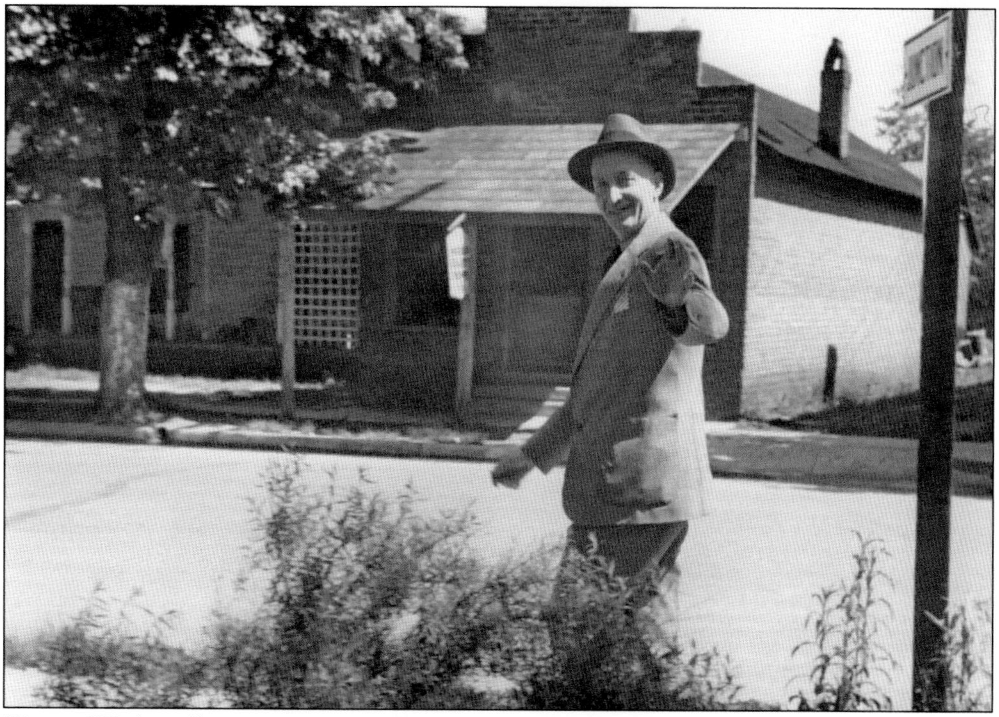

HELLO. While walking on Mountain Street across from the Cooke house and Lora Phillip's hair salon, Philip Körner Sr. offers a friendly wave to friends. (MVB.)

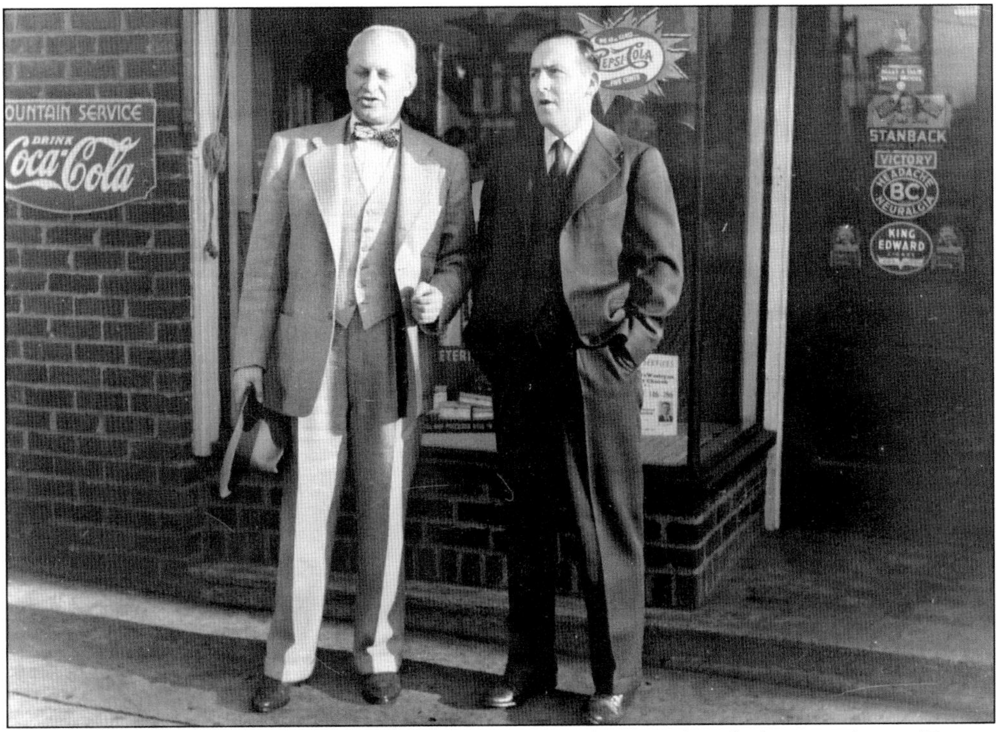

ANOTHER GATHERING PLACE. Joe Pinnix (right) visits with an unidentified man in front of Pinnix Drug Store. Note the Coca-Cola, Pepsi-Cola, Stanback, BC, and King Edward signs. (MVB.)

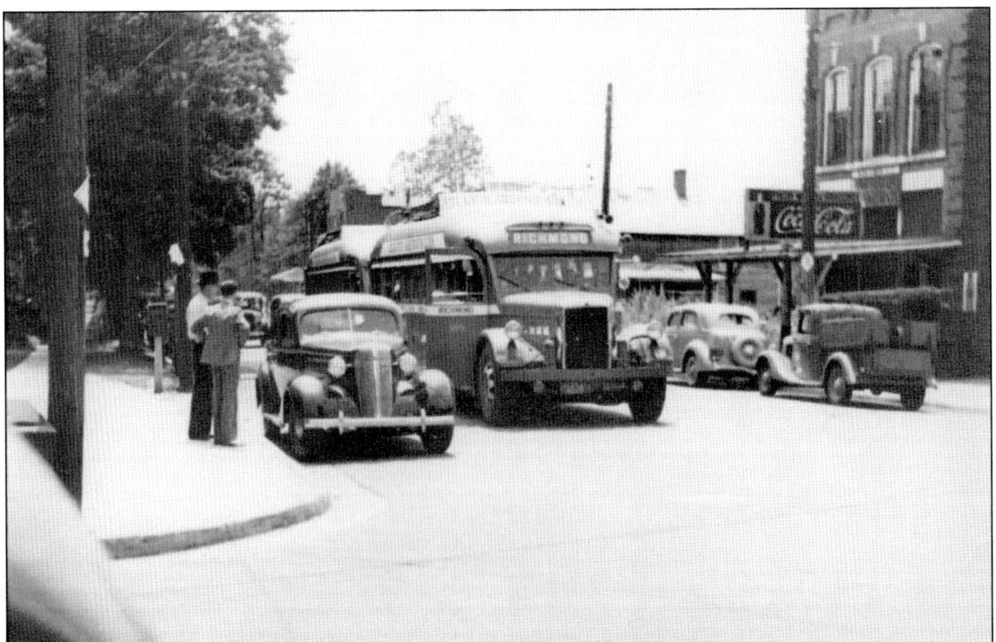

SAFETY FIRST. Two patient gentlemen visit as they wait on the corner of Main and Mountain Streets while traffic passes. The bus to Richmond waits at the intersection. (MVB.)

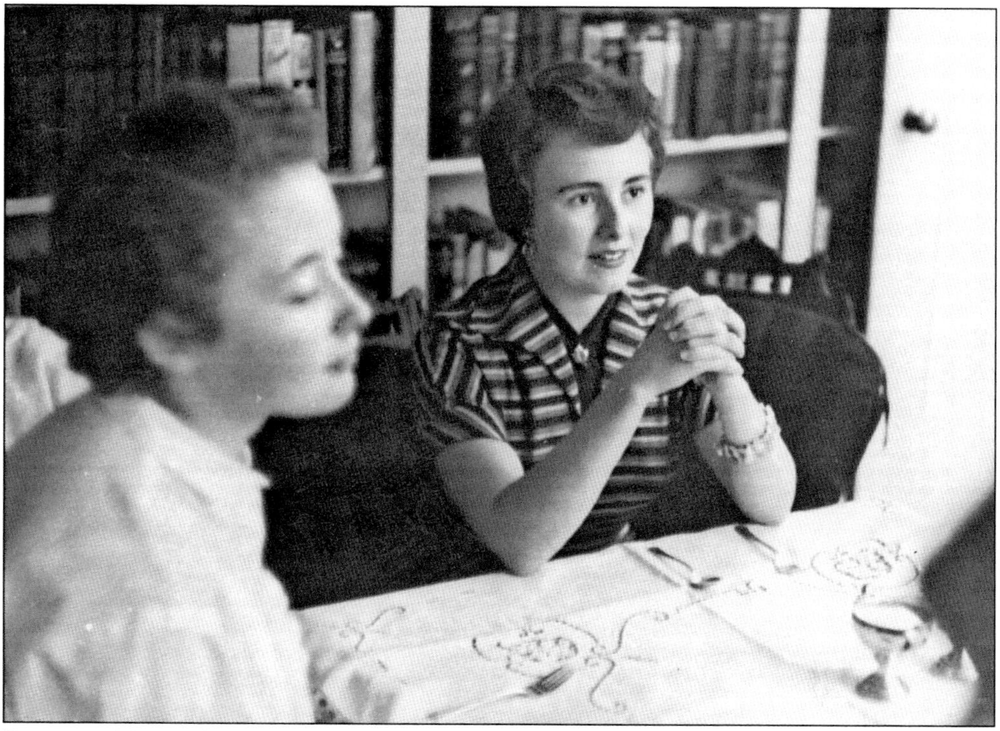

BEATRICE VANCE (LEFT) AND SALLY GREENFIELD. These two young ladies enjoy a meal at the Vance home. (MVB.)

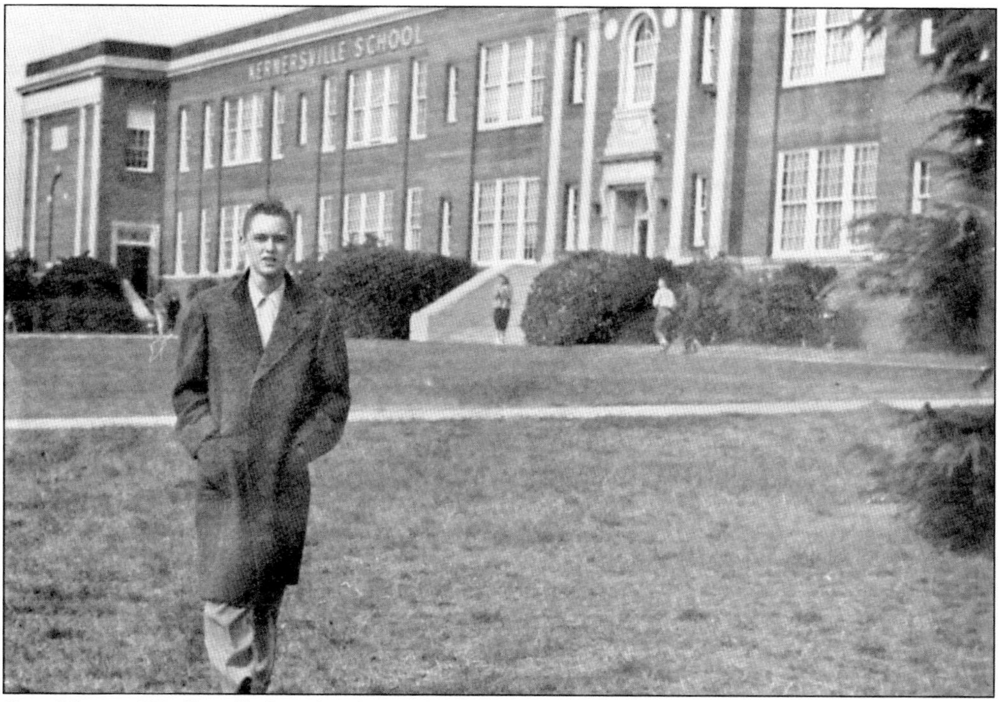

SAM VANCE III. Bundled up for the cooler weather, Sam Vance III strolls across the campus of Kernersville School. (MVB.)

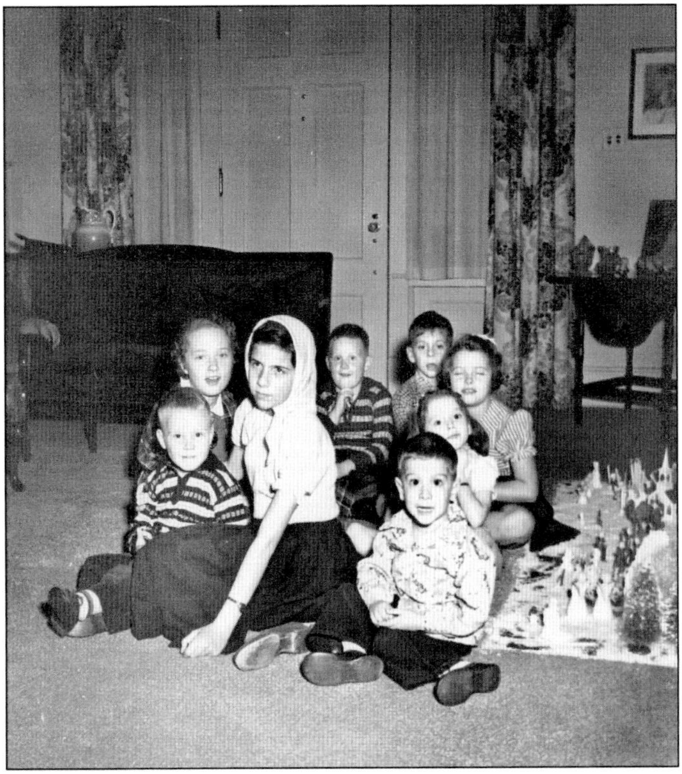

FAMILY GATHERING. The family gathers at Mrs. Clay Vance Ring's house. Among those present are David Cook, Beatrice Vance, Rebecca Pinnix, Tommy Cook, Joe Leak Pinnix, and Martha Vance. (MVB.)

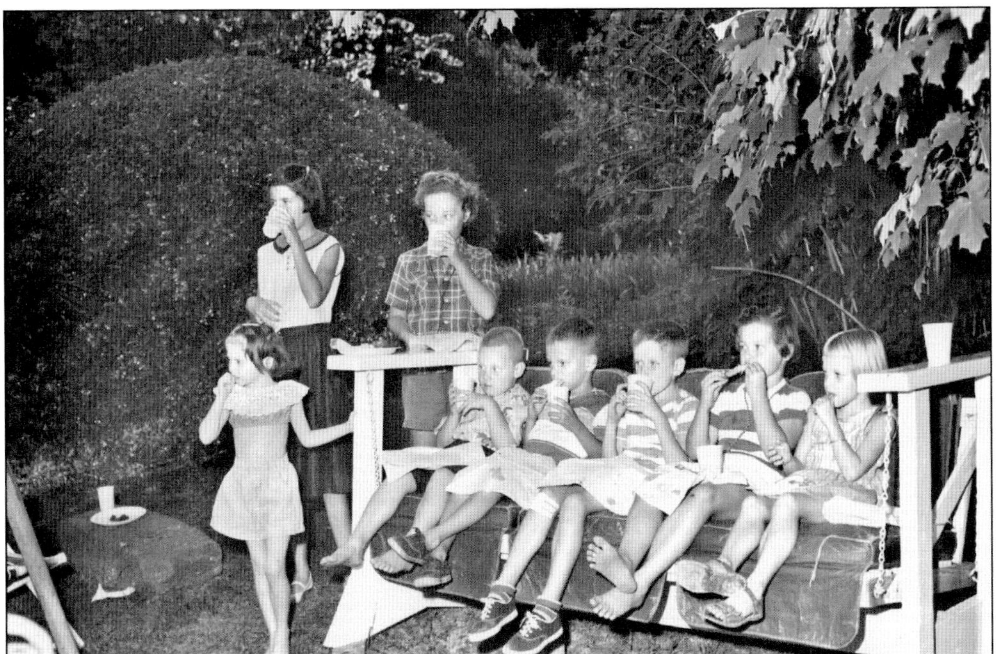

GARDEN PARTY. The Clay Vance Ring house was the setting for a lovely garden party. Among those present are Rebecca Pinnix, Beatrice Vance, Tommy Cook, Joe Leak Pinnix, David Cook, Martha Vance, and Jenny Stone. (MVB.)

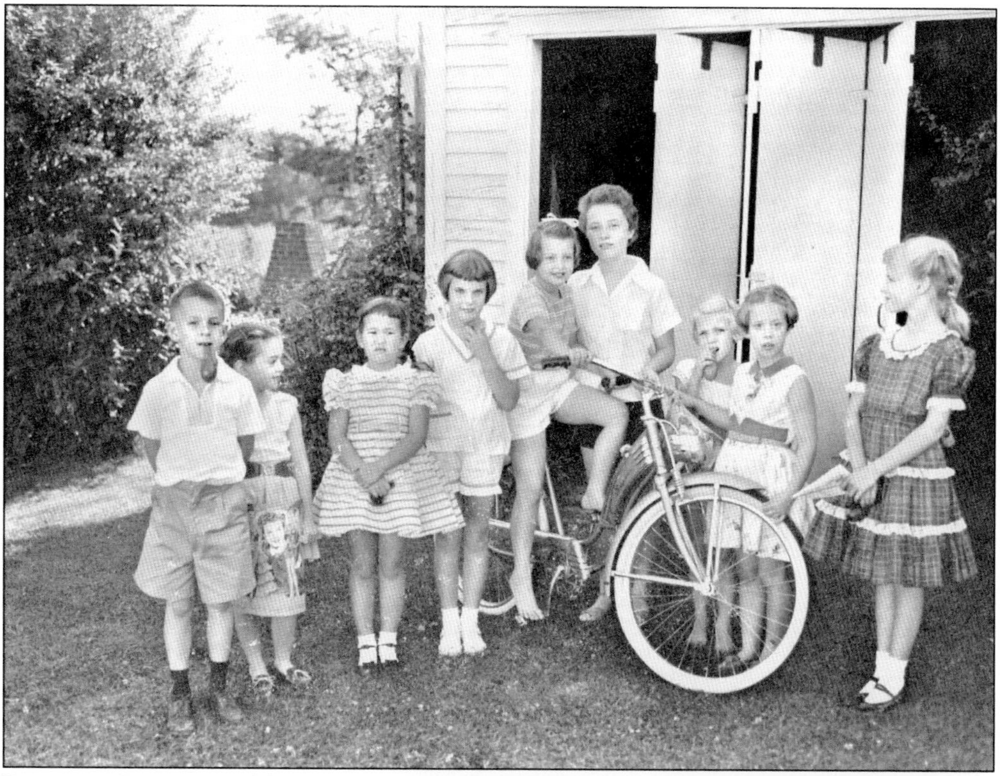

BIRTHDAY PARTY. A celebration honored Martha Vance's birthday at the Vance home on Salisbury Street. In front of the old garage are the following guests from left to right: Joe Leak Pinnix, Jenny Vance, Vickie Nelson, Jane Lasley, Martha Vance, Beatrice Vance, Jenny Stone, Sally Vance, and Connie Carter Ownesby. (MVB.)

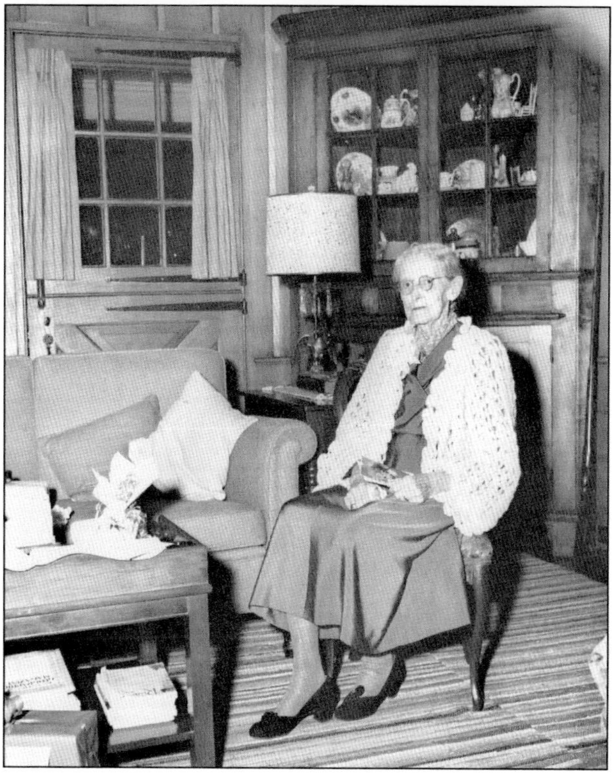

ADDIE KERNER ADKINS. All dressed up, Mrs. Adkins enjoys Christmas at the Ed Shore home. Addie, the daughter of Dr. Elias Kerner, lived next door to the Shores and celebrated holidays with them. She lived to be almost 100 years old. (MVB.)

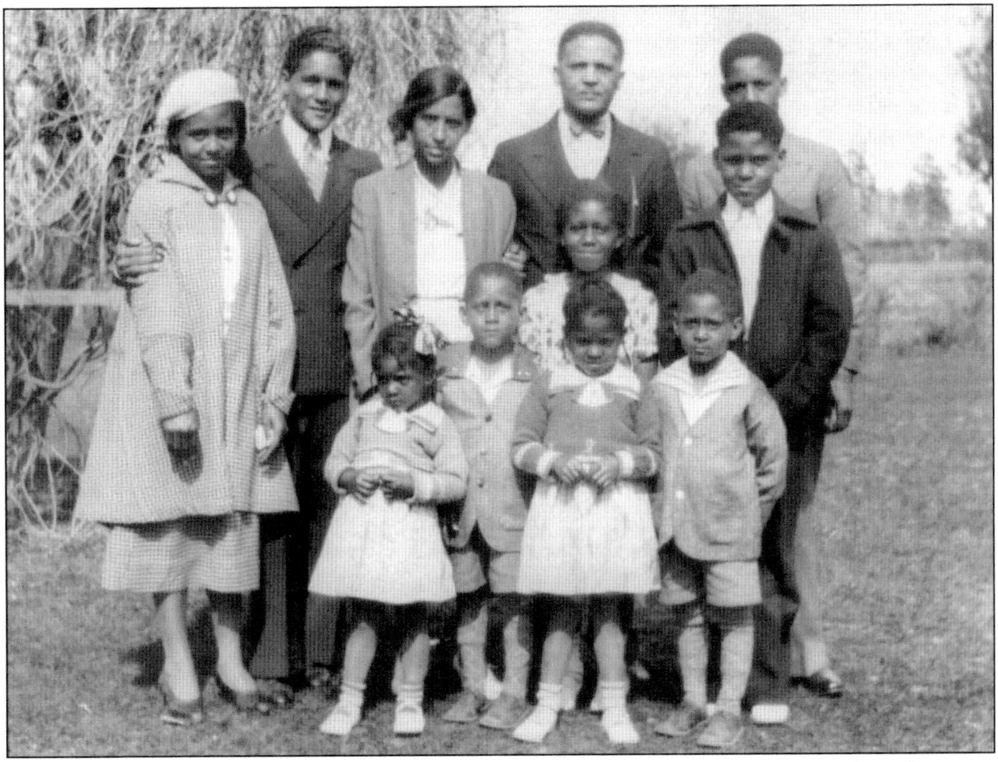

Martin Family and Triplets. Pictured here are members of the Bethania and Carl Martin family, including the first set of triplets born in Kernersville. On the first row, from left to right, are the triplets' sister Claudette, Jerry, Carrie, Evelyn (known as "Sis"), and John. (BM.)

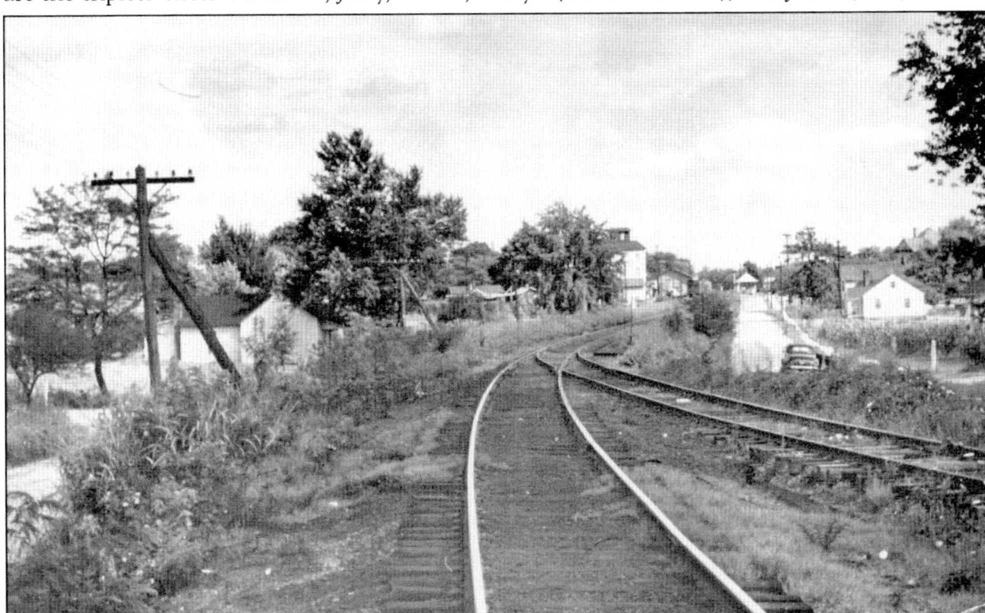

Looking East from Nelson Street. Captured here are the old Roller Mill, which is Farmer's Feed and Seed today, and the Old Depot. (MVB.)

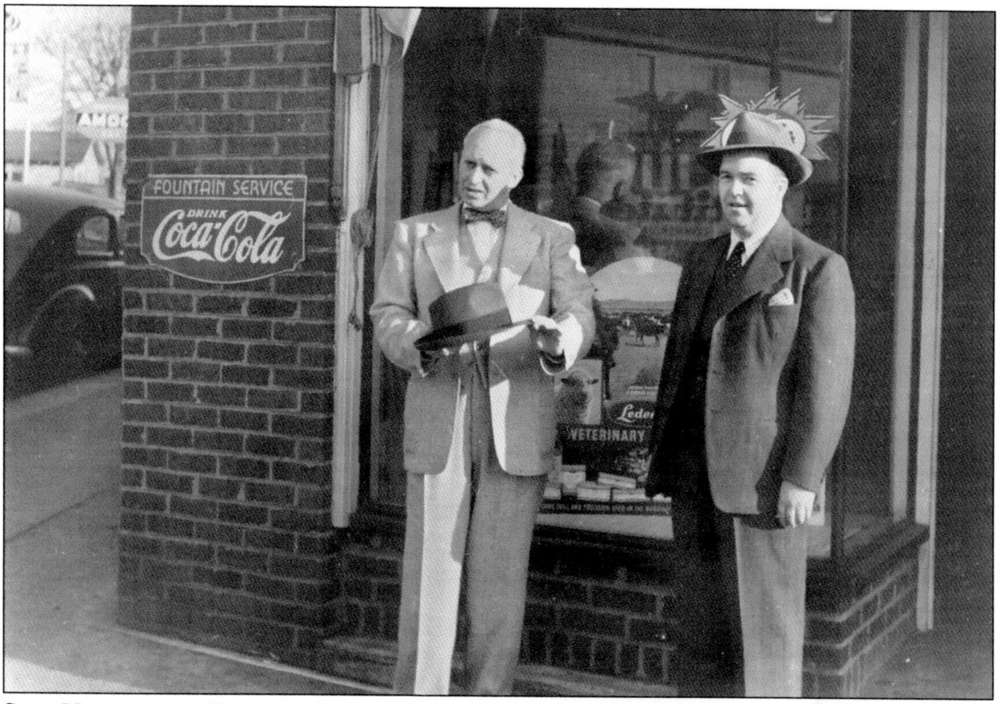

SAM VANCE AND FRIEND. Posing in front of Pennix Drug Store are Sam Vance (right) and an unidentified friend, probably a politician soliciting votes. Fountain service is offered inside. (MVB.)

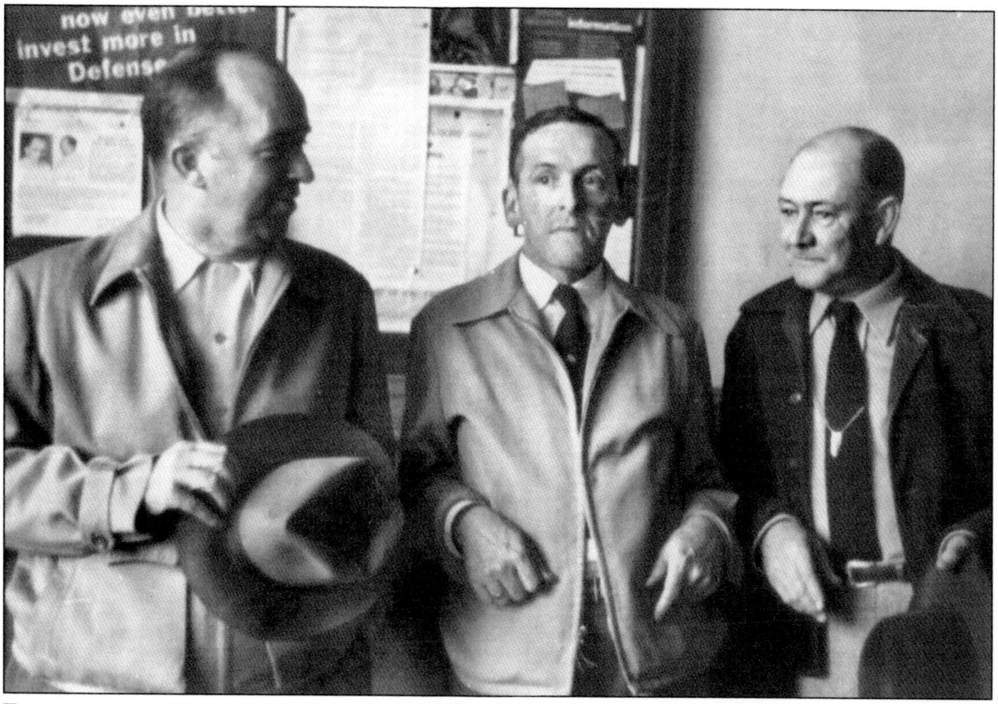

ENJOYING THE VIEW. From left to right, Fred Vance, Joe Pinnix, and James Justice enjoy the view. Note the Civil Defense Sign in the background. (SC.)

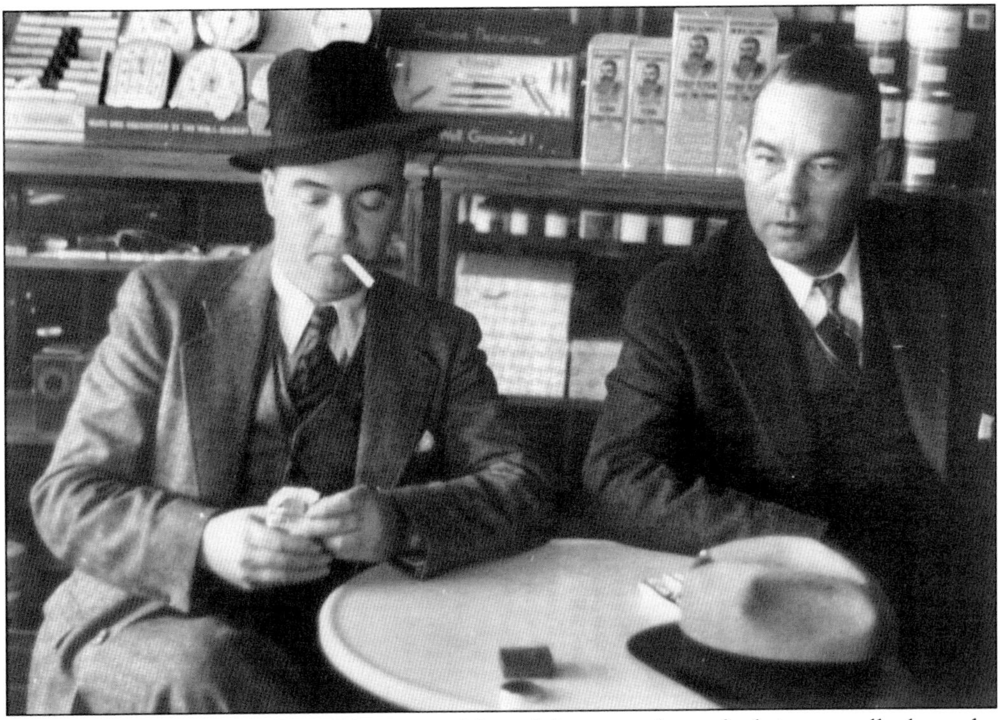

Sam Vance (Left) and Pete Hastings. Men of the town always find time to talk about the important events of the day as they enjoy a smoke. (SC.)

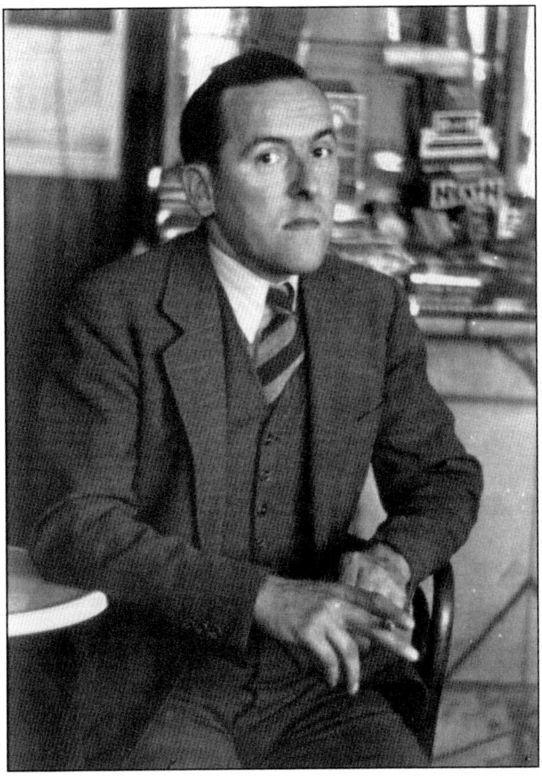

Joe Pinnix Sr. Joe's father, J. M. Pinnix, started Pinnix Drug in 1904. (SC.)

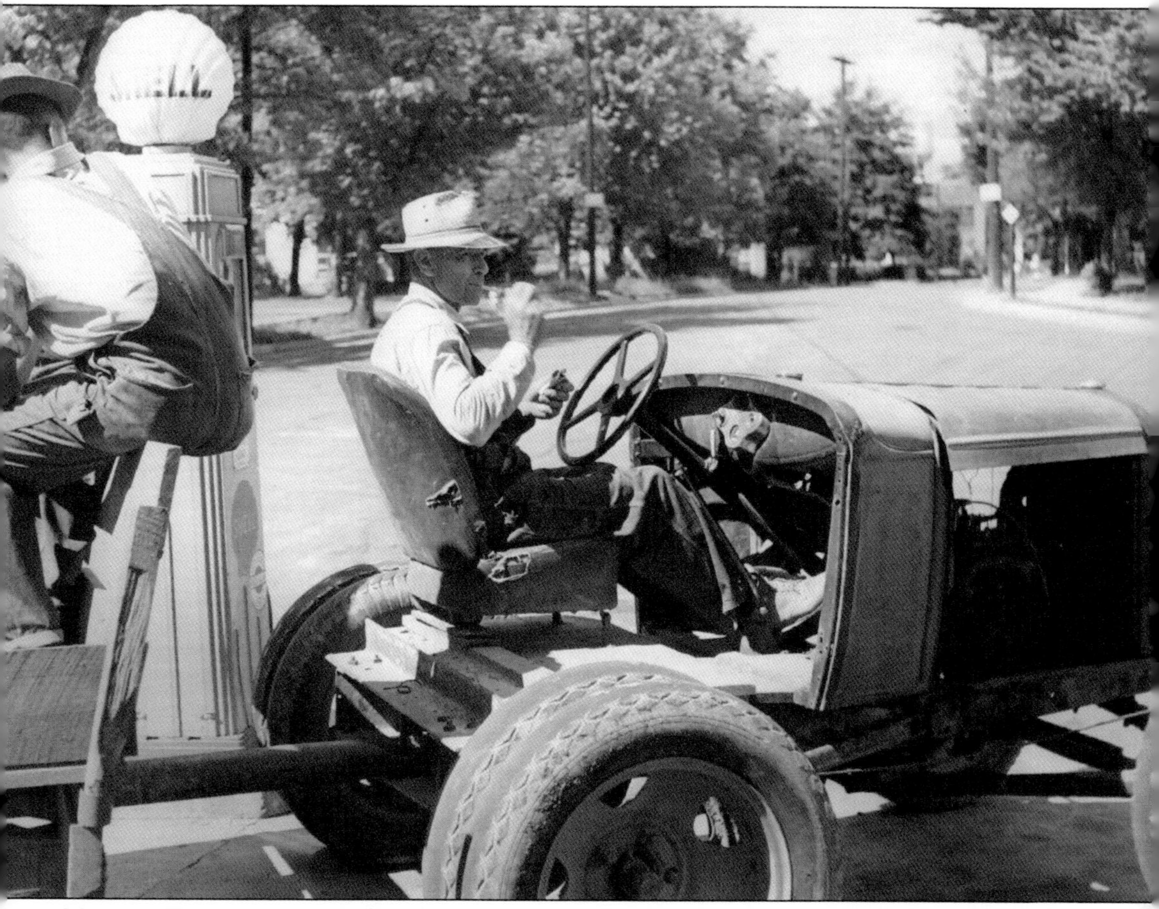

MAN ON TRACTOR. An unidentified farmer drives his tractor to refill at the Shell station and lights a cigarette at the pump. A bib-overalled worker waits patiently, resting on the side of a makeshift wagon. (MRK.)

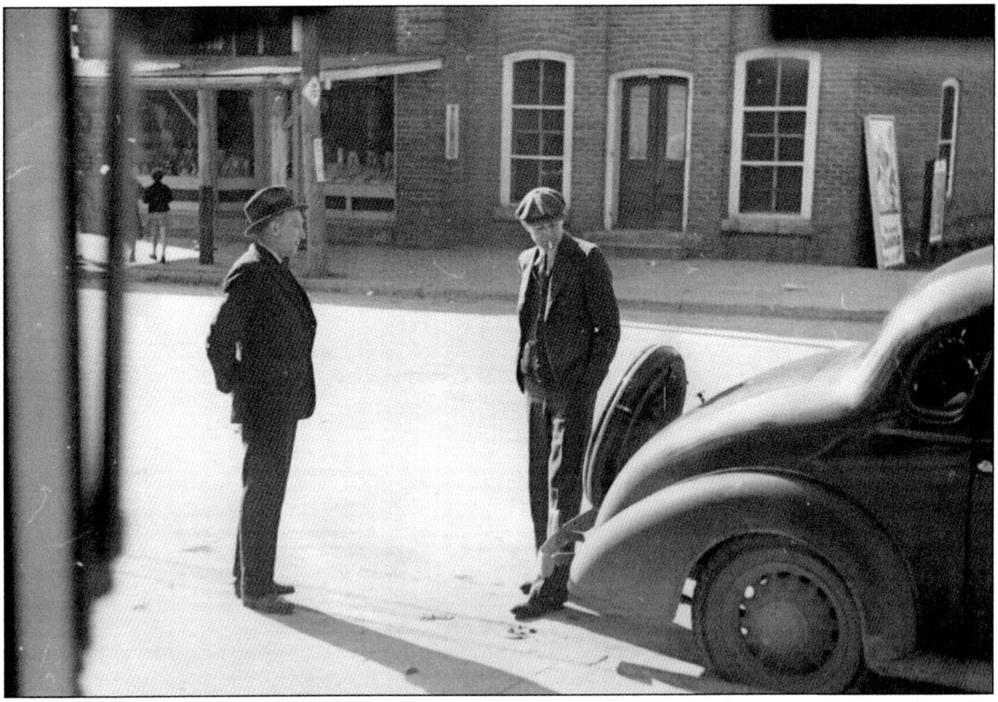

PHILIP KÖRNER SR. AND BILL MORTON. Kernersville is a town where everyone is friendly and has time to stop for a visit. Note the Bank of Kernersville and Linville Store in the background. (MRK.)

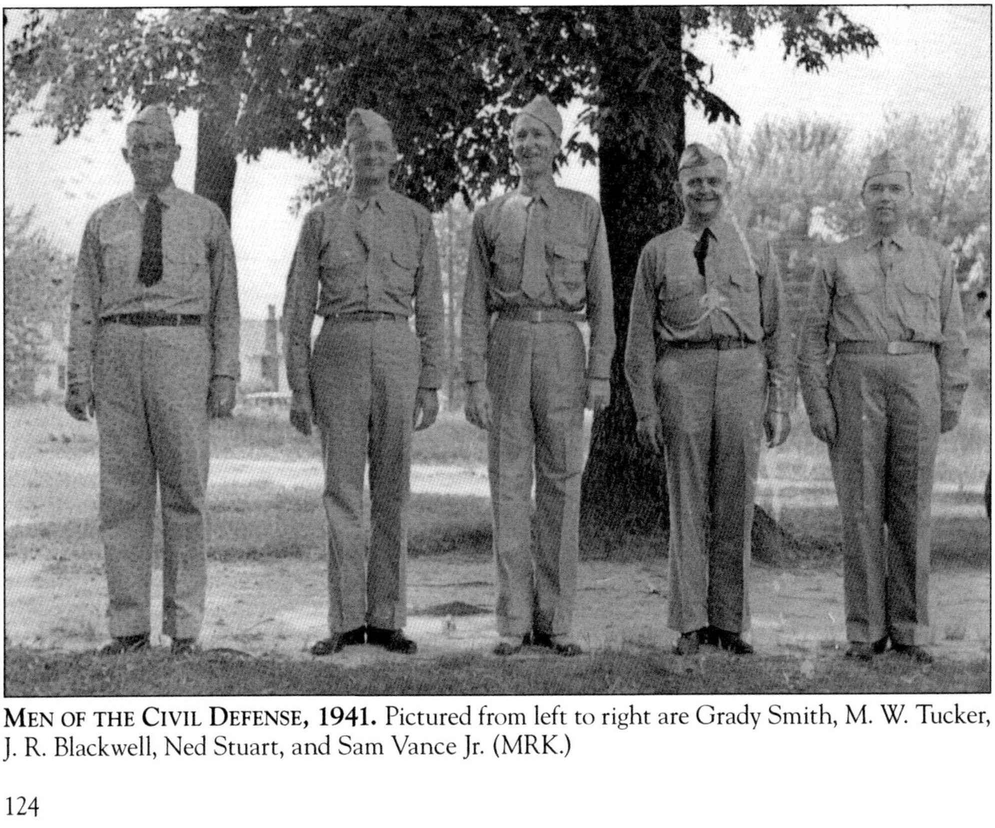

MEN OF THE CIVIL DEFENSE, 1941. Pictured from left to right are Grady Smith, M. W. Tucker, J. R. Blackwell, Ned Stuart, and Sam Vance Jr. (MRK.)

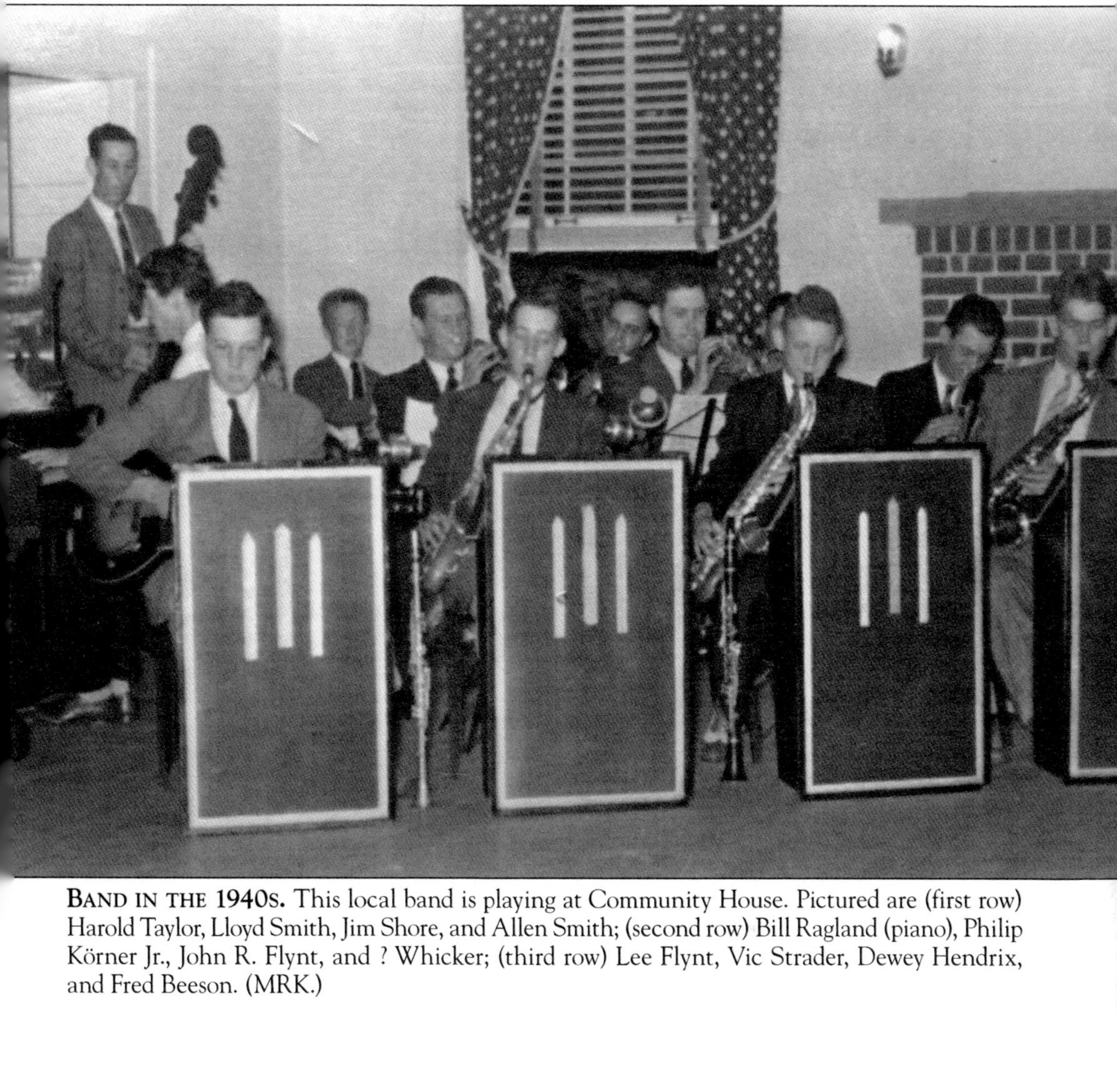

BAND IN THE 1940S. This local band is playing at Community House. Pictured are (first row) Harold Taylor, Lloyd Smith, Jim Shore, and Allen Smith; (second row) Bill Ragland (piano), Philip Körner Jr., John R. Flynt, and ? Whicker; (third row) Lee Flynt, Vic Strader, Dewey Hendrix, and Fred Beeson. (MRK.)

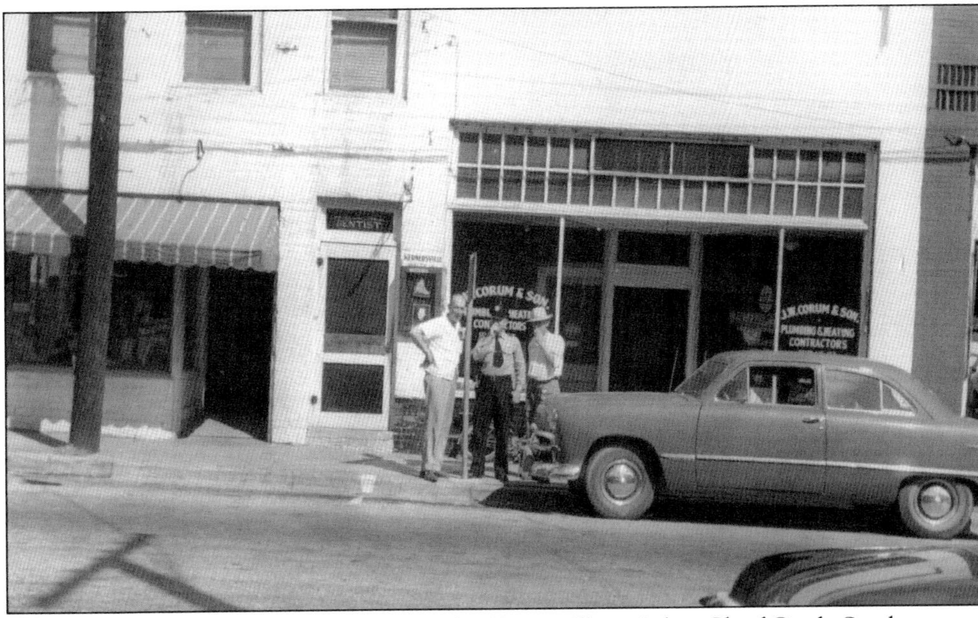

PATROLLING THE STREETS. From left to right, Eugene Flynt, Police Chief Grady Stockton, and Oscar Corum visit on North Main Street in the 1950s. (MRK.)

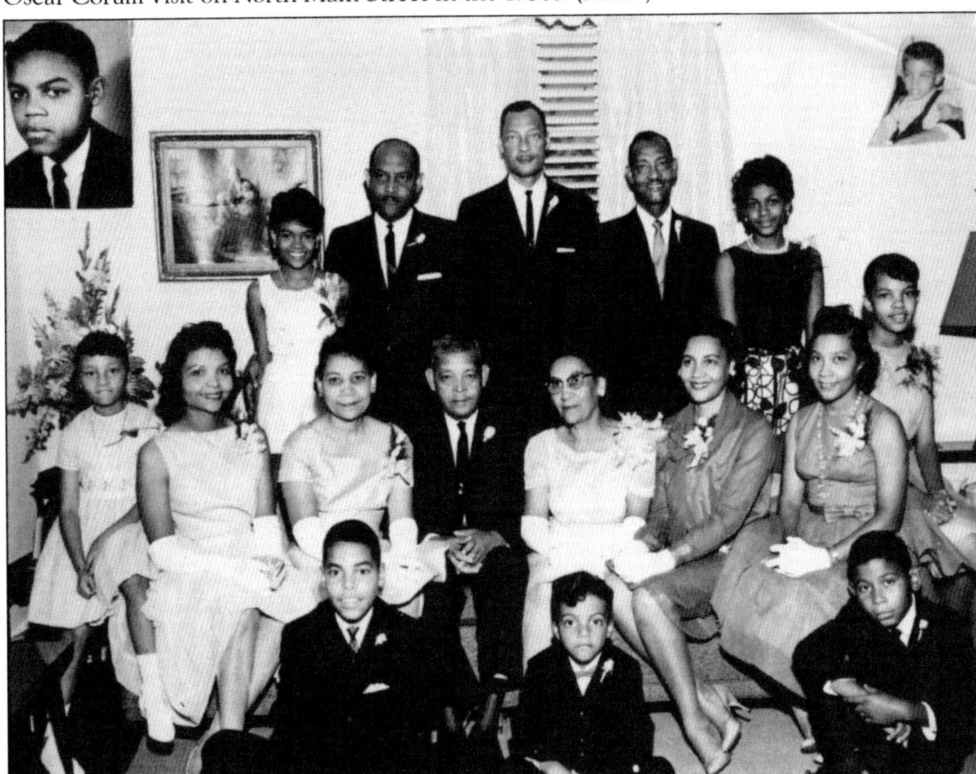

FRIENDE FAMILY. Mr. and Mrs. Walter Friende are pictured with children and grandchildren on their 50th wedding anniversary in September 1964. Six of the children obtained their master's degrees. (SH.)

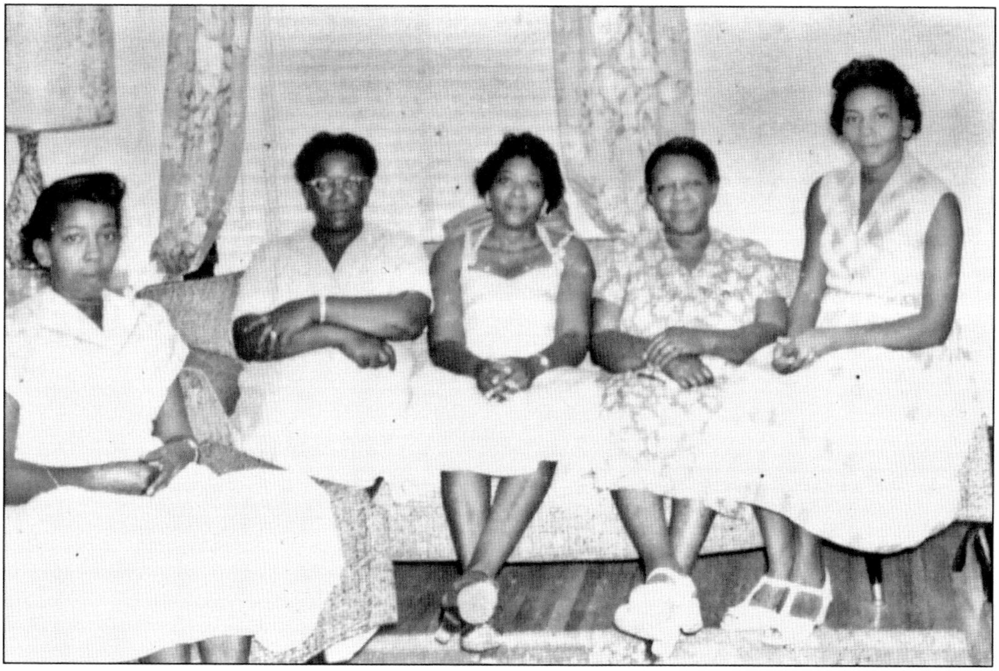

CHAMBERS FAMILY. The Inez and John Chambers family attended Providence Baptist Church. Inez was president of the Missionary Circle and president of the choir. John was a trustee. He also farmed, worked on the railroad, and ran the Little Sweet Shop on Church Street. Above is a picture of unidentified Chambers family members. (DW.)

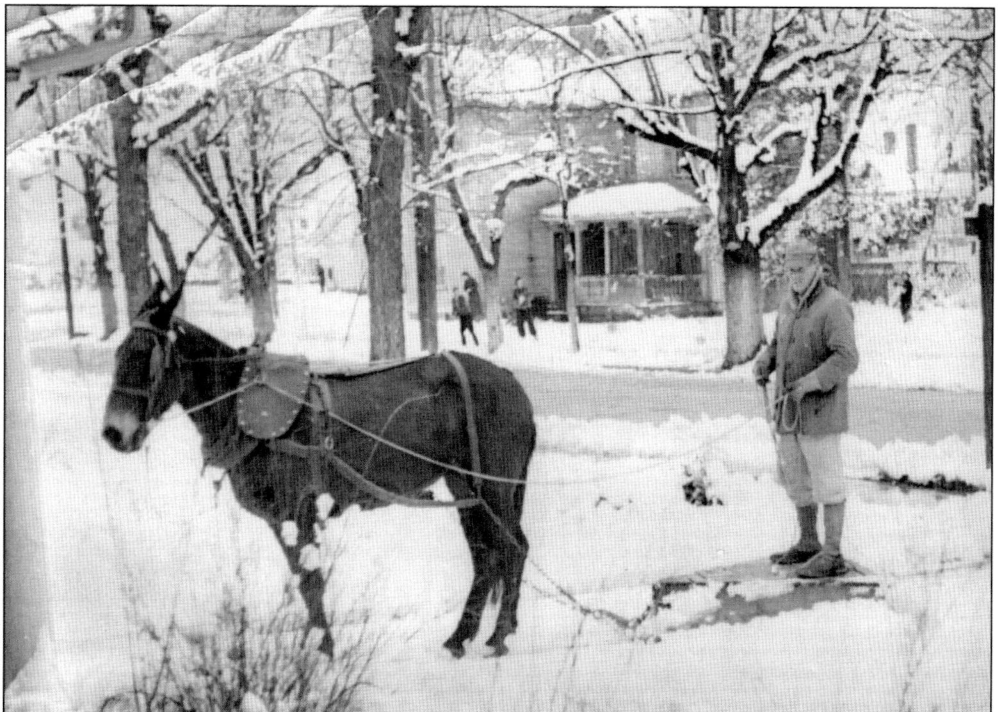

GILMER SMITH. After a heavy snow, Gilmer Smith cleans the downtown sidewalks. (MKH.)

BIBLIOGRAPHY

Kernersville North Carolina Bicentennial, March 1971.

Kernersville North Carolina (Revised Edition). Winston-Salem, NC: Hunter Publishing, 1976.

Kernersville Historic Preservation Society. "Kernersville, N.C.: A Walking Tour of Historical Homes."

Körner, Jules Gilmer Jr. *Joseph of Kernersville*. Durham, NC: The Seeman Printery, Inc., 1958.